Indexing Multimedia and Creative Works

INDEXING MULTIMEDIA AND CREATIVE WORKS

The Problems of Meaning and Interpretation

Pauline Rafferty
Rob Hidderley
University of Central England in Birmingham

ASHGATE

Published by
Ashgate Publishing Limited
Gower House
Croft Road
Aldershot
Hants GU11 3HR
England

Ashgate Publishing Company
Suite 420
101 Cherry Street
Burlington, VT 05401-4405
USA

Ashgate website: http://www.ashgate.com

British Library Cataloguing in Publication Data
Rafferty, Pauline
    Indexing multimedia and creative works : the problems of
    meaning and interpretation
    1. Cataloguing of nonbook material
    I. Title II. Hidderley, Rob
    025.3'4

Library of Congress Cataloging-in-Publication Data
Rafferty, Pauline, 1960-
    Indexing multimedia and creative works : the problems of meaning and interpretation /
    Pauline Rafferty and Rob Hidderley.
        p. cm.
    Includes bibliographical references (p.) and index.
    ISBN 0-7546-3254-7
    1. Information storage and retrieval systems--Multimedia (Art) 2. Multimedia
    (Art)--Abstracting and indexing. 3. Multimedia systems. 4. Semiotics. I. Hidderley, Rob,
    1959- II. Title.

Z699.5.A75R34 2004
025.04--dc22

2004043707

ISBN 0 7546 3254 7

Typeset in Century Old Style by Bournemouth Colour Press, Parkstone, Poole.
Printed and bound in Great Britain by MPG Books Ltd. Bodmin.Cornwall.

Contents

List of figures

List of tables

Foreword

We wanted to write *Indexing Multimedia and Creative Works: The Problems of Meaning and Interpretation* because we believe that existing approaches to multimedia retrieval, and multimedia indexing specifically, are limited because they do not generally engage with questions about the meaning(s) of documents – the 'subject analysis' in traditional librarianship terms. Like Mai (2000), we feel that this approach to issues relating to indexing is a matter of starting at the wrong place. A starting point for this book is the idea that indexing is not 'a neutral and objective representation of a document's subject matter but the representation of an interpretation of a document for future use' (Mai, 2000). For us, discussing 'the meaning of things' is a crucial prerequisite to designing and constructing multimedia information retrieval systems.

In this book we attempt to synthesize insights from writers in the fields of information science, computer science, communications and semiotics to explore subject analysis in multimedia documents, issues about interpretation and meaning, and issues relating to multimedia information retrieval. The book is written for people who are interested in communication, information and computer sciences, in the broadest of senses. The digitalization of documents and globalization of computer and communications networks means that information storage and retrieval are issues of significance for more groups in society than the computer and information professionals who were interested in such arcane matters in the past. In contemporary society there are very few institutions, including the home, in which the management, organization and retrieval of information and documentation is not of some concern!

Chapter 1 of this book provides an introduction and overview to studies of communication. In Chapter 1, conventional library-based indexing is situated within the broader context of human communication, which in turn is considered in terms of society, history and socio-political frameworks. This chapter explores traditional approaches to information retrieval, focusing on subject analysis and the 'challenges' of documents which are open to interpretation. Erwin Panofsky's 'levels of meaning' model is discussed in relation to image retrieval.

Chapters 2 and 3 provide an introduction to information retrieval and multimedia information retrieval respectively. In Chapter 2, information retrieval is discussed from two broad perspectives: the first approach might be called the theoretical approach of conventional library and information science; while the second approach might be described as the computer application viewpoint. In Chapter 3 issues relating to the principles and practices of contemporary multimedia retrieval systems are discussed.

Chapter 4 provides the reader with an introduction to some of the traditions of semiotics. Clearly the complete philosophy, methodologies and applications of the broad traditions of semiotics cannot be covered comprehensively in only one chapter, but the intention is to provide enough of an introduction so that the reader can engage with the semiotic-based rich readings of multimedia examples in Chapter 5.

Chapter 5 includes some descriptions of specific multimedia information retrieval tools, namely the Art and Architecture Thesaurus, Iconclass and the Library of Congress Thesaurus of General Materials I and II. Some multimedia objects are read using analytical and descriptive categories derived from the literature of semiotics. The multimedia information retrieval tools are used to index the multimedia objects. This exercise demonstrates the gap between the richness of interpretation using semiotics and the restricted description that inevitably results from using controlled vocabulary systems.

The argument which develops through the course of this book is that there are many approaches to multimedia indexing which we believe are limited in their scope because they are built on the assumption that communication is a straightforward process. Finally, in Chapter 6 we reflect on the issues which develop from this argument, and explore current computer-based research approaches; Democratic Indexing as an alternative approach to multimedia information retrieval; and the pragmatics of multimedia information retrieval.

We wanted to write this book because we felt that existing approaches to multimedia retrieval generally start at the wrong place and ignore important issues relating to meaning, communication and interpretation. We hope that the argument, which we build up in and through this book, demonstrates the validity of that position. We, at any rate, still hold the position!

Pauline Rafferty
Rob Hidderley
Birmingham

1 Information, retrieval, discourse and communication

INTRODUCTION

This book is about the indexing of multimedia objects. In the context of this book, the term *indexing* refers to the representation, in surrogate form, of information about:

- the *physical characteristics* of the multimedia object (for example, descriptive cataloguing)
- the *intellectual characteristics* of the multimedia object (for example, subject indexing).

Indexing is generally considered a crucial prerequisite for any effective information retrieval system. We use the term multimedia objects here to refer to a range of media within which information is stored. In this context information is assumed to be material, or in Michael Buckland's terms, information is treated as 'information-as-thing' (1991).

In this book multimedia information retrieval is information retrieval which is used to manage still images, moving images (with and without soundtracks) and sound recordings. The main focus of this book is on concept-based information retrieval which uses text to index and retrieve multimedia objects. Other forms of multimedia information retrieval will be described briefly to provide a perspective of the range of systems.

We believe that it is useful to situate multimedia indexing within a broader context. Our use of the term multimedia suggests that the objects with which we will be concerned are not textual but non-textual objects, yet many of the issues relevant to the indexing of multimedia objects, for example, subject analysis, are issues which are also relevant to textual objects. Our contention is that the issues are similar, but the nature of the communicative medium (for example, photography rather than written language) might result in additional difficulties in the indexing of non-textual objects.

1

We see indexing itself within the broader context of communication, and in turn, communication sitting within the broader context of human history and society. We believe that reaching an understanding of the issues involved in the indexing of multimedia objects is best done within a broader discussion of communication and culture, and the philosophies of communication and culture.

There are many approaches to multimedia indexing which we believe are limited in their scope because they are built on the assumption that communication is a straightforward process. In this book we hope to demonstrate that the issue is more complicated than this by drawing on models of communication and meaning from the domain of semiotics and communication studies as well as describing and critiquing information retrieval models drawn from the domains of information science and computer science. This first chapter provides the reader with an overview of the range of issues that we believe are of significance in multimedia indexing. Subsections in this chapter will examine the following topics:

- traditional approaches to information retrieval
- information retrieval and subject analysis
- information retrieval and discursive forms
- information retrieval and subjective discourse
- meanings, codes and conventions
- Erwin Panofsky and levels of meaning.

TRADITIONAL APPROACHES TO INFORMATION RETRIEVAL

For many years, librarians and information workers have designed and implemented information retrieval systems to help information seekers find exactly what they are looking for. Information retrieval involves the identification and representation of the information content of and about documents using descriptive and analytical systems which allow specific user requests for information to be matched up with the relevant information source(s). In the retrieval of textual documents the assumption is that the human indexer is able to decode the textual document and construct a representation of the significant information content using the codes and conventions of cataloguing rules and indexing languages, for example classification codes and controlled vocabularies.

Traditionally in libraries, information workers have focused on the document as the information-carrying vehicle. Documents, chiefly books, are organized in libraries on shelves according to subject through the application of appropriate notation derived from a library classification scheme. This practice allows books to be shelved in relative order and facilitates open access policies in libraries.

Catalogues are constructed to record information relating to the physical aspects of the document (descriptive cataloguing, author/title access points), and the intellectual aspects of the document (classification marks as indexing entries, controlled vocabularies).

The traditional process of information storage and retrieval depends upon human indexers and library users making decisions relating to the interpretation of, and representation of, meaning in media objects and indexing languages. These decisions can lead to success or failure in the implementation of the system and/or the subsequent search procedure. The human indexer must accurately describe the physical properties of the document using the appropriate cataloguing rules, and then form access points for author and title searches. How straightforward this part of the process is depends on how easy it is to identify relevant information and transpose it into the form demanded by the cataloguing code.

To subject index the document, the human indexer must first analyse the subject(s) of the document being indexed, and then choose the subject terms from the controlled vocabulary which best represents the subject of the document (the controlled vocabulary will be a standard, published externally or in house, which is often chosen or constructed by someone other than the indexer). To do this, the human indexer must interpret the meaning of the document, and interpret the meaning of terms in the controlled vocabulary.

The library users who seek information can perform an *author search* or a *title search* on the catalogue if they already have this information, but if the search is for an unknown item about a particular subject, then the search will take the form of a *subject search*. Such a search strategy is only possible because it is generally accepted that documents have fairly stable meanings which can be interpreted by readers and can be represented in other forms (cataloguing records, classification marks).

The information seeker has to decide which term in the controlled vocabulary best represents the subject of the information sought, and then hope that the subject of the document as interpreted by the indexer accurately represents the subject of the document as interpreted by the seeker. Thus analysed, it becomes clear that the information retrieval process is a communicative process in which meaning and interpretation are carried out by at least two agents, the object of interpretation having been encoded by at least one other agent, but probably more, given contemporary publishing practices.

The indexing process (Figure 1.1) as it applies to textual objects is considered to be one which needs specialist knowledge to implement successfully. This process has become professionalized in contemporary society. There are a number of textbooks devoted to information retrieval in general (for example, Chowdhury, 1999; Rowley and Farrow, 2000), and to specific aspects of the

3

The indexer
- Analyses and interprets the meaning of the information object (textual or multimedia object).
- Interprets the codes and conventions of the indexing language.
- Represents the meaning of the information object in the terms of the controlled vocabulary.
- Applies appropriate vocabulary to the information object, enters the indexing terms into the system.

The information seeker
- Approaches the information retrieval system to search for a specific subject.
- Represents the subject sought in conventional linguistic terms.
- Formulates the subject/meaning in the codified terms of the specific indexing language (controlled vocabulary).
- Chooses appropriate indexing term(s) and searches the system.

Figure 1.1   The subject indexing process

process (for example, Hunter, 2002; Langridge, 1989; Piggott, 1988). Computerized information retrieval has made it possible to focus search strategies on specific objects within documents (for example, text retrieval databases which facilitate searches for specific articles within journals, and hypertexts structures which allow access to specific nodes of information), but the principles of the process (analysis – representation – retrieval) are essentially similar.

INFORMATION RETRIEVAL AND SUBJECT ANALYSIS

Conventional information retrieval systems work on the principle that the textual object has meaning which has been encoded within the object by the author(s), and which can be decoded by the reader/indexer. The decoded meaning is assumed to be stable and 'naturally' transparent. The same principle works in relation to the indexing language which is also assumed to be 'naturally' transparent. Textbooks of librarianship have in the past given students scant advice about how to decode meaning in documents, and about how to deal with the perils of interpretation that lie before them. Derek Langridge, in *Subject Analysis* (1989), attempted a detailed exploration of the difficulties of establishing meaning of documents, and acknowledged that reading and interpreting meaning could very often require something more than the mechanistic 'technical reading' that Wyner referred to in passing (Wyner, 1980, p. 18). Langridge included many examples of difficult-to-interpret texts to illustrate the potential problems of interpreting meaning and deciding on primary and secondary subjects. The approach he took was to analyse and interpret these texts, thus showing the reader/student how it should be done. What is missing in this approach is the recognition that readers can interpret documents in a variety of ways. It may be that Langridge's interpretation would not be shared by all other readers who may bring with them different knowledge and different interpretative agendas.

Langridge held that the most obvious philosophical influence on indexing at the time that he was writing was the influence of philosophers whom he labelled 'the positivists'. He argued that the positivist definition of knowledge is a very narrow one, being limited to science and excluding a large part of written records (Langridge, 1989, p. 20). There are other philosophers who take a broader view about what counts as knowledge, but even those 'positivists' who favour a limited use of the term offer other terms such as 'modes of experience' or 'apprehension' to describe those written records which they do not view as knowledge. Langridge's point is that:

> [t]he fact that the positivists distinguish between the sciences and all else actually supports the view that there are different forms of experience on record, whatever name we use. Since they themselves are only interested in science, their writings can be no help in deciding how many distinct forms there are. (Ibid., p. 21)

There is much more of a debate about whether humans can ever claim that knowledge possessed at any given moment is immutable and absolute than is articulated in Langridge's treatment of the matter, and the similarities and differences between various epistemological positions in the modern world are not always as clear cut as he suggests. Langridge accepted that like Plato, the 'positivists' are concerned with distinguishing 'true knowledge from belief' (ibid., p. 22) rather than with the forms that either might take. This issue is of some interest to information management because the information manager must consider the problem of forms in relation to both knowledge and belief because there are 'written records' pertaining to both aspects of human culture. These records have to be organized because people may want to retrieve them whether they are 'true knowledge' or 'belief'. Subject coverage in conventional library classification schemes tends to be knowledge-based so that even aesthetic information objects are analysed and described from knowledge-based perspectives. The question that Langridge does not ask but might be of interest to multimedia indexing is whether there are approaches other than the knowledge-based academic discipline orientations of conventional retrieval tools. Could pleasure, ideology, or intertextuality form the bases of new approaches to indexing?

Langridge's own philosophical preference was for the idealist approach offered by R.G. Collingwood in *Speculum Mentis or, The Map of Knowledge* (1924). He believed that Collingwood's approach, which involved viewing different disciplines in their own terms because they are all 'rival ways of conceiving the whole' (Langridge, 1989, p. 22), and separating disciplines according to their own rules, offered an alternative way for librarians to think about 'knowledge' (ibid.). The various 'forms of knowledge' are treated as logically distinct because they are 'the ultimate classes of knowledge beyond which – we can make no further reduction' (ibid.).

Langridge's approach to meaning in documents seems to be based on the view that the meaning of the text resides entirely in the text; in other words, there is no recognition that individual interpretations of text might depend on the codes and conventions, the belief systems and world views that the individual reader at a specific historical juncture brings to the text. For Langridge, what the librarian indexer must do is to learn to read, or to decode, in the correct way in order to properly determine the meaning of any given document. Post-structuralist linguists and communication theorists might question whether the process is always quite so straightforward, and whether totally transparent meaning is to be found in all types of documents.

INFORMATION RETRIEVAL AND DISCURSIVE FORMS

Many of the traditional information and library studies textbooks of the 1960s and 1970s referred in passing to subject analysis. It may be that the relative neglect of subject analysis is due to the belief on the part of the writers that the subjects of documents are generally easy to determine and to interpret, but this is not necessarily the case for all documents at all times. There are many different types of discourse with different purposes and audiences, and while some types of discourse are constructed with transparency in mind, there are other documents constructed with other motivations. Moreover, discursive forms change over time. Decisions about how transparent or opaque the meaning of a document will be might be chosen freely by the author, or, as in the case of an author such as the imprisoned Italian communist writer, Antonio Gramsci (1971), whose sometimes cryptic writings, smuggled out of prison, were always in danger of falling into the hands of his enemies, such decisions might be imposed by circumstances.

Michel Foucault (1991), in essays such as 'What is an Author?' drew attention to the constructed and historically contingent nature of the communicative operations of authorship and textuality. In *The Order of Things* (1970), Foucault argued that each historical age has its own episteme, that is, its own system of knowledge constituted by recurrent patterns of signs and symbols, ways of speaking and seeing things, which are ascribed with the status of knowledge. The episteme determines what can be known at that moment. Like the notion of the scientific paradigm, each episteme is historically contingent and is dislodged from its position of power by the proceeding episteme. From this perspective, 'discursive practice' is a body of 'anonymous, historical rules' in and through which ways of seeing and writing and speaking are determined. For our purposes, the notion of determined discourse is of some interest in modelling types of text, which in turn is of interest in mapping textual transparency and opacity in social, political and institutional contexts.

In the contemporary modern world, the academy sets rules, codes and conventions about how scientific writings should be presented which privilege accuracy, proof, evidence, transparency and knowledge. This type of writing is motivated towards the reader, but is often difficult for lay readers to interpret because scholarly conventions demand that writers use professional language or jargon, and demonstrate their familiarity with, and knowledge of, writers within the scholarly tradition. Other types of writing, for example modernist and postmodernist fiction, and poetry, are not so heavily concerned with transparency; indeed, the authorial intention in such writings may be to obscure or complicate meaning: to create the self-consciously ambiguous text.

Linguists, philosophers and literary theorists have long been interested in identifying different types of writing (Figure 1.2). Roland Barthes distinguished between the 'readerly' and 'writerly' text by which he meant:

- 'writerly texts' – texts which invite the reader's involvement in interpretation
- 'readerly texts' – texts in which the writer keeps tight reign on the range of possible interpretations. The text tends to be representational. The reader is positioned as a relatively passive receiver and the text tends towards 'a' meaning (Barthes, 1974).

Umberto Eco differentiated between the 'open' and the 'closed' text (Eco, 1979). The point is that different discourses allow the writer different levels of freedom in establishing transparent meaning/opaque meaning, which in turn impacts on the freedom with which any reader might interpret the text. In a self-consciously wrought opaque text, the range of interpretations might be broad.

INFORMATION RETRIEVAL AND SUBJECTIVE DISCOURSE

Traditionally libraries focused on creating and implementing information retrieval systems which were based on rationalist or pragmatic positivist philosophical approaches to epistemology. The great classification creators of the

Scientific writing
- Transparent
- Detailed and specific
- Proof – evidence – objectivity valued
- Knowledge-based
- Reader-orientation but often specialist jargon
- Verification and peer review

'Opaque' writing
- Imaginative
- Suggestive of meaning, open to interpretation/subjectivity valued
- Affective dimension – intuition – belief
- Reader has to work to make meaning
- Value-oriented: experts decide on 'good'/'bad' texts and what constitutes the canon

Figure 1.2   Examples of types of writing

nineteenth century were particularly interested in the idea that knowledge can be ordered and organized and that there are 'orders of things' which classificationists can use to structure their classification schemes. Many of the classificationists of the 'golden age' of universal classification schemes believed in an objective, scientific approach to knowledge which was stable and which existed in the first place because of a dependable academic consensus.

Throughout the late twentieth century, the limits of objectivity have been much discussed in western philosophy, particularly by postmodern thinkers who question whether there is any such thing as 'objective' information and stable meaning in language. For our purposes it is enough to distinguish between discourses which aspire to objectivity and transparency, and discourses which are not subject to such aspirations. Traditionally, as we have already argued, the library profession have emphasized the management of knowledge-based discourses, rather than discourses of imagination and subjectivity, as the central focus of information retrieval systems. The treatment of fiction in libraries provides some evidence which supports such a view. In Dewey's Decimal Classification (DDC), fiction is organized using historical and geographical markers. There is no attempt to address the question of subject, of determining what the work of fiction is about. This is not an unreasonable way to deal with fiction if the focus of attention is organizing fiction for literary scholarship, where the fictional work becomes an object of research or criticism, traditionally read through the prism of 'literary history'. It is not a particularly useful way to subject index fiction for people who are interested in reading fiction for pleasure.

Establishing the meaning of some sorts of textual information is not always easy, for a variety of reasons, yet library-based information retrieval systems are built on the assumption that consensus about meaning can be reached and that human indexing can be consistent and accurate. Eugene Garfield's (1979) development of citation indexing as an alternative approach to managing and retrieving information was partly driven by a view that human indexing is often inaccurate and imperfect. Garfield was interested in finding a more accurate and objective way of establishing the relationships between texts and between ideas within texts. Citation indexing is based on the practice of scholarly discourse. It is the convention of the modern academy that scholarly papers contain references to other scholarly papers and research reports which suggests that there is some sort of link between these documents. Citation indexes work by linking up the references between papers. But as we have already seen, different types of discourse follow their own discursive codes and conventions. Scholarly practice such as that expected of scientific writing is not necessarily the rule in other kinds of writing. Even within scholarly practice there are differences in the normative practices of different disciplines.

MEANING, CODES AND CONVENTIONS

Determining the intended meaning of media objects where there is no text to stabilize meaning can pose even more of a problem. The production of textual discourse generally involves following the codes and conventions of the chosen discourse. In writing, this can mean adhering to grammatical and syntactical linguistic rules, choosing the appropriate register, choosing the appropriate textual structures and making decisions about paragraphs, chapters and sub-chapters, verses and other structural forms. The question is whether non-textual forms also work within their own codes and conventions.

Semioticians would argue that codes and conventions provide the framework within which signs have meaning. The individual is born into the specific linguistic, textual, social and ideological codes which structure their society, and although it may be possible to question or reject the societal codes, each individual is constructed, to some degree, through the codes and conventions of society, and the codes and conventions of subgroups operating within that society. The specific nature of that construction and its limits remain matters for debate. There is disagreement about the balance between individual agency and structural determinism and about the possibility of autonomous individuality. In this book it is enough to raise the issue, and to acknowledge that there is no settled agreement about matters relating to individuality and subjectivity. A radical anti-humanist argument might question the possibility of individual 'meaning' and agency at all, arguing instead that the creation of cultural and knowledge-based artefacts and the interpretation of cultural and knowledge-based artefacts are functions of society not of individual imagination.

The Italian semiotician and novelist, Umberto Eco (1976) stressed the importance of conventionality in the construction and maintenance of codes. There are conventions accepted by specific societies at specific historical moments which order and structure meaning within codes: in dress codes, for example, these conventions may cover 'formal' and 'informal' clothing and may be related to status and class, indeed, some commentators would argue that all codes and conventions are ideologically bound. Semioticians would argue that 'realism' in art or literature is essentially a diachronically shifting set of conventions about what kinds of representation are considered to signify the real world, for example, the German neo-realism of Fritz Lang was seen as neo-realistic in relation to earlier cinematic styles, while Stanislavsky's method acting was a reaction against the stylization of earlier acting styles. Views about 'realism' or 'stylization' relate to the codes and conventions of culture and aesthetics, not to the natural world or to the real.

There are writers who are interested in the use of semiotics as a micro-analytical method to explore the mechanics of meaning within cultural artefacts such as films, or musical works or, indeed, within novels and poetry, and who are also interested at a macro-level in critical perspectives which attempt to analyse the ways in which culture circulates and operates in contemporary society. Some of these writers and thinkers use Marxist frameworks of analysis through which to examine culture within society. Hodge and Kress's (1988) social semiotics, for example, is materialist and is orientated towards analysing power relationships manifested in and through communicative practices.

For the Marxist-orientated semiotician, specific societies at particular historical moments construct and maintain codes and conventions relating to all aspects of the 'superstructure'. Some of these codes and conventions will be relatively autonomous (for example, the operation of the camera to construct specific filmic conventions), and some will be more general, concerned with the maintenance of the broad ideological codes and conventions necessary to support the economic 'base'. These might include narrative and generic conventions. Using the base/superstructure metaphor offers a framework for analysing the way in which society operates. The *base* refers to the economic base of society which is made up of the mode of production, that is the forces and relations of production. The *superstructure* refers to the political, cultural and social institutions, codes and conventions which operate to reproduce, at the level of culture, the economic base. Elements of the superstructure include the political system, religion, philosophy, morality, art, science, education and library systems.

For Marxist-orientated critical and cultural theorists the codes and conventions which operate within the superstructure are always ideological, that is, they reproduce the stories and ideas through which the ruling class produces its economic dominance at the level of everyday culture. For such thinkers the meaning of a document is always ideological, and the meaning of an individual document can only be determined with reference to the broader codes, conventions and ideologies of the given society within which it was produced, and within which it is consumed.

Ideology is not simply imposed from above and accepted by people without any question, however. For many cultural studies practitioners, the significance of popular cultures and subcultures is that these cultural forms offer space for people to resist and criticize dominant ideologies through the construction of cultural artefacts which have critical meaning encoded within them. The question of making meaning and interpreting meaning in this context becomes almost political. The songs of The Clash and The Manic Street Preachers are obvious examples of cultural artefacts whose meaning is established in the broader context of resisting capitalist ideology. Cultural studies writers have analysed youth subcultures such as the British punk scene in the late 1970s in the same cultural-political terms.

Within any given society there may be a variety of sub-codes and conventions, some of which critique and subvert the dominant codes and conventions. Some cultural commentators use the Gramscian notion of hegemony to describe the relationship between dominant cultural practices and resistant counter-cultural practices. For Gramsci, *hegemony* refers to the way in which dominant ideologies circulate in and through societies with fairly strong social stability, such as British society, to maintain the moral and intellectual leadership of the ruling class. In Gramsci's model, *counter-hegemonic* subversive ideologies emanating from subordinate classes are also allowed to circulate, at least to a degree that the dominant classes can bear. The Manic Street Preachers may write songs full of subversive left-wing lyrics, but they are also a commercial pop band signed up to EMI, a company which is happy to allow the band to peddle subversive lyrics as long as they continue to make money not only for themselves, but also for the record company.

Viewed from this perspective, the full and complete interpretation of a multimedia object is only possible if the interpreter has an understanding and knowledge of societal and aesthetic codes and conventions which operate at the point of production. Moreover, the reading undertaken by any individual reader will be to some degree determined by the codes and conventions of the society and the historical moment in which the reading is taking place. Theorizing the interpretive process in such a way enables us to think about the creation and the interpretation of multimedia objects as being similar to the creation and interpretation of textual objects.

Within the literature of structuralist social theory there are a number of studies which use semiotic frameworks of codes and conventions to analyse the operations of a variety of superstructural forms. An early example of studying non-textual codes and conventions can be found in the work of the structuralist anthropologist, Claude Lévi-Strauss, who used the notion of cultural codes and conventions as a framework through which to analyse the food systems of the Murgin people of North Australia in his study *The Raw and the Cooked* (Lévi-Strauss, 1986 [1964]). Elizabeth Wilson's study of fashion as a modern commodity examined the dress codes which operated in specific subcultures of modern western capitalism at specific historical moments (Wilson, 1985). An earlier fashion-based study is to be found in the work of always innovative philosopher and cultural critic, Roland Barthes, who in 1967 attempted an analysis of the codes and conventions of fashion journalism in his study *The Fashion System* (1985 [1967]).

Music, too, follows its own sets of forms, codes and conventions. Music listeners in western culture have become familiar with the scales and forms of western classical music; however, different cultures have different musical forms. Indian music, for example, is based on its own set of musical scale-modal structures called 'ragas', while Indonesian music is based on two main scales, the five-note slendro, and the seven-note pelog. Recently popular music has used the techniques of sampling and mixing to produce new forms constructed from the remixing of older forms. Such techniques oppose the conventional western capitalist traditions of originality and novelty, and bring with them new ways of listening to and interpreting music, as well as forcing debates about intellectual property issues, which in turn forces examination of the societal codes and conventions of capitalist commodification. A recent advertisement on the music television station *Kiss* promoted a disc jockey (DJ) mixing competition by inviting budding DJs to send in their creative and 'original' mixes. In this cultural environment the meaning of the term 'original' is itself being 'twisted'.

A number of film theorists have discussed the 'constructedness' of film, arguing that the structure and features of film are based on specific codes and conventions created and maintained by generations of film-makers. The argument is that film is not so much a reflection of reality as we experience it in the material world, but the implementation of film codes and conventions so that what we, as filmgoers, identify as verisimilitude is a matter of codes and conventions that we have come to read as 'real'. Daniel Chandler makes the point that what was considered 'real' in silent film is quite different from the 'real' in contemporary film (Chandler, 2002, p. 162). Christian Metz (1974) argued that while filmic codes and conventions are not of the same nature as language, lacking the equivalent of phonemes, the arbitrary sign and the double articulation of language (double articulation refers to the fact that the minimal sign units in language, sounds or letters have differences which give them meaning and these units can be connected together at the level of words to produce units which have difference and meaning in relation to other words), nevertheless, film is discourse with signifying practices. Metz argued that meaning in film comes not from individual units but from the ways in which these units are connected together to form plot order and story order. The process of making a film depends on the selection and combination of images and sounds, and the viewing and interpreting (reading) of photographs and film are, for Metz, learned processes.

PANOFSKY AND LEVELS OF MEANING

In the domain of image indexing and retrieval, writers have acknowledged that establishing the meaning of images is a complex business (for example, Brown and Hidderley, 1995; Burke, 1999; Enser, 1993b, 1993c, 1995b; Enser and Cawkell, 1994; Enser and McGregor, 1992; Fidal, 1997; Krause, 1988; Layne, 1994; Rasmussen, 1997; Shatford, 1984, 1986; Shatford-Layne, 1994; Svenonius, 1994). Enser and Burke in particular have referred to Panofsky's 'levels of meaning' model as a way of thinking about the operation of meaning in images. In his essay 'Iconography and iconology' (1993 [1955]), the art historian Erwin Panofsky identified different types of meaning in art and constructed a framework of meaning which he then applied to the interpretation of Renaissance art. Panofsky distinguished between three different levels of meaning which are:

1. *Primary or natural subject matter:* which are subdivided into *factual* and *expressional* subject matter. This is the pre-iconographical level of art:

   It is apprehended by identifying pure forms that is: certain configurations of line and colour, or certain peculiarly shaped lumps of bronze or stone, as representations of natural objects such as human beings, animals, plants, houses, tools and so forth; by identifying their mutual relations as events; and by perceiving such expressional qualities as the mournful character of a pose or gesture, or the homelike and peaceful atmosphere of an interior. The world of pure forms thus recognised as carriers of primary or natural meanings may be called the world of artistic motifs. (Ibid., pp. 53–4)

2. *Secondary or conventional subject matter:* identifying the male figure in the painting with the knife as St Bartholomew (ibid., p. 54). This level of subject matter depends on cultural knowledge and is called the iconographical level of art. The artist would have consciously wanted to depict the specific

13

character. Panofsky argued that expressional qualities might well be unintentional.

3. *Intrinsic meaning or content*: 'It is apprehended by ascertaining those underlying principles which reveal the basic attitude of a nation, a period, a class, a religious or philosophical persuasion – qualified by one personality and condensed into one work' (ibid., p. 55). The compositional and iconographical features are interpreted as more particularized evidence of 'something else'. This level of meaning depends on the viewer synthesizing information gathered at the first two levels of meaning with additional information which might include information about the artist and the socio-political cultural moment of production. A work of art might be interpreted as evidence of Leonardo's personality, or 'of the civilization of the Italian High Renaissance, or a peculiar religious attitude' (ibid., p. 55). It involves historical, psychological or critical approaches to art. Achieving iconological interpretation depends on having 'synthetic intuition', according to Panofsky, an attribute which might be more often found in the talented layperson than the erudite scholar. Where this level of meaning depends on 'subjective and irrational' sources it is all the more important that 'objective' correctives relating, for example, to documentary sources and history are applied.

Panofsky's model has been used by information theorists interested in mapping the specificities of meaning in images. Peter Enser (1995b) related Panofsky's levels of meaning to images in general, arguing that iconography refers to specifics, pre-iconongraphy refers to generics and iconology refers to abstract meaning, while Mary Burke constructed her own version of Panofsky's table of levels of meaning (1999). Both Burke and Enser emphasize the subjective interpretational aspects of iconological content, but it is worth remembering Panofsky's own insistence that the more such interpretation is based on individual psychology and '*Weltanshauung*' or world-view, the more crucial it is that objective correctives be applied.

At the first level of meaning, Panofsky wrote about the 'natural' subject matter which included expressional content. He assumed that qualities such as mournfulness or homelike atmospheres as represented in art forms are 'natural'. A critical theory approach would ask whether such qualities are learnt rather than given. Determining such qualities as a viewer might be fairly subjective. A comparative and historical approach to art forms might begin to offer some empirical evidence about whether expressional content is natural or cultural.

Earlier in this chapter it was argued that traditional textbooks of librarianship have often downplayed the complexities of reading texts and establishing the meanings of texts. The adaptation of Panofsky's model is evidence that as information professionals have had to engage with issues about managing multimedia documents, so they have become interested in debates about meaning, interpretation and communication. Panofsky's levels of meaning are clearly of some interest but there are other approaches to modelling communication and interpretation. Later in the book we will focus on using semiotics to analyse the mechanics of meaning and communication in multimedia artefacts. In the next chapter we provide an introductory overview to information retrieval in general.

2 An overview of information retrieval

INTRODUCTION

In this chapter the nature of information retrieval (IR) is discussed from two broad perspectives: the first approach is one which might be described as the theoretical approach of conventional library and information science (LIS), the principles and practices of which do not necessarily depend on computer systems; while the second approach might be described as the computer application viewpoint. Information professionals and their theories and practices have influenced many of the computerized IR applications, and significant overlaps are apparent between the two viewpoints. The main aim of this chapter is to identify key themes in mainly text-based IR that are useful in a discussion about multimedia information retrieval (MMIR) in Chapter 3.

Subsections in this chapter will provide introductions to the following topics:

- knowledge organization in libraries, specifically cataloguing and classification
- information retrieval: a systems perspective including text-based information retrieval systems; computer indexes of documents created by human intervention and computerized bibliographic records
- bibliographic approaches to web resources including Dublin Core
- other approaches to IR and aspects of computerised, text-based IR
- key questions for computerized IR.

WHAT IS IR?

Information retrieval systems operate on the assumption that information is a thing (Buckland, 1991) that can be stored, organized, described, catalogued, classified and retrieved. Reference was made in Chapter 1 to the traditional approach to subject indexing (Berwick Sayers and Maltby, 1967; Wyner, 1980) which often takes the view that the communication process is relatively straightforward, and that an understanding of the meaning of any recorded information is shared by encoders (indexers) and decoders (retrievers), and is relatively static. Views about the communication process and the operation of meaning in and through recorded information are important as they can facilitate and limit the design and construction of information retrieval tools.

The proliferation of texts in the modern age of print and electronic culture, and the growth in demand for instantaneous access, has increased the need for information retrieval tools to mediate between the text (information-as-thing) and the user. Within the literature of library management there has been a tendency to write about the tools of managing information as if they are universal and almost 'natural', which in turn suggests that the assumptions on which they are based are equally universal and absolute. But this is not the case. The tools which have been developed to manage information and knowledge are historically determined. This implies that the assumptions on which the management of information and knowledge are based are also historically determined. The literature of hypertext suggests that this hypothesis is reasonable.

KNOWLEDGE ORGANIZATION IN LIBRARIES

Traditionally, librarians have been the curators of information held in documents, and to varying degrees, depending on specific historical and geographical junctures, facilitators of access to information in documents. Sources of information managed by libraries are based on the document as the dominant medium of communication. Many representations of human knowledge are not textual, for example photographs, images, art, other aesthetic forms, music, sound recordings of human voice, film, television programmes and filmed versions of drama. The approach in librarianship to managing non-textual documents has been to adapt the codes and conventions originally developed to manage access to textual documents for non-textual information. In cataloguing practice, the Anglo-American Cataloguing Rules (AACR) (Joint Steering Committee for Revision of AACR, 2002) includes chapters dealing with the specific needs of a range of non-textual media, for example, music, sound recordings, maps and cartographic materials. The real challenge for information retrieval theorists and practitioners is to develop indexing methods which properly address the question of subject access.

CATALOGUING: THE DESCRIPTION AND NAMING OF THINGS

Definitions about the purpose, structure and function of the library catalogue can be found in a number of textbooks. Hunter and Bakewell (1991, p. xx) defined the catalogue as 'a list of documents and other materials in a collection or collections'. Mary Piggott wrote that:

> Such a list is necessary because the librarian cannot store in his [sic] memory all the information about the books and other materials in the library which is likely to be wanted by his readers, nor can he be available personally to conduct the readers to all the books they need to see. The catalogue stands in as his permanent substitute to answer all the simpler questions about what is in the library and where it is to be found. It is a medium of communication, necessarily formal, but not necessarily formidable. (Piggott, 1988, p. 1)

Underlying the principles and practice of cataloguing lie the assumptions that:

- information is a 'thing' which can be recorded and stored in an appropriate media form (document) to facilitate access and retrieval
- the document is complete, finished and in the public domain
- the materiality of the document can be described
- the description can be transcribed on to some sort of surrogate – the catalogue record.

Information in this context is that which can be captured in some medium and which can be exchanged and shared with other humans. Information storage and retrieval activities within the library and information profession are thus socially orientated activities. This approach limits the domain which is of concern to the library and information science discipline and profession. Conversation, for example, contains information, but it can only be managed if it is captured and stored on some sort of storage medium. It can only become the object of interest for library and information professionals when it is recorded materially in a form which abstracts it from its human origins.

Behind the catalogue lie the notion of the 'document', and the notion that information is somehow a 'thing'. Information becomes objects and, because constructed as objects, it can be bought and sold: it can be exchanged. In our society, within which library and information professionals have specific roles as curators, facilitators and managers, information becomes commodified objects. This in turn leads to the emphasis placed in our society on notions of individuality, authorship and originality, as well as the associated issues relating to copyright, intellectual ownership, plagiarism, copying, referencing, acknowledgement and citation.

The assumption in library cataloguing and in the management of library documents is that the document is complete and finalized. To a certain extent the philosophy of cataloguing is one which reifies the document – documents are treated as products, finished objects – constructed, final, whole and complete, while less emphasis is placed on the social processes of publishing – the production and reception regimes in society. Clearly an important aspect of this traditional philosophical approach is that information is assumed to exist in the shape of complete and finished documents that are assumed to be whole entities which can be described and which have a recognizable identity.

Library and information science writers agree that the purposes of a catalogue are to:

- record stock
- describe physical aspects
- facilitate user access to stock through 'access points' (usually author, title and subject access points)
- help in housekeeping functions
- function as the 'living memory' of a library. The catalogue record is a record of the document which will be permanently in the catalogue even if the document is out on loan.

The catalogue provides information about the location of the resource and about collocation by showing what the library has by a given author, on a given subject and in a given form. Moreover, library cataloguing codes and conventions enable the library to provide information which can help a library user make decisions about specific editions and about the subject or form of the document. The library catalogue entry is made up of both descriptive elements and what are called access points, or index entries.

The Anglo-American Cataloguing Rules (2002) remains the 'cataloguers' bible'. These rules consist of codes and conventions for the description of a wide range of media types and the formation of appropriate access points. There are separate chapters within the AACR for a broad range of media: sound recordings, film, maps and cartographic materials, and so on. Each specialist chapter contains rules about exactly how to describe the medium in question, with specific and particular rules pertaining to the physical form of each medium.

The widespread acceptance of information retrieval standards such as International Standard Bibliographical Descriptions (ISBDs), International Standard Book Number (ISBN), International Standard Serial Number (ISSN), machine-readable cataloguing (MARC) and Dublin Core, has been an important catalyst for the commodification of information retrieval products and services in the LIS field. Standardization means that it is easier to exchange information about resources. Standardization of cataloguing rules and conventions has also facilitated the commercialization of the cataloguing process. As early as 1902, the Library of Congress realized the commercial potential in providing centralized cataloguing services, at a price, to American libraries, and sent out a circular which offered printed catalogue cards at 'generous prices'. Large commercial bibliographic suppliers such as OCLC now provide not only cataloguing services, but have also diversified into related information management services and products.

The catalogue record traditionally contains information recording the description of the document being catalogued, the main entry heading and added entries, the subject headings and the classification mark or call number. The codes and conventions in the AACR are used by librarians to construct the bibliographic descriptions and main and added entries. Main and added entries are used to provide access or retrieval points which allow library users to access the whole catalogue record. Codified standards such as Sears List of Subject Headings (SLOSH) or the Library of Congress Subject Headings (LCSH) may be used to assign subject headings to text-based documents. General library classification schemes such as Dewey Decimal Classification (DDC) or Library of Congress Classification (LC) might be used to assign an appropriate classification mark.

The AACR provides explicit detailed rules about exactly how to set out descriptive information pertaining to various types of documents, and these rules include using highly conventionalized symbols in the form of punctuation marks to separate and introduce specific information fields. An AACR-based catalogue record might look something like that in Figure 2.1.

In contemporary catalogue practice it is usual for libraries to adhere to the MARC standard. The MARC format is a set of codes and content designators defined for encoding bibliographic records. The MARC format is primarily a communications medium allowing the exchange of bibliographic records and thus facilitating shared cataloguing. The most recent implementation of MARC standard codes is MARC 21 which is defined by the Library of Congress as:

> MARC 21 is an implementation of the American national standard, *Information Interchange Format* (ANSI Z39.2) and its international counterpart, *Format for Information Exchange* (ISO 2709). These standards specify the requirements for a generalized interchange format that will accommodate data describing all forms of materials susceptible to bibliographic description, as well as related information such

---

Olson, Hope.
The power to name: locating the limits of subject representation in libraries / by Hope A. Olson. – Dordrecht, London : Kluwer Academic, 2002.
261 p. – 10 in.
Includes bibliographic references and index.

ISBN 1-4020-0776-0

Figure 2.1   AACR2 rev. edn catalogue record

as authority, classification, community information, and holdings data. The standards present a generalized structure for records, but do not specify the content of the record and do not, in general, assign meaning to tags, indicators, or data element identifiers. Specification of these elements are provided by particular implementations of the standards. (MARC 21, 2000)

LIBRARY CLASSIFICATION: IMPOSING ORDER ON KNOWLEDGE

In his textbook on cataloguing and classification, Wynar defined a classification scheme as 'an orderly distribution of the universe into groups of main subjects or classes. A class is, broadly speaking, any group of entities exhibiting one or more common characteristics or traits' (Wynar, 1980, p. 391).

The 'subject approach' to information retrieval is based on the view that to create a complete information retrieval system, surrogates (catalogue records) which consist of a physical description of the document (author, title, number of pages, size) are not enough in themselves: surrogate summary records of the meaning of the document – both the 'ofness' and 'aboutness' of the document – need to be recorded and used as possible retrieval access points. Traditionally, the 'subject approach' in LIS seeks to satisfy two requirements in an information retrieval system within a library:

- to provide subject access points in the catalogue
- to organize the physical documents on shelves.

The classic nineteenth-century general or universal classification schemes were created specifically with the physical organization of documents in mind. Open access to library shelves was facilitated through the use of general classification schemes which could be used to shelve documents in subject order.

Classification proceeds from the assumption that 'knowledge' can be mapped within a mental space, and the resulting structure made material in the form of a classification schedule which contains lists of subject terms and accompanying notations.

General classification schemes for libraries are concerned with mapping knowledge so that subjects are differentiated from each other and the relationships between subjects are spatially represented. Classification theorists believe that there is some sort of 'order of things' and that the order, which relates to the abstract world of ideas, can be made material in the form of highly conventionalized, symbolically annotated classification schemes. The general library classification system developed into a tool consisting of a system of classes, made up of main classes, each of which was divided into increasingly specialized sub-classes; a series of symbols, called notation, which operate as signs signifying the classes; and an index which links subject terms and the notational signs (Rafferty, 2001).

Library classification schemes are usually made up of three components: schedules, notation and index.

1. *Schedules*: subjects are listed systematically showing relationships. In many textbooks from the 1960s and 1970s onwards the tendency has been to downplay the importance of philosophical frameworks and foundations in influencing creators of classification schemes to organize knowledge in particular ways, and to emphasize the pragmatic purposes of classification theory. But classification schemes were created by specific individuals who were the products of their societies and their times.

   The philosophical framework through which the creator of the classic enumerative library classification scheme viewed knowledge determined the ways in which the order of subjects and the relationships between subjects were represented in the schedules. There is no one 'natural' structure of knowledge: the order of things as determined by creators of library classification schemes is constructed and historically contingent. H.E. Bliss, the creator of the Bibliographic Classification scheme, took the view that 'knowledge should be organized in consistency with the scientific and educational consensus, which is relatively stable and tends to become so as theory and system become more definitely established in general and increasingly in detail' (Berwick Sayers, 1955, p. 190). What is of interest in the context of this book and this argument is that the focus for Bliss, whose main class order is considered to be particularly successful, is clearly on 'knowledge' which is seen as the domain of scholarship, but a scholarship which is based on a positivist, scientific world view. There are few solutions in this knowledge-based approach for dealing with aesthetic and cultural information except through the prism of knowledge.

2. *Notation*: the notation is the 'artificial language' constructed to represent the subjects recorded in the schedules. Some classification theorists, for example Paul Otlet and S.R. Ranganathan, viewed the artificial language of classification as being in some ways 'purer' and better suited to international communication than what Ranganathan called 'natural language'. Otlet used Dewey's decimal notation as a natural language that he could use to attach to the 'facts' which he believed were to be found in even the most opinionated and subjective document. These 'facts' in the form of artificial language would be stored on catalogue cards in a huge index which covered all documents in all languages in the world. Otlet's world view, like that of Bliss, was positivist, and for him there was a clear distinction between subjective 'opinion', which he was not interested in for his International Institute of Bibliography, and 'fact'. He believed that fact could be extracted from documents and captured on catalogue cards inscribed in an international language based on the DDC,

but developed to encompass syntactical relationships as well as representational relationships.

S.R. Ranganathan believed in the notion of international language, but he also believed that there were phenomenological experiences which the individual could not communicate in existing 'natural languages' but which could be contextualized and described in his notational language. Ranganathan, too, viewed the notational language that he developed for the Colon Classification scheme as a translation tool, but translation in this context was not Otlet's positivist reductionism of extracting fact from opinion, subjectivity, perspective and bias as if there was no relationship between all of these elements; it was about translating from the subjectivity of consciousness to a public discourse using notational language. Ranganathan's world view was idealist and metaphysical. He believed that individuals can have metaphysical experiences, related often to spiritual or religious domains or the domain of aesthetic experience, which cannot be expressed in 'natural' language, but had to be expressed through what Goethe called a divine language. This metaphysical 'meaning' cannot be expressed in its 'bareness and purity' but when the idea is considered in the context of different subjects, its different 'contextual transforms' can be expressed by different words (Ranganathan, 1951, p. 70).

Through the faceted approach of Colon, which unlike the rigidity of enumerative schemes attempts to create a flexible organization of subjects which can be fitted together like a Meccano set, and through the notation that he developed, Ranganathan sought to create an expressive language which could represent the metaphysical 'meaning' of the most subjective idea. Of all the classic library classificationists, Ranganathan alone attempted to construct a system which goes beyond the bounds of positivist science-based knowledge. His system is not much used in libraries, partly because his world view was so very different to the approaches taken by western library scientists, but Ranganathan is considered by theorists and philosophers of information to have been possibly the most influential classification theorist and philosopher of the twentieth century. For the purposes of this book, he is of interest because of his attempt to represent the aesthetic, the metaphysical and the subjective. One might, after Volosinov, wonder whether ideas and even metaphysical subjectivity are formed through and in the language of specific historical societies, through dialogue, but nevertheless, Ranganathan's acknowledgement that information retrieval schemes should deal with more than knowledge as it is defined and accepted by western positivist science was, and still is, an interesting contribution to the field.

3. *Index*: the entry point to the scheme. The index comprises a list of subject terms alphabetically organized with a location mark beside each term.

The schedules of the general classification schemes consist of main classes which are systematically subdivided into increasingly specific subject terms. Main classes are determined by the creator of the scheme and are always constructed, and historically determined. The DDC consists of 10 main classes and a numerical notation; Henry Evelyn Bliss (1939) used both numbers and alphabetic notation to represent main classes; the Library of Congress classification scheme has 26 main classes and uses a notation based on alphabetical symbols. A comparison of the order of classes in Bliss's Bibliographic Classification (Figure 2.2) and the People's University of China's library classification (Figure 2.3) clearly shows the constructed and ideological nature of main classes in library classification schemes.

The classic general classification schemes were created to manage 'knowledge' in libraries. The approach to subjects is academic and scholarly in nature. This approach means that traditional library classification schemes are not flexible enough to deal with the subject approach in relation to information which is not knowledge based, that is, based on interpretation and/or multiple viewpoints. We have already seen that many of the issues of interest to the domain of non-textual information, particularly where that information is cultural

---

Classes 1–9 – Universe of knowledge, Communications

Class A – Philosophy; Logic; Mathematics; Statistics

Class B – Physics; Physics-based technology

Class C – Chemistry; Materials technology

Class D – Astronomy and space science; Earth sciences; Geography

Class E–G – Biology; Botany; Zoology

Class H–I – Health sciences; Psychology

Class J – Education

Class K – Sociology; Customs; Folklore; Ethnography

Classes L–O – History

Class P – Religion; the Occult; Morals and Ethics

Class Q – Applied Social Science and Ethics

Class R – Political science

Class S – Jurisprudence and Law

Class T – Economics; Management

Class U – Arts: useful, industrial and less scientific technology

Class V – Fine arts

Class W/Y – Philology, languages and literature

Class Z – Bibliobiology, Bibliography and Libraries

Figure 2.2   Bliss's order of classes

Part 1. Theory of Knowledge
1 Marxism, Leninism, Mao Tse-tung thought
2 Philosophy and materialism, historical and dialectical materialism, religion, atheism

Part 2. Knowledge of the Class Struggle.
3 Social science, political science
4 Politics, Economics.
5 State defence, Military science
6 State and law
7 Culture and Education
8 Arts
9 Language
10 Literature
11 History and History of the Revolution
12 Geography

Part 3. Knowledge of the Productive Struggle
13 Natural science
14 Medicine
15 Technology
16 Agriculture

Figure 2.3   The main classes in the Classification Scheme of the People's University of China

rather than knowledge based, have been debated within the literature of fiction indexing (Beghtol, 1989; 1990; 1994; 1995; Pejtersen, 1978; 1979; 1993; Saarti, 1999; 2000a; 2000b; 2002) and it is in the area of fiction that a number of information retrieval approaches have been developed which seek to deal with cultural information in ways which are not knowledge based and scholarly but which recognize the cultural, leisure and pleasure aspects of fiction.

There have been many attempts to develop fiction retrieval systems to deal with the topical or subject access to works of fiction in the absence of suitable approaches in general classification schemes. Petjersen's Bookhouse graphical user interface (GUI)-fronted catalogue was built on the Analysis and Mediation of Publications (AMP) framework which Pejtersen developed to represent the multidimensional indexing needed to achieve rich subject access to fiction (Pejtersen, 1978; 1979; 1993). This project is among the most scholarly of all the fiction retrieval projects.

The GUI-fronted, interactive Bookhouse system was built on empirical research undertaken by Pejtersen to determine the types of requests options that fiction readers would find useful in a fiction retrieval system. The design brief which resulted from the research was to design an OPAC (Online Public Access Catalogue) system which would incorporate the following framework for subject analysis:

1. Author's goals and values
   (a) Author's intention
   (b) Author's affiliation and attitudes
2. General and specific topic content of the book
   (a) General frame/time content
   (b) General frame/setting content
   (c) Subject matter content
   (d) Living beings, institutions and artefacts
3. Communication and presentation of book format
   (a) Literary form
   (b) Accessibility level
   (c) Physical characteristics
4. Publication attributes
   (a) Bibliographic data and identification numbers
5. Library attributes
   (a) Library goals and policies
   (b) Local library conditions (Pejtersen, 1994).

Bookhouse was first implemented in the late 1980s. More recently, library users have been encouraged to write annotations in some Bookhouse libraries, not least because indexing a book using the Bookhouse template takes a long time. Although the system includes a thesaurus of controlled terms and rules for indexing which were developed to ensure a consistent and suitable vocabulary, and to reduce as far as possible the subjectivity of judgements within categories such as 'author intentions', the issue of interpretation is still debated. Even with its detailed indexing template, the question of individual interpretation of fictional texts by indexers and by readers still remains an issue.

Librarians in the UK have begun to become interested in fiction retrieval and in 'reader development' promotional activities which provide subject access to fiction and encourage fiction reading, perhaps influenced by the sophisticated retrieval tools created and implemented by Amazon.com, a commercial site which sees the value of investing in information (bibliographic information) and interpretation (for example, readers' reviews) for material and economic ends (Rafferty, 2001). Branching Out, a reader development scheme supported by public libraries in England and Wales developed a fiction retrieval system, Book Forager, now relaunched as whichbook.com, which attempts to facilitate access to fiction through effective subject searching.

Branching Out's whichbook.net (2003) runs on software developed by Applied Psychology Research. The philosophy underpinning the whichbook.net fiction retrieval system is that as the 'subject approach' to fiction is multidimensional, fiction retrieval systems should allow readers to search for fiction using a form of affective dimension searching rather than confining searches to known-item searching or to genre-based searching. The books which make up the project's data-set are read by a team of 150 people drawn from public libraries and literature organizations who have been trained to create entries. The system has been built on the assumption that it is possible to train people to interpret both the fictional texts and the controlled vocabulary of the whichbook.net indexing language in a relatively standard way. It has been designed on the principle that meaning resides (almost) entirely within the text and that its representation within the artificial language of the indexing system is fairly straightforward and unproblematic.

The initiatives developed by fiction retrieval workers are of particular interest to those involved with the development of retrieval systems for non-knowledge-based multimedia documents, for example, certain types of photographs and images, moving and still, and music. Traditional library classification schemes developed for knowledge-based documents are of limited use for dealing with non-knowledge-based documents, despite the ironic fact that current LIS and philosophy scholarship identifies the scope of informational objects of interest to LIS as being broader than that which counts as knowledge for the epistemology of social knowledge (for example, Floridi, 2002).

FACETED CLASSIFICATION

The universal schemes created in the late nineteenth century were based on the assumption that knowledge could be represented in the form of hierarchical subdivisions, the order of which could be arrived at rationally. Ranganathan's Colon Classification was the first universal classification scheme based entirely on faceted principles. Contemporary classification schemes, including the revisions of the great nineteenth-century schemes, now routinely include faceted principles, and specialist classification schemes tend to be constructed using faceted principles.

Faceted classification schemes develop from a different philosophical approach than the assumptions and philosophy of enumerative schemes. In the faceted approach, distinct subject areas are analysed into facets, or aspects of the subject, and within those facets, single concepts, or isolates in Ranganathan's language, are identified and listed. The facets and isolates are arrived at rationally, based on literary warrant; in other words, the single concepts are drawn from the literature of the subject. To build a classification number the analyst synthesizes the single concepts to construct a class number. This is sometimes called the analytico-synthetic principle. Using faceted analysis to deconstruct a subject area can act as a useful basis for the identification of vocabulary from which to construct a thesaurus. Indeed, the Thesauro-Facet is an example of a hybrid retrieval system which combines the hierarchical organization and display of a classification scheme with the alphabetical representation of a thesaurus.

The notion of faceted classification forms the basis of the development of most contemporary classification schemes which are constructed to deal with specific subject domains. In the domain of image retrieval, Enser and Orr's (1993) classification scheme developed for Hulton Deutsch is a faceted classification scheme. This scheme includes facets relating to people, places, activities and emotions. Such a scheme might work very well in terms of dealing with concrete known aspects of images. It is reasonably easy to identify persons if they are persons who have lived their lives in the public domain. What becomes more difficult to establish is exactly what emotions might be represented in an image. Accompanying text can help, but, of course, accompanying text itself can be misleading. An image which lacks accompanying text, such as newspaper captions, is open to interpretation by the indexer. It is probable that agreement becomes more difficult as the facets become more abstract.

IR FROM THE PERSPECTIVE OF COMPUTER APPLICATIONS

Information retrieval applications are not new. Since the 1960s computer systems have been constructed to automate or enhance the work of information professionals. These systems have reproduced the methods and approaches used to classify, organize and retrieve information developed in pre-computer times. Over the last 40 years the opportunities to apply the work capacity of computer systems have led to new approaches to IR problems that would have been prohibitively expensive or physically impossible without such systems; such approaches include full-text analysis and retrieval (Salton, 1989). With the advent of computer-mediated information networks, such as the Internet and the World Wide Web (the Web), not only have the opportunities and demands for IR-like systems grown but so have the search for new solutions to the problems of IR. An example of such a solution is the 'markup language' (standard generalized markup language – SGML: extensible markup language – XML) efforts currently being applied to web pages and digital archives.

INFORMATION RETRIEVAL: A SYSTEMS PERSPECTIVE

In the world of computer systems data, information and knowledge are often difficult to distinguish and the focus tends to shift to technical issues of representation and processing. An example of this can be seen in the way information (or data) is stored and processed.

Traditionally in the computer application world there have been two, fairly distinct, approaches to data management. The first, and most common approach, is the data-processing orientated approach which began with files and programs and is currently with relational database management systems (RDBMSs). The world view of such systems is one of a highly structured and defined environment, a 'structuralists' dream. In many ways the meaning of the contents of these structures is incidental: it is only important, from the computer application developers' perspective, in determining the structure of the containers (relations in the RDBMS) and the processing which might be applied to them. This is not to criticize the value of such systems, they clearly satisfy a whole range of data-processing problems common in today's business world and without them most companies would cease to function. This approach to data and information has its IR parallel, in the 'card-index', rigidly structured catalogue record of library systems. Indeed, such computerized reproductions of library systems were among the earliest computer applications in the IR area and are still produced today.

The second approach takes the text as the primary focus of a (text-based) IR system. This approach, sometimes referred to as a 'full-text' approach, recognizes that the richness and subtlety of the meaning of a text may be lost in its translation into a five-line index entry. Such systems often try to improve the user access to the collection of texts so that users may better express their needs and gain improved, more relevant, results from their use of the system. However, the key difference between this approach and the preceding one is that the contents are of paramount importance to the system rather than the structure. Of course the contents have structure, being written in some natural language, and so one finds systems that attempt to understand the language so that retrievals based on the meaning of the contents may be made.

As far as computerized IR is concerned there are four key questions to consider in any system or approach, irrespective of what software, programming language or computer theory is applied. These are:

1. What is stored (what is the 'item' in the system)?
2. How is the item, 'taken on'?
3. What is the user able to ask for and how (query language/interface)?
4. How is the item indexed?

There is overlap between these questions; for example 'How is the item indexed?' has a close relationship to the answer to 'What is the user able to ask for?' but the focus of the question remains distinct and leads to different aspects of the system being assessed. It is often the case that a system may have, for example, a particularly comprehensive set of stored items (the complete text of every book recorded) but the user interface only facilitates searching by author and title.

There is a fifth question that, in part, is implied by the answers to the first four but which is of particular concern to the computer scientists creating the software, namely:

5. How is 'matching' performed between user query and stored item?

The answer to this question may be facilitated by the answers to the first four questions and it may limit the scope of the answers to the same questions. Software engineers like to treat programs and processes in a 'black box' fashion (encapsulation) so that a 'user' of the process does not need to know how the process performs the activity but simply that it is reliable and the method of communication (its interface). This should only be of concern if the driving force for a system's design is the fifth question rather than the first four. This issue is discussed further in Chapter 3 in relation to systems dealing with image retrieval.

INFORMATION RETRIEVAL SYSTEMS (TEXT BASED)

There are good overviews of text-based IR in both Chowdhury (1999) and Baeza-Yates and Ribeiro-Neto (1999) the latter being more orientated to computer science than the former.

Chowdhury's (1999, p. 14) taxonomy of databases provides a useful starting point. He describes two major types of database, reference and source databases. Reference databases are subdivided into bibliographic, catalogue and referral types. Source databases are generally of less interest here but include full-text databases that are discussed below. Chowdhury's taxonomy, then, focuses on the questions of 'item' and 'index' (questions 1 and 4 above).

Baeza-Yates and Ribeiro-Neto (1999, p. 20) describe a taxonomy of IR models (as opposed to databases). Their emphasis is on the approach to retrieval adopted in an IR system. Their taxonomy has three broad types; Boolean, Vector and Probabilistic. These types refer to the way a user query is compared to a set of documents using keywords as the primary method of description. All three approaches rely on statistical methods to compare user queries with document descriptions (index entries). The Boolean approach is the oldest and is considered to be the least effective, the Probabilistic the most complex. However, the Vector model is generally the most popular and possibly the most effective approach. It is this approach that is often used in web-based search engines. Their taxonomy, it is worth observing, focuses on the fifth question, that of the 'matching process'.

Rather than repeat the taxonomies outlined above, a further analysis based on identifying where index entries are derived from and how those index entries are generated is outlined below. Three main approaches to computerized index generation may be identified. These are:

1 Index of documents created by human intervention.
2. Index entries created by a computer program without (much) human intervention.
3. Fully automated indexing.

Why is this important? First, there is an issue about what is being indexed. Is the index representing the items or the interpretation of those items? If the former, then an automated approach may be adequate if the item contains information in a form that facilitates the direct mapping between itself and the index. However, if the item only indirectly includes indications of relevance to the index, then human intervention is increasingly likely, for example, the interpretation of some poetry might demand more than the index of the words used in the text. Secondly, what is the purpose of the index? If it is for use by computer systems then an automated approach is more than likely to be successful but if it is for human use then some human mediation (by the indexers and/or by the users) is very likely to be required. Finally, is the index a model of a 'single truth' or 'multiple interpretations'? If it is the former, then an automated system may be sufficient; if the latter, then an automated system is unlikely to be satisfactory.

However, these broad approaches may overly simplify a range of variations that may have a significant effect on the performance of a retrieval system. The issues that are important in determining the scope and performance of a text-based IR system include:

- index structure (often determined by human intervention)
- keywords used (or codes used)
- the focus of the software (that is, *what* is indexed? – title, author, contents?)
- user needs (what retrievals are anticipated)
- how are queries expressed? (effort and may they evolve? – feedback)
- how easy are modifications made to the index and index entries? (retrospective updates?)
- relevance of responses (retrieved items – for example, *Recall & Precision* – Baeza-Yates and Ribeiro-Neto, 1999, p. 75).

These issues mirror the factors that affect the performance of non-computerized indexing systems. The use of a computer system by no means guarantees the elimination of problems caused by poor choices.

COMPUTER INDEX OF DOCUMENTS CREATED BY HUMAN INTERVENTION

We might characterize this approach as the computerization of a card-index based catalogue. This approach offers some advantages over the physical card indexes that were so common in libraries until relatively recently. First, the index may be searched on attributes like author, title and publisher relatively quickly; such queries may even be expressed in a Boolean query language. Entries are unlikely to be lost or defaced (unlike cards) and may be corrected very quickly. Additionally, the card-index space is saved and access to the index may be provided from a variety of locations via computer networks (worldwide if linked to the Internet). These advantages have lead to the replacement of physical card-based indexes in almost all major libraries.

There are, however, some limitations. First, a simple system based on cards, that may even be handwritten, is replaced by a complex computer system that will require maintenance and resources (money, space, equipment and so on) for it to continue. Secondly, almost no attempt is made to 'add value' to the index, so it is not uncommon to find computerized catalogues reproducing the limited author, title, subject (single subject often based on a Dewey-like classification structure) paradigm. Finally, these systems rely on human input to maintain the index, for example new acquisitions and index structures, and to decide how the individual item is to be classified based on the index and knowledge of the item's contents.

This approach offers a limited number of benefits for index users and relatively little for providers (except, perhaps, availability). A significant problem with this approach is the relatively static nature of the index; any modifications needed owing to new acquisitions or new knowledge are time-consuming to apply retrospectively to the existing items. This process is essentially dependent on the same people who originally classified the items.

COMPUTERIZED BIBLIOGRAPHIC RECORDS

An important sub-category of this general approach is the use of specialized bibliographic formats to encode bibliographic data, possibly with the intention of sharing the information with other organisations.

Chowdhury (1999, pp. 26–55) describes bibliographic records in some detail. Typically there are three major components of bibliographic data:

1. Physical structure (essentially, a technical specification of the format of the computerized data).
2. Content designators (codes to identify the different data elements, like the tags in hypertext markup language – HTML).
3. Content (the 'stuff' of the entry, closely tied to the designators and possibly limited by type, for example jpeg files for images, .pdf files for documents).

The essence of this approach is one that mirrors the 'card-index' approach. People determine the entries within a relatively rigid structure. The advantages of this approach are that standards are available (for example, MARC and Universal Machine Readable Cataloguing – UNIMARC), databases exist based on the standards and, therefore, their contents may be accessible by a wide audience (wider than the host organization).

BIBLIOGRAPHIC APPROACHES TO WEB RESOURCES

It is interesting to observe that the bibliographic approach has echoes in the Markup Language approach that we will meet later when we discuss multimedia indexing.

Dublin Core is an initiative which has been developed to facilitate at least a basic level of 'ordering' to web-based resources which can be much more fluid and changeable than the types of documents which libraries have traditionally dealt with. The original information resources for which Dublin Core was developed were called document-like objects (DLOs) written in HTML as simple web pages. The idea was that metadata informational elements would be embedded within these DLOs and would remain static and complete in themselves like the traditional card catalogue (Lagoze, 2001).

The Dublin Core Initiative takes the view that the Dublin Core framework for the description and 'ordering' of digital document-like objects is a 'prominent candidate' for resource discovery systems because of its:

- *Simplicity*: the Dublin Core is intended to be usable by non-cataloguers as well as resource description specialists. Most of the elements have a commonly understood semantics of roughly the complexity of a library catalogue card.
- *Semantic Interoperability*: in the Internet Commons, disparate description models interfere with the ability to search across discipline boundaries. Promoting a commonly understood set of descriptors that helps to unify other data content standards increases the possibility of semantic interoperability across disciplines.
- *International Consensus Recognition* of the international scope of resource discovery on the web is critical to the development of effective discovery infrastructure. The Dublin Core benefits from active participation and promotion in some 20 countries in North America, Europe, Australia and Asia.
- *Extensibility*: the Dublin Core provides an economical alternative to more elaborate description models such as the full MARC cataloguing of the library world. Additionally, it includes sufficient flexibility and extensibility to encode the structure and more elaborate semantics inherent in richer description standards (Dublin Core Metadata Initiative Home Page, 2003).

The basic elements which the Dublin Core Initiative suggest should be included as metadata reference description are: title, creator, subject, description, publisher, contributor, date, type, format, identifier, source, language, relation, coverage and rights. The full set of Dublin Core terms includes Section 3: Other Elements and Element Refinements which includes: audience, alternative, tableOfContents, abstract, created, valid, available, isVersionOf, hasVersion, isReplacedBy and so on. Section 4: Encoding Schemes includes elements for LCSH, Medical Subject Headings (MeSH), DDC, Universal decimal classification (UDC), Dublin Core Metadata Initiative (DCMI) Type, the ISO 639-2 standard for the representation of language terms and URI, the Uniform Resource Identifier. Section 5 covers DCMI Type vocabulary.

Lagoze (2001) argues that Dublin Core works as a cross-domain discovery tool but that it has some limitations as a detailed resource description. To demonstrate the limitations of the current Dublin Core elements set in detailed description, he discusses as an example an image created by George Castaldo called *Mona Lisa in Curlers* which is a modified version of Leonardo's original. Lagoze makes the point that although:

> This example may seem contrived, but resources that mix intellectual property in this way are common – for example, Alfred Stieglitz's famous photograph of Daniel Burnham's Flatiron Building – and will become more common due to the malleability of digital objects. As shown in Figure 2, this derivation is the product of several agents, tools, and events. A 'complete descriptive record' for such a resource might document, for example, that a Nikon digital camera was used and that the photograph was altered using Adobe Photoshop. (Lagoze, 2001)

Lagoze argues that specific details such as these 'are not particularly useful for cross-domain resource discovery' (ibid.), which is more appropriately served by simple statements about common attributes such as title and creator. However, Lagoze argues that there may be institutional or application-specific requirements which could mean that a resource description of this document might well need to include details about related photographer, camera type, software or computer artist and that, even with the RDF: Value approach, it is not clear that Dublin Core:

> provides the best framework on which to hang such descriptive complexity. Because of the document-centric nature of Dublin Core elements, this manner of attachment models the document as 'first-class' and the remaining entities (agents, events, etc.) as subsidiary to the document. Rather, the need for richer descriptions suggests a need for more expressive data models and vocabularies able to define and delimit multiple entities. (Lagoze, 2001)

His own research project entitled the 'Harmony Project' argues that 'event-awareness' is an important part of resource description. He makes a distinction between *work* and *expression* which is facilitated through a composing event. To make these events explicit in metadata would mean including clear attachment points for agency, dates, times and roles. Using event attachment points would make it possible to specify attributes which led to the composing event of adding curlers to Mona Lisa that George Castaldo undertook in 1994 (Lagoze, 2001).

The illustration used by Lagoze gives some flavour of the complexities that might be involved in describing and cataloguing contemporary multimedia objects, even at the relatively straightforward level of physical description.

INDEX ENTRIES CREATED BY A COMPUTER PROGRAM WITHOUT (MUCH) HUMAN INTERVENTION

The major difference between this approach and the one outlined above is that a computer program determines how the entry will appear in the index rather than relying on the (possibly variable) decision of a human indexer. Salton and McGill (1983) and Baeza-Yates and Ribeiro-Neto (1999) provide good summaries of the kinds of textual analysis algorithms used to index documents.

In this kind of system the computer system processes text from the item, possibly including title, abstract and part (or all) of the text, and automatically adds references from identified keywords in the index to the item. So, for example, if a book was titled *Media Engineering: A Guide to Developing Information Products* (West and Norris, 1997), index entries may be generated for significant words and phrases such as 'Media Engineering', Information', 'Information Products' rather than relying on a human indexer to identify an index code or entry (like 070.5797).

This kind of system then facilitates retrievals using one or more keywords in combination – probably using some form of 'Boolean'-based language (featuring operators like 'and', 'or' and 'not').

Human intervention is likely to be limited to the maintenance of the index structure – words and phrases used in the index. It may be likely that every new item may generate a list of possible index entries and the indexer's role is to identify meaningful words and phrases that can usefully enrich the index. For example, the phrase 'Media Engineering' may never have been used before and so a decision needs to be taken about its appearance in the index – is it too specialized to be of use? Equally, a variety of words and phrases may be too common to be useful and these need to form a 'stop list' which the indexing program uses to eliminate candidate phrases for the item's entries. Indexers have tools to help them manage the index, for example, statistical analysis of the frequency of words and phrases and the number of entries per item. It may, for as long as the original material on which the index entry is retained in digital form, be relatively easy to modify the index (add new terms and phrases) and ensure that this is retrospectively applied to all the existing items.

Systems of this type may be quite sophisticated in their analysis of the words in an item, and work on systems like this drove early research on 'natural language understanding'. Some systems attempt to analyse more representative parts than just the title of an item, for example, an abstract or even the whole body of the text. This can lead to systems that resemble 'full-text' systems.

Systems of this kind do offer users some benefits, mainly the use of a Boolean-based language to describe their needs. Thus, queries may be constructed that enable the enquirer to focus a search on the subject they have in mind and be more confident that the response will include items that are relevant to their needs.

There are limitations to systems of this kind. First, the analysis of text is statistical and therefore makes assumptions about words and phrases that may not be supported by the meaning of the text. Secondly, the amount of processing required to 'take-on' a new item (unless all the material is available in digital form) is much more than a basic 'catalogue' approach.

There are many IR systems that use some human input to maintain computer-generated index entries. Yahoo, for example, uses web-crawler software created by Google and then enhances (some of) the entries with human-indexer 'editing'.

TO INDEX OR NOT?

The 'index' could be considered to be the root of many IR problems. How information is organized to facilitate retrieval is the first major problem; the second is identifying associations between items and the index. The 'index' acts as a mediator between the items and the 'information seeker'. So the inevitable question must be asked: if the index is a source of difficulty, confusion and potential inaccuracy, would it not be better to simply eliminate it altogether?

Computerized IR systems use an index to improve the performance (retrieval speed) of query processing. It is the activity of matching a user's query against the stored items that is time-consuming. If 'response time' was eliminated from the problem then a computer system need not use an index at all, each time a user requested a document containing some combination of words and phrases all of the documents in the store could be searched (similar to the way Microsoft Windows Explorer's 'search' works). The key issue then becomes one of the interface – how are queries described – and the 'matching' process. However, although this may be a theoretical possibility, in practice such an approach is prohibitively time-consuming and, so, computerized IR needs indexes that map user terms to stored documents that facilitate the retrieval of relevant documents.

OTHER APPROACHES TO IR

Chowdhury (1999, pp. 317–32) describes the use of artificial intelligence (AI) approaches, in particular expert systems (ES), to the problem of IR. The ES approach is an attempt to combine knowledge of two areas, the users (that is, their retrieval needs) and the document collection, so that retrieved documents from the collections are more likely to satisfy the user's retrieval needs. The addition of knowledge of a user's needs (however and whatever may be recorded) is a step beyond simply expressing a query using keywords and Boolean operators. For example, users may be asked to provide feedback on what retrieved items were useful to them or their retrieval behaviour (documents retrieved and used) may be recorded as a model for their needs. The Internet retailer Amazon (2003) uses a simple form of user modelling in that it produces recommendations based on previous customer purchases and other customers' purchases.

Natural language processing (NLP) is an attempt to construct software that can understand the meaning of language in the way that a person might understand the meaning of some text. Chowdhury (1999, pp. 333–56) briefly describes the approach. Natural language processing requires knowledge of language syntax (language structure), semantics (meaning of words and phrases) and pragmatic knowledge (how meaning applies in different contexts) to begin to understand language.

The approach may be characterized as one that attempts to *understand* the contents of the item (book, article) and thus when a query is posed only those items that are *about* that topic will be retrieved. Systems have been created which, for example, analyse news stories (Kuhns, 1988) and chemical information (Cover, 2002e). Although these experimental systems work effectively in their areas, the areas themselves are relatively limited. A generalized system to understand a broad domain (any subject area) is still to be achieved. Systems that do attempt to cover a broad domain only manage a relatively superficial analysis. The difficulties include the breadth of world knowledge and probably the variability of human interpretation required for such analyses.

OTHER ASPECTS OF COMPUTERIZED, TEXT-BASED IR

Although the main focus of this book is multimedia indexing there are some general aspects of text-based IR not directly linked to the problem of indexing which should be borne in mind. These issues include user modelling, interfaces, item take-on and 'interoperability'.

User modelling in IR systems is about improving retrieval performance for individual users. In a 'classic' system a user expresses their requirements through some kind of interface, usually a language (such as a Boolean query language like the DIALOG interface or through some kind of forms-based interface like the Yahoo or Google interfaces. Both types of interface are essentially ignorant about their users and every new query is the first that user has ever made, even if they have selected items from the retrieved lists of previous queries. A simple enhancement would be to remember previous 'retrievals' by the user; an example of such an approach is that of the Internet retailer Amazon where previous purchases and other user purchases are displayed for the user, as are other 'of interest' items. This use of the user's recorded behaviour to enhance the service provided to its customers could be extended to more generalized IR systems. Ultimately, however, 'user-modelling' is still likely to be limited by the kind of index that exists in the system and, although such features may improve the service to users, they are only likely to improve retrieval performance if users participate in the interpretation of the contents of items and thus enrich the general index.

Interfaces to text-based archives are inevitably text based! Interfaces include query language – both structured (Boolean based) and natural, forms (text entered in named fields) that may be thought of as simplified language interfaces, catalogues (subject index hierarchies) and browsing in some order (author, title and so on). It may also be possible to specify a query through the concept 'similar to … ' based on a known or retrieved item providing the model for the required items. The essence of all these interfaces is to provide a way for users to express their needs. Inevitably the interface is limited by the index that mediates the stored items, so if codes are the only way items are recorded then the interface will be limited to those codes.

'Item take-on' is a phrase that names the process through which the system stores the item and has entries made in its index so that the item may be retrieved. This process may have a number of separate activities depending on the scope of the system. The simplest form of 'take-on' would be the creation of a card index-like entry describing the item's bibliographic details. More complex systems might require the digitization of the entire text followed by some text analysis to create index entries in addition to the description of bibliographic details. These activities are likely to include human and computer time and resources. Take-on is relatively well defined in any system and is usually a hidden, housekeeping role but, of course, is absolutely essential for the system to function. It is likely that take-on is easier in more sophisticated systems if the material to be indexed is already in digital form, as then most of the activities can be automated, but there may be a danger in favouring computerized material over non-computerized material.

Interoperability is a term describing the ability of a computer system to interact with another computer system. In terms of data and IR systems, interoperability is about the ability of a system to be interrogated by another system and to supply responses that the other system can understand. Why is this important? If a user queries a system, for, say, items on 'X' then they can expect to find all the items in the systems archive on that subject, but no single archive has all the items ever written on 'X'; it would be unreasonable to expect comprehensiveness except in very narrow domains. There may well be many other archives that include items on 'X'. The user has the option of visiting each and requesting those items separately from each system: the user may be lucky and find all the archives that include relevant items or may not. Interoperability offers the objective of allowing a system to take the user's request for 'X' and automatically interrogating all the other systems that are interoperable, thus saving the user's time and offering a much more comprehensive coverage. How interoperability is achieved is not of particular concern here (Date, 2000, pp. 678–83, 'DBMS Independence' provides a database perspective) but clearly queries need to be translatable and query terms must be mapped between interoperable systems.

KEY QUESTIONS FOR COMPUTERIZED IR

The following is a list of key questions which might be asked in reviewing and evaluating computerized IR systems in general:

1. What is stored and retrieved?
   (a) Whole item/surrogate?
2. What is available for searching?
   (a) Whole item/surrogate?
3. How is the content represented?
4. How do users express their searches?
5. Are there other ways of interrogation?
   (a) Navigation by network?
   (b) Examples?
   (c) Browsing?
6. Are changes retrospective (to search/index)?
7. Who/what describes content?
8. Is the system for general or specific needs?
9. Is the language specialized?
10. Is the system a gateway to other systems?
    (a) Heterogeneous systems?
    (b) Interoperability?
11. Economics?

This chapter has provided a generic overview of information retrieval principles and practice preparatory to focusing on the specific concerns of multimedia information retrieval. We will return to many of the issues that have been discussed in relation to generic IR systems in our discussion of multimedia information retrieval systems in Chapter 3.

3 Multimedia information retrieval

INTRODUCTION

In this chapter general issues relating to multimedia information retrieval (MMIR) are discussed. An initial discussion about general problems with multimedia is followed by an examination of the aims of MMIR systems. The principles that might govern a good MMIR system are reviewed, followed by a brief outline of some of the approaches to indexing multimedia information as a prelude to Chapter 5 in which indexing approaches are discussed in more detail.

Subsections in this chapter will provide introductions to the following topics:

- the problems of 'multimedia documents'
- user warrant in image retrieval research, and users and facets
- multimedia (information) systems and multimedia languages
- the aims of multimedia information retrieval: including source of information; analysis of contents; representation of objects; matching user queries against stored (indexed) objects; data modelling and data retrieval
- the ways in which MMIR systems satisfy the aims: including helping human beings find the things they are looking for; helping human beings find things that are useful to them without them even knowing the item existed; replacing human beings within the indexing/retrieval cycle; sharing items between the largest possible group and preserving the items
- digital libraries and archives
- MMIR and the Internet.

THE PROBLEMS OF 'MULTIMEDIA DOCUMENTS'

In the first chapter we explored the insights of communication and cultural studies writers who contextualize the communicative process, and considered information retrieval as a communicative practice. One of the debates in communication and cultural studies relates to the locus of meaning in documents: whether meaning generally resides in the document which is decoded by the receiver, whether meaning is a function of the reading process and resides entirely with the receiver, or whether meaning is an operation in which meaning, already encoded by the author, is constructed, or reconstructed, by the reader in the reading process. Different views on this matter can lead to different views about where the focus should be in multimedia retrieval research.

Similar issues are debated in the literature of fiction indexing. Clare Beghtol (1994) explicitly discussed the concept of the 'warrant' for classification systems in relation to fiction classification explaining that 'the "warrant" for a classification system is the set of rationalizations and justifications that are invoked to govern judgements about what classes and concepts are to appear in the system and how they are to be structured in relation to each other' (ibid., p. 91).

Beghtol concluded that the warrant for a fiction classification scheme might be drawn either from the fiction itself or from the requirements of the readers of fiction, clearly expressing her own preference for a warrant drawn from the literature. Anneleise Pejtersen's Bookhouse system (Pejtersen, 1993) is built on the concept of reader warrant. Content-based image indexing projects generally draw warrant from the documents themselves and limit themselves to describing physical attributes of specific ranges of images, while concept-based image indexing systems often attempt to draw warrant from viewers or users.

The discussion of subject indexing issues in multimedia information retrieval has been most developed in the area of image indexing. In 1989, Michael Krause speculated on whether it was possible to distinguish between 'soft' and 'hard' indexing of images. He analysed a number of images and concluded that the distinction between 'hard' and 'soft' meaning is difficult to maintain in practice, because meaning is more fluid and complex than such a distinction would suggest. Sara Shatford Layne (1994) argued that images can do some things that text cannot, and can differ from text both in content and in what they convey. She identified three subject attributes:

1. Ofness/aboutness.
2. Simultaneously generic and specific.
3. Classifiable into four facets:
    (a) Time
    (b) Space
    (c) Activities/events
    (d) Objects.

For Shatford Layne, what an image is 'of' is likely to elicit an objective response, while what an image is 'about' is likely to elicit a subjective response. Burke

(1999) relates Shatford Layne's 'of' category to 'hard' factual iconography and the 'aboutness' category to 'soft' subjective iconology, however, Svenonius (1994), like Krause, was sceptical about whether the issue is quite so straightforward with non-textual documents. The difficulty is in interpretation, in the fact that meaning is constructed. Fletcher (2000), in an MSc dissertation on the subject of the indexing of digital skating images, argued that in a wordless medium it might be difficult to state definitively that snow is white. How absolutely white must the snow be to be classed as white? Could a viewer find it more useful to be directed to a picture of grey snow? If so, how grey must the snow be to be considered grey snow? These issues might suggest that combinations of content-based and concept-based retrieval could offer fruitful ways of solving the problems of dealing with documents which are not textual and often not what might conventionally be considered as knowledge based.

Discussion about multimedia systems is likely to be coloured by a variety of different views about what constitutes a multimedia information system or even what multimedia actually means! A convenient definition might be 'all computerized data except text' but, of course, there is no reason not to include text within such a definition, it is data after all. Sometimes multimedia is thought of as being text, still images, moving images (with and without soundtracks) and sound recordings. This more or less includes all digitized, computer-processable data, but it has the weakness of focusing on computer technology rather than the data or information.

If a definition of multimedia is attempted that is based on the content rather than the means (digitization and computer processing) then matters hardly become clearer. For example, multimedia could include a television programme in digital form. This leads to a view of multimedia which is entirely dependent on the subject of the media; for example, medical media like X-rays, CT scans and ultrasound scans would be multimedia for doctors and medical workers but almost too specialized to consider for web designers. Specialist definitions like these are useful within the specific domain but are confusing in a wider discussion about MMIR because, almost certainly, specialist software and applications will be required to deal with such data; for example, software to manipulate and retrieve CT scans is likely to be very different to software that does the same kind of job for aircraft inspection systems.

Why does this issue of definitions matter? In relation to people who understand what is happening, it probably matters little. However, many researchers and authors are using the terms multimedia and IR separately and together to mean very different things, from specialized software to spot tumours in medical imaging through software to do text-like IR on image collections. The approaches, assumptions, user needs and applicability of these systems are often entirely different and yet the same terms are used to broadly describe them. This may well lead to unrealistic expectation of what multimedia IR systems can achieve as well as, at least, disappointment in published articles. Baeza-Yates and Ribeiro-Neto (1999, p. 325) refer to the range of such systems as 'Multimedia Information Systems'.

USER WARRANT IN IMAGE RETRIEVAL RESEARCH

Research in concept-based image retrieval tends to focus on establishing user needs with a view to constructing systems built on user warrant. In 1992, Enser and McGregor undertook a project to explore the form and content of user requests for visual information retrieval by surveying requests for still images addressed to the Hulton Deutsch photograph library. This work led to the publication of a British Library report and to the development of an indexing system for Hulton Deutsch. Their approach was to focus on user warrant rather than the 'literary' or document warrant. A collection of 1000 request forms, embodying 2722 individual requests, was made available by the Hulton Deutsch Collection Limited. These requests were analysed in terms of subject content (using concepts of uniqueness and refinement), specificity of request terminology, user type and search output. The results of the investigation suggested that queries for image-based information tend to be more specific than for text-based information and the majority of the requests were for specific instances of general categories.

Goodrum (2000) discussed specific difficulties relating to image retrieval, drawing on the work of Shatford-Layne (1994) and James Turner (1990). Manual indexing is time-consuming and inconsistent, and there is little agreement between indexers and user queries. Automatic indexing is possible if accompanying text exists, but many images do not have accompanying text. Goodrum cites Enser and Orr's (1993) analysis of queries put to the Hulton Deutsch archive, noting that the results suggested that queries for visual materials tend to be more specific than requests for textual materials, and that the majority of requests were for specific instances of a general category. She also reports Armitage and Enser's (1996) extension of this initial research in the form of a survey and subsequent analysis of seven picture archives. This work resulted in the construction of a framework for queries consisting of four main categories (who, what, when, where) and three levels of abstraction (specific, generic, abstract). Goodrum asserts that research examining users' interactions with electronic information systems was still quite sparse. Investigations carried out by Goodrum and Spink (2001) analysing 33 149 image queries put to Excite suggested that users input very few query terms and most query terms occur only once. Users also used terms which modified a 'general request' such as 'girls' to a 'specific visual request' such as 'pretty girls'.

Goodrum (1997, p. 65) noted that users tend to construct narratives to describe images when 'unconstrained from a retrieval task' quoting from O'Connor, O'Connor and Abbas (1999) who discovered that when image descriptions were elicited, users created short narratives or stories for images that went well beyond describing the objects depicted. This high level of connotation associated with images was also noted by Enser (1993a) in his investigations of the meanings that users derive from images. We discovered the same behaviour in our much smaller investigation (Brown (Rafferty) and Hidderley, 1995). Goodrum's conclusion is interesting in that it clearly points to the continued lack of agreement about fundamental aspects of image retrieval. She argues that even criteria of evaluation need to be established in relation to image retrieval:

> Fundamental questions remain in areas such as indexing and classification, vocabulary control, user needs, relevance, similarity measures, granularity of indexing, economies of scale and presentation of retrieval results. There is strong indication that the combined use of both text and image features may result in improved VIR system effectiveness, but when should textual attributes be present: at the time of indexing, at the time of searching, during query reformulation, or all of these?
>
> Finally, in contrast to the evaluation of systems for text retrieval, which have been conducted for more than 30 years (Cleverdon et al, 1966), image IR has suffered from the lack of research analyzing the effectiveness of various systems. This state of affairs is compounded by the lack of a large image test bed and disagreement about what constitutes effective image retrieval and how to measure it. An image version of the TREC text retrieval experiments has been called for in the multimedia research community, and several test beds have been proposed (Schmidt & Over, 1999; Slaughter & Marchionini, 1999 [sic]). For image retrieval effectiveness to be studied we need to establish large test collections of images and benchmark queries, and the adoption of a set of evaluation measures such as the pooling methods used in the TREC experiments. (Goodrum, 2000, p. 66)

The difficulties that Goodrum notes in relation to visual retrieval systems are equally true for other non-textual information retrieval systems.

USERS AND FACETS

Information retrieval systems, like information systems in general, are not created in isolation, they are open systems. They are created for one or more purposes usually for a group of people. Sometimes the purposes or aims are in themselves clear and well defined, but sometimes the aim may be clear but the definition of how to achieve it may not be. The focus of this book is generally on describing the content and meaning of items, particularly non-text items. However, it is easy to forget that the meaning and content of an item is only one 'category' of information recorded about items. Other data, like when it was created, its resolution and format (for computerized images for example) and its location, all contribute to the collection of information about an item. The complete collection of information about an item may be described as its metadata. Besser (2002) describes metadata issues in relation to database development.

Ideally the user group for an IR/MMI system would have entirely predictable needs. Sometimes, for groups who share a common purpose (for example, students seeking books by author name), it is relatively easy to construct systems that meet their needs. Sometimes, however, the needs of the prospective user group are very diverse, sometimes it may not be possible to survey all the different types of user of the system or, worse, there may be one or more user types who do not even exist yet! For such situations systems construction is much more uncertain.

It is relatively straightforward to construct systems that store information about items, such database systems have existed for many years. There are technical problems to resolve, particularly in a networked environment (Besser, 2002), such as those relating to interoperability. However, these problems are likely to be solved but the problem of content and meaning is more difficult, in Besser's terms 'Discovery Metadata'. The difficulty of content and meaning discussed elsewhere in this book are not resolved by computer systems that mimic their manual equivalents.

A key feature of a faceted system is that each facet and the possible entries in each facet is predicted in advance (in the case of the facet) and is predictable in terms of range of values (for the facet's contents). Faceted classification schemes are generally based on the principle of literary warrant. In relation to textual domains, facets are not so much a product of abstract rational prediction as the identification and organization of meaningful elements drawn from the literature of the subject domain. If a faceted scheme is to be developed for collections of documents that are non-textual, then the issue is further complicated. Difficulty immediately arises if a user wishes to retrieve items based on a facet or concept that is not part of the faceted structure. Intuitively it seems unlikely that someone could construct a completely comprehensive set of facets that will satisfy all current and future needs but that has not stopped people trying (for example Ranganathan's Colon Classification).

The issue of analysing user needs has been a significant problem faced by information scientists and systems analysts since system construction began. There is no simple solution; in a sense there may be no solution at all as the essence of the problem is an attempt to predict the uncertain! Does this mean that this is a 'non-issue' and that a faceted system will do?

In terms of any information retrieval system or multimedia retrieval system the system designers must make choices about what they can provide and how the system will provide it. Performance and cost are also likely to be factors that influence the design. Let us assume for all intents and purposes the system has unlimited resources and instantaneous response. Would it be possible to build a perfect IR/MMI system based on a faceted approach, a system that could support all current and future items and search requests?

The faceted approach has been discussed in Chapter 2. From the perspective of system analysis and design and data analysis, issues such as the overlap of facets, duplication of meaning and the relevance of a facet to an item (that is 'do all items have an entry in the facet or not?') are paramount. In addition, large numbers of facets may well lead to user confusion about where a particular piece of information is recorded and how it is recorded in the facet(s).

It may be possible to include a facet that is deliberately 'general' in its scope, for example a 'description' facet. Here all the information to describe an item is recorded in a single text facet with free-form contents. More importantly, the indexer must be able to anticipate all the things any user might be interested in within the item – an almost impossible task! The contents of this facet would be very broad and could facilitate the inclusion of, as yet, unrequested information. However, there are many problems with an approach such as this, for example, controlling the format and contents of such a facet is inherently difficult in addition to the problem of how the contents for such a facet are derived. A generic 'description' facet might lead to long text descriptions of each image but still not satisfy, in any consistent way, the needs of users of the image collection. A text description will also encounter the same problems that a text-based IR system faces in terms of the analysis of the text and the resolution of user queries against the text but with the added, and significant, difficulty that the text is not the original item but a 'model' of the information content of the item described by some third party (human or machine).

MULTIMEDIA (INFORMATION) SYSTEMS

A distinction should be drawn between computer systems designed to manipulate a variety of media and systems designed to act as storage and retrieval systems. It would be a mistake to think of Microsoft Word as an example of a conventional (text-based) IR system, similarly it is mistaken to think of image or video editing software as multimedia retrieval software. Sometimes this distinction is not always evident in the literature and the research! As has been stated above, there is a range of systems that deal with digitized media other than text and undertake IR-like operations; for example, a medical application, where a system might be asked to detect images containing suspected tumour sites (Faloutsos, 1999).

The phrase 'multimedia information systems' does cover a wide spectrum of application systems. There are a number of distinctions that may help to understand the scope and usefulness of such systems.

First, there is the issue of purpose. Is the system designed with a single application in mind or a generalized system to deal with unforeseen data or queries? There is a huge difference between a system designed to search for tumours in x-rays and a photo-journalism archive. Equally, is the system a multimedia system or a monomedia system that just happens not to be text based? It would be hard to conceive of a system that did not include text in some way, so perhaps the minimum 'multimedia' system would be text plus one other media?

Secondly, is the system based on generalized software (like Oracle) or has it been specially written? While this issue may not be so important for the functionality or indexing scope of the system, it will inevitably affect the ability to share data between (external) systems and may limit the lifespan of the system and its 'database'. These issues have faced the commercial database community for many years and are often characterized by debates about heterogeneity, interoperability, version control and standards (Date, 2000). There are also the 'management' or 'housekeeping' roles, such as backup and recovery functions, encompassed within commercial database management system (DBMS) which may be costly or even overlooked in one-off systems.

Thirdly, is the system a repository of knowledge or is it designed to automate analytical functions as well as the 'IR'-like functions? At one, primitive end of the scale, we might have a system that is essentially a card index plus media. At the other extreme we might find a system that can interpret a user query, possibly expressed in visual or aural forms, and analyse the contents of its database to find similar items. This could be thought of as a kind of 'full-media', 'natural-media' equivalent of a full-text, natural language text-based system.

MULTIMEDIA LANGUAGES

In general, (text-based) IR uses language to describe user queries (Baeza-Yates and Ribeiro-Neto, 1999, pp. 99–116). The language often includes Boolean operators (for example 'and', 'or', 'not') and keywords recognized by the system. Sometimes the language may be close to natural language. This approach is suited to text-based systems and is clearly related to the data in the indexed documents. However, multimedia provides different challenges. In a picture or a video, significant content (sometimes all the content) is visual without text or words. Thus there is a problem about describing the contents (and meaning) of multimedia. The same issue but perhaps more obviously, applies to music, without words how is the content described?

In recent years languages have been developed to describe contents. Some of these languages have their origin in text applications (SGML) and some with specific media (music for example: Huron, 1999) in mind. In these cases the language is not used to describe user queries but, rather, to describe the contents of the item.

The need to express queries does not disappear from multimedia systems and keyword-based interfaces are very likely to be needed and provided. However, multimedia queries may need to be expressed in other forms, for example by sound or picture examples (a kind of visual or aural 'query by example', Baeza-Yates and Ribeiro-Neto, 1999, p. 335; Date, 2000, p. 233). The interpretation of queries in a multimedia environment are much more likely to be based on 'quality of match' rather than an 'absolute' match, so issues like 'relevance' and 'feedback' are likely to be necessary functions of MMIR.

THE AIMS OF MULTIMEDIA INFORMATION RETRIEVAL

There are two main aims of any MMIR system (adapted from Baeza-Yates and Ribeiro-Neto, 1999, pp. 328–42):

1. Data modelling.
2. Data retrieval.

Chowdhury (1999, p. 3) identifies seven major functions of an IR system (although not specifically an MMIR):

1. To identify the information (sources) relevant to the areas of interest of the target user's community.
2. To analyse the contents of the sources (documents).
3. To represent the contents of the analysed sources in a way that will be suitable for matching users' queries.
4. To analyse users' queries and to represent them in a form that will be suitable for matching with the database.
5. To match the search statement with the stored database.
6. To retrieve the information that is relevant.
7. To make the necessary adjustments in the system based on feedback from the users.

The two lists reflect their respective author's preoccupations namely computer science and information science respectively. For the purposes of this discussion about MMIR a review of the combined aims is in order, we will take as broad a view as possible.

SOURCE OF INFORMATION

Any 'object' – image, speech, music score, text, video recording and so on – is potentially a multimedia object in an MMIR. From a systems perspective, we may not be particularly concerned with the quality or source of the object, but this lack of concern is not typical of the professional 'information community' which takes particular note of the source as well as the object because the source's quality may well determine the value and authority placed on the object.

However, it is worth considering this aim by thinking about the source of the 'object's meaning or contents'. In a text document the source of its meaning might come from the document itself or from some human interpretation (the indexer), sometimes from a combination of the two. This is the kind of differentiation between full-text indexing (from the document's text) and conventional cataloguing and classification (mainly from human intervention).

Multimedia information retrieval systems dealing with objects other than text documents may adopt similar approaches to those devoted entirely to text-based documents. The question, 'does the meaning of the object come from the object or from a human interpretation or a mixture?' is crucial in determining what information is recorded about an object, how it is represented on a computer system and, in turn, how humans may interrogate the system.

ANALYSIS OF CONTENTS

This aim describes a process by which 'meaning' is attributed to objects. There are significant philosophical and practical problems with this activity even with the relatively straightforward area of text-based objects. These issues have been discussed in depth elsewhere in this book. However, such problems have not stopped MMIR systems being developed that attempt to record meaning.

As far as MMIR systems are currently concerned we should ask the question 'What is the basis and scope of the object-content analysis?' rather than 'How does the MMIR system do content analysis?' For example there are image oriented MMIR systems that analyse the representation of the image in terms of colours, light/dark, colour changes and so on, IBM's QBIC system (Flickner et al., 1995) being one example. The 'Computer Vision Homepage' at Carnegie Mellon University (Huber, 2002) links to examples of recent research in the area. Such analysis may be very relevant for some purposes like that of finding similar (in a colour sense) images or for the purposes of image reproduction but has limited use for journalists. Equally, a system that records the names of any people in the image (most likely via human intervention) is of little value to satisfying the request for 'coloured like a Canelletto'!

Ultimately we should not be concerned if a human or a computer constructs the index entries for an object per se. However, the same philosophical problems about meaning and interpretation will be faced by the computer system as they are currently faced by human indexers, even if the computer system eventually becomes as good as (or better than?) the humans that they replace.

REPRESENTATION OF OBJECTS

This issue might, mistakenly, be considered to be an entirely technical issue. Those MMIR systems that store a digital representation of the object (accepting that some objects may only exist in a digital form, for example a photograph taken with a digital camera) must do so using a technique that best serves their purpose. It is not necessarily compulsory for an MMIR system to store a digital representation of an object in the same way that not all text-based IR systems record the entire text of the document to which they refer, but many authors see MMIR systems including a digital representation as the *de jure* standard.

The process of storing a digitized object has its own, technical, issues, for example the space required to record the object, the software required to save and 'replay' the object, the quality of the reproduction (and any loss of quality from the original) and the 'universality' (how common is the software used to access the object) of the software are some of the more important factors in choosing a digital representation.

For Chowdhury (1999), though, the issue of representation follows on from the preceding aims, namely, it is an issue about facilitating the retrieval of stored objects by users not necessarily about being able to read them via a system. So the question here, then, might be 'In what form does the user of the MMIR system express their query?' For most people used to conventional IR (both manual and computerized) the answer is, naturally, in words. Therefore, the representation or at least the index entries, needs to be in words. In text-based IR this is both natural and expected but when one considers music or images, for example, it is less so. Therefore some systems use the digitized representation of the object or an abbreviated version of particular parts as the index entry and the query language is not one made up of words but of image or sound 'tokens' that the system is then able to match against the index entries.

In the multimedia (MM) world the issue about representation is a complex one if only because the objects stored in the system are more than words. If words are used to represent non-textual objects (which of course is what language is very well suited to do), it should be remembered that they form an abbreviation of, and are one step removed from, the original. In some circumstances language will prove to be an inadequate medium, for example in describing a precise shape, colour hue, tone or pattern of music, and in these cases a 'language' possibly visual or auditory would be the more appropriate medium to express those needs.

However, it is dangerous to generalize; for example, just because an MMIR system deals entirely with sound recordings does not mean that a text-based interface is inappropriate. If a substantial number of the recordings included the spoken or sung words of people then an interface that facilitated searching for those words rather than simply musical or tonal changes would be appropriate.

The key to this issue is to primarily consider who the users of the system are. So if the objects are sound recordings and the audience will use the recordings in their own compositions, then it is likely that a sound-based interface will be more useful than one based on words. In the spirit of interoperability and sharing archives across the Internet, however, one can only argue for *all* relevant interfaces to be included in every archive (making the assumption that if an 'index' entry does not exist for an object it is only because nothing useful can be stated in that entry about the recorded objects).

MATCHING USER QUERIES AGAINST STORED (INDEXED) OBJECTS

This issue might be considered to be the 'black box' of MMIR systems. In a sense it does not matter *how* a system actually finds the relevant objects stored in the database so long as it does! The definition of *relevance* is crucial in this aim.

Relevance, like beauty, is 'in the eye of the beholder', ultimately it is the human consumer of the retrieved objects who determines whether their needs are satisfied or not. Rather than attempt to define how users are satisfied, it is worth imagining causes for their dissatisfaction (with retrieved objects). First, the language they are expected to use to express their needs might not let them adequately state their needs or they may not understand the language sufficiently. Secondly, they may misuse the 'language' or use it differently to the indexer (manual or automated). Thirdly, items may be inaccurately indexed, leading to relevant items not being retrieved and irrelevant items being retrieved. Fourthly, there may be no way for users to understand why an object has been retrieved at all (and so cannot modify their query). Fifthly, users may not be able to usefully describe 'relevant' items to the system in a way that the system can then use to re-evaluate its search.

There is, of course, an even more insidious problem, namely, that objects exist in the database that precisely match the user's needs but because of problems, like those described above, are never retrieved by the system for the user. How, then, would they know if the system had performed well or not and that they should now stop searching?

DATA MODELLING

For Baeza-Yates and Ribeiro-Neto (1999) data modelling is about the ability of a system to represent the multimedia objects. Their discussion of object representation is interesting because they recognize the relatively 'unstructured' (or variable) nature of multimedia. However, they believe that the flexibility offered by object-oriented database systems (OODBMS) offers the opportunity to develop models that can represent such a varied range of objects. They go on to further identify 'semi-structured' objects, those that have some elements in common with a general structure but other features that are unusual or unknown.

Their discussion is from the perspective of computer science and, although informed and relevant to that domain, appears to avoid the issue of the 'meaning' of the objects entirely. It is a little like having a discussion about text-based documents, recognizing the complexity of the language, layout and the grammar of documents, and then stopping there. Models are developed to enable those features to be recorded, but then the words (and their meaning) are left uncommented within the structure.

This may be a harsh analysis of data-modelling approaches to this problem. Baeza-Yates and Ribeiro-Neto (1999, p. 333) describe a structure for a business letter and it is clear that the structural components identified are at a higher level than simply names or words (including receiver's name, address, company logo and so on). Apart from using a text-based example to illustrate a multimedia object discussion, one might ask how many photographs, even from a photo-journalism archive, have even that shared structure?

The modelling approach taken by computer scientists is reflected in the markup language approaches (SGML/XML) that identify document structures within which objects (both text and other media) are recorded. These approaches are further discussed later.

DATA RETRIEVAL

For Baeza-Yates and Ribeiro-Neto (1999) data retrieval is about query specification, query processing and optimization, query answer and query modification. All of these issues are relevant to any MMIR system. They recognize the difficulty of dealing with multimedia objects but come to the problem from their technological perspective. So, for them, the issue about retrieval is driven by the objects that are recorded rather than how meaning comes to be taken from an object. Therefore their solutions, relevant as they are to the performance of MMIR systems, offer little in a discussion about meaning and 'content'.

WAYS IN WHICH MMIR SYSTEMS SATISFY THEIR AIMS

HELP HUMAN BEINGS FIND THE THINGS THEY ARE LOOKING FOR

Computer systems are often developed to assist human activities. In IR systems this is often described as finding items of *relevance*. An item is relevant if the human seeking information judges that it satisfies their need in some way. Clearly this is a measurement, although probably not always an objective one. This concept has been discussed earlier, in the chapter about text-based IR (Chapter 2).

Systems to assist this activity pre-date computer systems and are likely to have existed soon after people began to collect things. In the context of multimedia, people have developed indexes and languages to help them record and, later, find music, recordings of sounds and images before computer systems were developed. However, as soon as images, sounds and moving image began to be stored digitally, so the need to develop computer systems to classify and retrieve them grew. The Internet has added a new dimension to the purpose of developing systems to retrieve items because those items are likely to be stored (indexed and kept) by third party providers anywhere in the world in a variety of languages.

One of the features of multimedia is that sounds and images form some kind of universal language independent of the country of the producers or the (spoken or written) language that they may use. Therefore, if someone in England wishes to find images of happy children it should not matter what nationality they were or where the images were recorded or the language in which the image was indexed. If these things did matter (for example, pictures of happy Chinese children) then a system should find those images irrespective of the fact that no one had described such a picture in English but maybe had in French, Chinese (Mandarin or Cantonese!). The Internet may well provide the technical link to enable one to download such images from any connected machine in the world but, as yet, the ability to find all the relevant semantic links is not yet possible.

HELP HUMAN BEINGS FIND THINGS THAT ARE USEFUL TO THEM WITHOUT THEM EVEN KNOWING THE ITEMS EXISTED

Early cataloguing systems adopted the approach of naming the items, possibly describing the title and author of an item. This approach is adequate in so far as the title is an accurate description of the content and/or the author is known. Such entries are useful in finding the location of an item but are limited otherwise. For someone seeking information, such an index is of limited value unless the collection is relatively small so that they could be expected to know of all the works of interest. Therefore, almost all libraries soon developed a method of conveying information about the content of the items, a simple approach being the subject index found in many card indexing systems.

The most important issue with this aim is how is knowledge of the content to be conveyed? There are many approaches to this problem including hypertexts (Keep, McLaughlin and Farmer 2001), user modelling (for example, Amazon's (2003) display of 'other customers also purchased' and 'recommendations'), lexical approaches (thesauri like Art and Architecture Thesaurus – AAT) and more sophisticated indexing approaches including faceted approaches (Iconclass). Ultimately, this requires more information to be collected from the user (by feedback as to relevance, describing their needs in more detail than single words, from their earlier queries and the items they have retrieved), from the items (by more detailed classification, possibly including 'full-text' analysis) and from other users (their queries and the items they retrieved).

This aim is achievable through the use of computer systems where it would be prohibitively expensive and time-consuming without, but it is not without a cost. Users of the systems must be prepared to allow their needs to be recorded (even if those needs are perfectly legal and legitimate) and may have to spend more time interacting with a system. Indexers may have to spend more time (and the consequential expense) describing items that may never be retrieved. Clearly it would be attractive to develop computer systems that could automate as much of that activity as possible.

REPLACE HUMAN BEINGS WITHIN THE INDEXING/RETRIEVAL CYCLE

This may sound a bizarre requirement because what possible use could a multimedia IR system be, if it does not provide something for a human being? Humans introduce a number of factors which computer systems are designed to moderate or even eliminate. For example, people are a relatively expensive resource, particularly when one considers expensively educated and trained information professionals. Therefore any system that could reduce or eliminate their use, no matter how much it cost to develop it, might be considered to be beneficial. Additionally, these expensively educated and trained individuals are unlikely to be consistent, let alone perfect, performers (measured over the complete set of such people) and, therefore, unacceptable variations are very likely to creep into the index, resulting in a less than perfect system.

In practical terms systems that can repeat the same operation over and over again are likely to be better than human beings doing the same task. So, theoretically, a computer system to recognize human faces should be able to identify particular faces more competently than a human simply because a computer does not get bored or tired. It should be noted, however, that although face recognition systems have been, and are being, developed their actual performance is not yet considered to be useful for the situations where it may be put into practice (Greene, 2001; Heo et al., 2003).

Government intelligence agencies are very interested in sifting communications circulating around the world. In times past it was a relatively simple matter to intercept the mail and read it (even if coded). With the advent of electronic communication this activity soon exceeded the capacities of governments and the volume of email and telephone communication would make any non-computerized sifting impossible.

The elimination of humans from the indexing/retrieval cycle can be seen to be sensible or even necessary in some circumstances, but we should never lose sight of the fact that humans can never be eliminated entirely from the cycle without we imagine some world where computer systems have their own needs and purposes entirely independent of human society. So humans will be involved in the description of needs and analysis of results because those are for them not for the machine.

SHARING ITEMS BETWEEN THE LARGEST POSSIBLE GROUP AND PRESERVING THE ITEMS

Indexing and classification schemes have been developed in media libraries and museums long before computer systems were developed. Media libraries are generally more specialized and have a much more specialized user group than 'ordinary' book-orientated libraries. Unlike book-based libraries that have broadly accepted standards to refer to (like Dewey or Library of Congress), media libraries tended to evolve procedures and descriptions specifically for their user groups. So, for example, a picture agency's catalogue might focus on date, title, key subject (often a character) and photographer because their 'clients', mainly journalists, would primarily request pictures using those terms.

The idea that one day, someone in the world might request an image from any one or all of the world's picture agencies in his or her own language and terms probably never occurred to media libraries. The Internet has changed all that! Media libraries may respond to the Internet by putting their collection online (The Hulton Archive (Hulton, 2003) and British Pathe (Pathe, 2003) are examples of such archives) and, although that is better than not providing access online at all, it is far from adequate. For example, the interface may be different on each system with the result that a user may have to visit each site in turn and repeat their query. Also, the structure of the catalogue, including facets, terms and language available, may all be different.

Preservation is a separate but closely allied issue to multimedia IR. Multimedia information retrieval does not necessarily have to include the 'actual item': it may include a reference to it. For example, is a piece of music the score, a performance, an original recording of a particular performance or a recording of any performance? Clearly the answer depends on the purpose of the archive and the user's needs. Preservation, however, is a much more loaded term and the issue of the 'replacement' of items otherwise held by an archive is fundamental to the way the issue is perceived. Hedstrom (2002) reviews some of the motives and problems with digital preservation. No one would say that a photograph of Constable's (1821) *Hay Wain* is the same as the original. The oil painting has quality and presence in itself that, no matter how high the quality of reproduction, the photograph cannot replicate. However, if a digital (sound) recording of a performance is made it is generally considered to be the best technical recording possible at the moment and it can easily be faithfully reproduced. There are many film archives that are in danger of losing their films because the physical medium has deteriorated and this issue could be reproduced in almost any physical archive. Controversially, some archives are funding their digitization projects, and, they would claim, the acquisition of new items, through the sale of the very items they are digitizing! There are also possible benefits with digitization such as accessibility (by making the digital archive available over the Internet, for example the Text Encoding Initiative (TEI, 2001), (UML 2000a, 2000b) which are independent of the retention of the physical objects, but these advantages depend on MMIR delivering access.

DIGITAL LIBRARIES AND ARCHIVES

The Institute of Museum and Library Services (IMLS, 2001) describes a framework for measuring the quality of digital collections. The framework includes seven principles for the collections themselves (Table 3.1), six principles for the objects in the collections, six principles for metadata and three principles for the projects to develop the digital collections.

In this framework, the *collection* might correspond to a library, the object to books in the library, the *metadata* to the indexes and catalogue in use in the library, and the *project* to the process by which the original library was created.

The collection principles are, as one would expect, related to the overall aims of the digital collection. However it is worth considering principles 3 and 7 in particular. Principle 3 related to the lifespan of the collection. Computer data, in general, has not had a particularly long lifespan. Computerized data suffers from two factors that other records do not: first, the hardware on which the data is recorded has a limited operational lifespan and as time progresses so the likelihood of needing to transfer the data to a newer medium increases. Think of paper tape or magnetic tape: very few computer systems have the hardware to

Table 3.1   Principles for collections in digital archives

Collections

Collections principle 1. A good digital collection is created according to an explicit collection development policy that has been agreed upon and documented before digitization begins.

Collections principle 2. Collections should be described so that a user can discover important characteristics of the collection, including scope, format, restrictions on access, ownership, and any information significant for determining the collection's authenticity, integrity and interpretation.

Collections principle 3. A collection should be sustainable over time. In particular, digital collections built with special funding should have a plan for their continued usability beyond the funded period.

Collections principle 4. A good collection is broadly available and avoids unnecessary impediments to use. Collections should be accessible to persons with disabilities, and usable effectively in conjunction with adaptive technologies.

Collections principle 5. A good collection respects intellectual property rights. Collection managers should maintain a consistent record of rightsholders and permissions granted for all applicable materials.

Collections principle 6. A good collection provides some measurement of use. Counts should be aggregated by period and maintained over time so that comparison can be made.

Collections principle 7. A good collection fits into the larger context of significant related national and international digital library initiatives. For example, collections of content useful for education in science, math and/or engineering should be usable in the NSDL (National Science Digital Library).

Source: IMLS (2001). Reprinted with permission from the Institute of Museum and Library Services (IMLS).

read data stored on these media now. Therefore, unless the data is to be lost, it needs to be transferred to a newer medium. There is no reason to believe that the development of new storage media has reached the end or that optical devices like compact discs read-only memory (CD-ROMs) are the ultimate storage medium. Secondly, software is continually changing, either to 'improve' it or because standards change or vendors cease to exist. Thus a digital file may be accessible today but difficult or impossible to access some years later. Again, this may not be catastrophic if remedial action (updating the files or ensuring that software exists to read the data) is taken regularly but without such action there is a danger of inaccessible data.

It is also worth remembering that archives are intended to store items for posterity, over tens, hundreds and, possibly, thousands of years. The techniques to store and preserve physical objects, including documentary data, are well established and books and papers exist that are well over 1000 years old. However, the preservation of more modern materials like early film and early computerized records is much less successful. Already much material has been lost. The lifespan of digitized material on magnetic and optical media has not yet been proven over time. Although an advantage of digitized data is that its existence is as electronic data and that in itself enables continual migration to newer (and possibly more reliable and long-life) media, this has to be done to ensure that the data does not simply disappear – which will take time and resources (space and money).

Principle 7 is particularly interesting because it relates to the changing audience for an archive. Generally, it was only physical visitors to an archive who could gain access. This often involved an expensive journey, possibly residence at a remote location and, even, 'privileged' access. One of the great opportunities that digital archives can deliver is access to all from 'anywhere' (with access to the Internet?). However, the issue is not simply one of providing a digitized collection and making it accessible through a web interface, although it is better than nothing at all! The issues of the archive's structure, its metadata and conformance to standards are all crucial and are discussed further below.

The word 'object' refers to artefacts that are only digital (for example, a digital recording of someone's speech) and a digital representation of some other object (for example a digital representation of a photograph).

Object principle 2 (Table 3.2) echoes the third principle for collections and the same issues raised above generally apply.

Object principle 3 recommends the conformance to standards but, worryingly, would allow deviations from a standard. While freedom of expression and special requirements may be arguments in favour of non-conformance, those arguments would have to be very strong as non-conformance inevitably reduces accessibility and interoperability.

Object principle 7 is interesting because it is a key focus of this chapter and it leads in to the principles about metadata.

Metadata principle 3 is interesting because of its implicit belief that the use of standard controlled vocabularies is sufficient to deal with content-based indexing. The issues of meaning of both the content and the vocabulary are significant issues and are likely to be magnified across a worldwide audience. Additionally, the potential for miscommunication between indexer and retriever are not likely to be resolved through a standardized vocabulary, even if it is published in the form of a dictionary or thesaurus.

Metadata principle 2 is important because it is through metadata that interoperability is partially delivered. For example, the use of markup languages

Table 3.2 Principles for objects in digital archives

Objects (IMLS, 2001, cites principles 1, 2, 3, 5, 6, 7 only, presumably a numbering error)

Objects principle 1. A good digital object will be produced in a way that ensures it supports collection priorities.

Objects principle 2. A good object is persistent. That is, it will be the intention of some known individual or institution that the good object will persist; that it will remain accessible over time despite changing technologies.

Objects principle 3. A good object is digitized in a format that supports intended current and likely future use or that support the development of access copies that support those uses. Consequently, a good object is exchangeable across platforms, broadly accessible, and will either be digitized according to a recognized standard or best practice or deviate from standards and practices only for well documented reasons.

Objects principle 5. A good object will be named with a persistent, unique identifier that conforms to a well-documented scheme. It will not be named with reference to its absolute filename or address (e.g. as with URLs [Uniform Resource Locators] and other Internet addresses) as filenames and addresses have a tendency to change. Rather, the filename's location will be resolvable with reference to its identifier.

Objects principle 6. A good object can be authenticated in at least two senses. First, a user should be able to determine the object's origins, structure, and developmental history (version, etc.). Second, a user should be able to determine that the object is what it purports to be.

Objects principle 7. A good object will have and be associated with metadata. All good objects will have descriptive and administrative metadata. Some will have metadata that supplies information about their external relationships to other objects (e.g. the structural metadata that determines how page images from a digitally reformatted book relate to one another in some sequence).

Source: IMLS (2001). Reprinted with permission from the Institute of Museum and Library Services (IMLS).

and data type definitions (DTD – a model of the structure of a collection of objects) enable very varied, independently constructed software to access and process varied archived data (see section below for a discussion about markup languages).

Interestingly, the other metadata principles are related to issues regarding archive and object management rather than content and classification of objects. This implied focus is possibly too narrow as it identifies with the idea of the

Table 3.3   Principles for metadata in digital archives

Metadata (the sixth principle is less clearly identified in IMLS (2001))

Metadata principle 1. Good metadata should be appropriate to the materials in the collection, users of the collection, and intended, current and likely use of the digital object.

Metadata principle 2. Good metadata supports interoperability.

Metadata principle 3. Good metadata uses standard controlled vocabularies to reflect the what, where, when and who of the content.

Metadata principle 4. Good metadata includes a clear statement on the conditions and terms of use for the digital object.

Metadata principle 5. Good metadata records are objects themselves and therefore should have the qualities of good objects, including archivability, persistence, unique identification, etc. Good metadata should be authoritative and verifiable.

Metadata principle 6. Good metadata supports the long-term management of objects in collections.

Source: IMLS (2001). Reprinted with permission from the Institute of Museum and Library Services (IMLS).

'object' and may therefore be questionable because insufficient attention is placed on the 'meaning' of the objects in the collection.

The European Visual Archive (EVA) (van Horik, 2001) is a European Commission funded project to produce a web-based system to access historical photographic archives. Two archives, the London Metropolitan Archives and the City archives of Antwerp are participating in the initial development. The system uses Dublin Core description elements as its metadata foundation. Content-based indexing is limited to a free-text descriptive field of what is 'visible' in the image. Subject/keywords that were used in the original archive are also recorded in the computerized archive.

A key feature of the archive, as with many European funded projects, is the multilingual capabilities of the system. Therefore, not only has the system to cope with variation in meaning attributed by indexer and retriever, but also the problem of language translation in addition to cultural variations.

COMPUTER SCIENCE APPROACHES TO MMIR

Two significant areas of computer applications are briefly examined: first, those approaches (loosely) driven by computer science techniques and, secondly, those driven by the 'markup language' approach.

Computer science may offer, in the future, a substitute for human indexing thus making large-scale indexing practical. Artificial intelligence techniques have been applied to IR problems for some time (Chowdhury, 1999, pp. 326–9; Salton, 1989, pp. 405–10). Automating the indexing and to a certain degree the retrieval process through the application of AI techniques has not changed the nature of what is indexed from that of human indexers. There are three areas of research which may become significant for multimedia indexing: vision, neural networks and genetic algorithms. These are relevant to any discussion about multimedia because they represent a different approach to the problem of 'understanding multimedia content'.

Markup languages are a very popular way of encoding knowledge so that computer applications may access (retrieve and process) all suitably 'marked up' documents as if stored in a huge database of knowledge. This is particularly relevant in a networked environment (the Internet, for example). The application of markup languages is inherently orientated to computer systems and the Web in particular and, therefore, the best sources of information are web-based (see Cover, 2001a; W3C, 2003).

COMPUTER SCIENCE – VISION

For a human this is a mundane task. All people who can see make sense of visual stimuli every waking second, although this statement grossly oversimplifies the enormous amount of processing the brain undertakes to both visually sense 'the world' and to interpret those sensations against its knowledge of the world. Vision research is concerned with the creation of a computer system to understand visual stimuli with, presumably, the ultimate aim of producing systems that perform at least as well as human beings.

Eakins and Graham (1999) highlight the difference between content-based image retrieval (CBIR) and vision systems:

> CBIR draws many of its methods from the field of image processing and computer vision, and is regarded by some as a subset of that field. It differs from these fields principally through its emphasis on the retrieval of images with desired characteristics from a collection of significant size. Image processing covers a much wider field, including image enhancement, compression, transmission, and interpretation. (Ibid., s. 2.5)

Although vision research is not new, spanning more than the last 20 years, the work is still relatively limited when compared with human performance. For example, vision systems to recognize faces or to assist a robot navigate around objects are now practical. However, from the perspective of a generalized picture interpretation and *understanding* perspective, vision systems are currently only figments of the imagination.

In order to provide machines with the ability to interact in complex, real-world environments, sensory data must be presented to the machine. One such module dealing with sensory input is the visual data processing module, also known as the computer vision module. A central task of this computer vision module is to recognise objects from images of the environment.

There are two different parts to computer vision modules, namely segmentation and recognition. Segmentation is the process of finding interested objects while recognition works to see if the located object matches the predefined attributes. Since images cannot be recognised until they have been located and separated from the background, it is of paramount importance that this vision module is able to locate different objects of interest for different systems with great efficiency. (Wong and Wong, 1996b)

There are many applications of vision recognition. Fisher (2001) provides a survey and links to a range of current applications. It may be a crude simplification, but the focus on many of the systems appears to be that of object recognition within a narrow domain. So the idea that current vision systems are able to deal with generalized image classification problems (discussed earlier in the book) such as 'photographs containing unhappy people' is not realistic. Wieblut (1995) points out that a range of user needs can be met by vision-orientated approaches and that applications in science and medicine, for example, are likely to be better served by image content (meaning lines, colours, shapes) rather than interpretive content. However, it is not inconceivable that vision systems will eventually be able to perform in a similar fashion to human viewers in determining content/meaning. Of course, at this point the debate about 'single truth' versus 'multiple truths' (also discussed earlier in the book) comes in to play.

It is sometimes surprising to discover that 'content', especially when used in the phrase 'Content-based information retrieval', means something different to that of the library/IR world. For vision researchers, 'content' means the qualities of individual pixels making up an image, how those pixels can be analysed with their neighbours so that shapes may be perceived and what those shapes and lines might actually represent in terms of real-world objects. Clearly there is potential for confusion between the two communities. The vision community tends to dismiss text (that is, words) as being a time-consuming and inadequate method of describing content (Wieblut, 1995). On the one hand, from the perspective of an information scientist it is difficult to imagine how an analysis of pixels, shapes and so on will lead to a system able to describe in human terms the content and meaning of, for example, newspaper photographs. On the other hand, as soon as this 'semantic gap' is noted it should be reasonably straightforward to propose and design systems that can merge the two areas together to produce efficient and effective content and meaning multimedia information retrieval systems.

COMPUTER SCIENCE – ARTIFICIAL INTELLIGENCE

There are many branches of AI, some of which are currently being applied to vision systems and information retrieval (for example, Chen, 1993). Neural networks (NN) and evolutionary computing (Heitkötter, 2000), of which a genetic algorithm (GA) is an example, are likely to be the most relevant AI approaches.

Neural networks and GAs may be thought of as computerized mechanisms that function in analogous ways to the human mind. Vision systems are constructed to recognize the visual world; NNs and GAs are components of these systems that correspond to the memory and analytical components of the mind. The general approach is to mimic the way a human brain makes links between neurones in a computerized system thus creating a system that may learn and adapt to a range of inputs and respond accordingly.

An (artificial) neural net may be described thus:

> A neural network is a processing device, either an algorithm, or actual hardware, whose design was motivated by the design and functioning of human brains and components thereof. Most neural networks have some sort of 'training' rule whereby the weights of connections are adjusted on the basis of presented patterns. In other words, neural networks 'learn' from examples, just like children learn to recognize dogs from examples of dogs, and exhibit some structural capability for generalization.
> …
> In practice, NNs are especially useful for mapping problems which are tolerant of some errors, have lots of example data available, but to which hard and fast rules can not easily be applied. (Neural-net-faq, 1995; 2001)

Neural networks are often components of vision systems and are useful in determining conclusions from incomplete or 'noisy' (that is, for example, images containing unclear or confusing components) data. This may, in the future be of relevance to multimedia systems in the classification and retrieval of multimedia objects. For example, a computer system that could reliably identify objects within a photograph would enable large volumes of images to be quickly and easily classified for the purposes of indexing and retrieval.

Genetic algorithms are part of a branch of AI called 'evolutionary computing' (see Heitkötter, 2000).

> Genetic Algorithms (GA) were introduced as a computational analogy of adaptive systems. They are modelled loosely on the principles of the evolution via natural selection, employing a population of individuals that undergo selection in the presence of variation-inducing operators such as mutation and recombination (crossover). A fitness function is used to evaluate individuals, and reproductive success varies. (Wong and Wong, 1996a)

The idea that a system could learn and adapt to a set of stimulus is of relevance to vision and information retrieval systems, particularly in the area of user modelling, that is, to identify the characteristics of a user's interests and thus be able to find similar 'texts' without user intervention (Chen, 1993). Artificial Intelligence systems have much to offer and the approaches, applications and results of AI research are likely to continue to grow in the future.

It is, possibly, interesting to question whether an AI approach could ever be (provably) better at interpreting the meaning/content of images than any single human being even if the system learnt from a larger set of images than any single person. The first problem is to define the meaning of 'better' in this context. It might be possible to interpret 'better' as meaning a system that can more accurately identify 'red London buses' more often than most human viewers. However, if a system were to be asked to identify 'unhappy people' then the qualitative judgement is not simply 'true or false'. Even if the system responded as the majority of human indexers performed this would not mean that it performed better than the minority because an interpretation like 'unhappy people' is open to a wide range of acceptable (and justifiable) responses. One might speculate that even if such a system were developed its output could only be a single perspective on the content/meaning of an image and thus could never be 'better' than the collection of people on which its responses were based.

MMIR THROUGH THE USE OF MARKUP LANGUAGES

Markup languages have their origins in text-based applications, as Burnard (1996) states:

> The objectives of those who designed SGML were simple. Confronted with an increasing number of so-called 'markup languages' for electronic texts, each more or less bound to a particular kind of processing or even to a particular software package, they sought to define a single language in which all such schemes could be re-expressed, so that the essential information represented by such texts could be transferred from one program or application to another.

and goes on to state:

> Generalizing from that sene [*sic*], we define markup, or (synonymously) *encoding*, as any means of making explicit an interpretation of a text. At a banal level, all printed texts are encoded in this sense: punctuation marks, use of capitalization, disposition of letters around the page, even the spaces between words, might all be regarded as a kind of markup, the function of which is to help the human reader determine where one word ends and another begins, or how to identify gross structural features such as headings, and syntactic units such as dependent clauses or sentences. Encoding a text for computer processing is in principle, like transcribing a manuscript from *scriptio continua*, a process of making explicit what is conjectural or implicit. It is a process of directing the user as to how the content of the text should be interpreted. (Ibid.)

The XML (Cover, 2002a) may be thought of as a simplified version of SGML that nonetheless facilitates the creation of application specific languages so that particular kinds of documents may be 'marked up'. There are hundreds of different XML applications for document types as varied as e-journals, court (legal) documents, Petri nets, image metadata and music to name five randomly selected types (Cover, 2003a; Martinez, 2001). It is not surprising that there has been such a rapid growth in the number of applications because individuals and groups have specific information processing needs and therefore look for tools that offer the possibility of solving their specific problems (generally storing, retrieving and communicating).

Markup languages offer the possibility of solving both presentation problems (one of the original aims of SGML) and IR problems (Cover, 1999) by virtue of the software that is written to process the marked up files. The range of information that markup languages have been developed for includes still images (Cover, 2001b; 2002c; Lober, 2000; Thomas, 2001), moving images (Cover, 2002b; 2003b) and music (Cover, 2002d).

Are, therefore, markup languages a solution to the IR and MMIR problem? Consider a text document. Marked up this document will include tags that bracket parts of the text. The tags are like structure codes (for example, a tag in a business letter might identify the sender's address). Thus when the document is stored there is additional 'structural' information encoded within the document that describes the 'meaning' of the text within the tags. One might then search the collection of business letters for those whose 'sender' is 'Bloggs' and expect the system to be able to use the tags to find only those documents that include 'Bloggs' between the relevant tag thus improving retrieval performance (rather than simply searching for 'Bloggs' anywhere within all of the business letters). Markup approaches to multimedia are a little less satisfactory because the non-text media is not susceptible to markup in the same way as text is. Therefore marked-up multimedia tends to include the multimedia item as a complete object and the tags exist to add metadata 'around' the object. Moving Picture Experts Group (Mpeg-7), a parallel but related development for the encoding of metadata in moving image files, essentially takes this approach (Cover, 2002b).

A marked-up document collection, whether text only or multimedia, contains more information than non-marked-up text and is thus likely to be retrieved better than a collection without (depending on the quality of markup, purpose of the application and quality of the software). However, there are two issues facing markup language approaches that are difficult to overcome. The first is entirely pragmatic: the cost involved in marking up the text and documents and maintaining the quality of the encoding. Secondly, each application may have its own definitions and, although all the documents that share the application's definition can be easily shared, sharing between different applications is difficult. Problems about naming (same name for different concepts and different names for the same concept are two simple difficulties) and conflicting structural definitions are likely to make sharing documents between applications very difficult. This is an issue of interoperability: just because XML, an approach based on a standardized language, has been used does not mean interoperability is guaranteed. The application problem in XML (interoperability) is similar to that of dialects in natural language, it used to be said that the UK and the USA were divided by a common language! This problem has been known in the database community for many years (see Date, 2000, pp. 678–83 in 'DBMS independence') and is still difficult to resolve by technology. In fact the most likely way to resolve the problem is by the imposition of standards (not just for writing XML but for content, tag names and meaning and so on) – highly unlikely to be accepted in practice! Finally, one can think of markup as being a kind of large-scale 'faceted' approach, one still has problems about choosing and naming tags and entries within tags!

Although it can be argued that the development of many XML applications reflects the complexity of available information and is therefore to be welcomed because the individual XML document type definition (DTD) is better suited to marking up a specialized item than a very broad, general set of tags (like HTML for example), there are pitfalls. Interoperability has been discussed earlier: the development of myriad DTDs makes interoperability harder to achieve. The markup approach tends to lead to a 'once only' indexing activity. For some tags and texts this may be acceptable but there are a range of indexing activities that are likely to demand maintenance and review. Generally, software tools are used to make marking up a text easier, however there has to be considerable knowledge on the part of the encoder about the tags, their meaning and syntax within the DTD as well as detailed knowledge of the source documents. These skills are similar to those of information professionals, not typists!

MMIR AND THE INTERNET

Multimedia is, of course, not limited to specialist databases of multimedia. Perhaps one of the motivations for the development of multimedia indexing and search tools is the provision of multimedia data on the Web.

Some search engines attempt to search (and index) non-text data in 'ordinary' HTML based pages. Google (2002) has an image search facility described as follows: 'Google analyzes the text on the page adjacent to the image, the image caption and dozens of other factors to determine the image content. Google also uses sophisticated algorithms to remove duplicates and ensure that the highest quality images are presented first in your results.' It is difficult to imagine what the 'dozens of other factors' are but the Advanced Images Search page on Google does not appear to offer further possibilities in terms of content indexing apart from, perhaps the rendition (colour, black and white and so on) of the image.

TOWARDS THE IDEAL MULTIMEDIA RETRIEVAL SYSTEM?

What would an ideal multimedia information retrieval system be like? Obviously it would be one that retrieved the images (or multimedia) that satisfied the user's need! However, as can be seen in the previous discussion, there are many different ways of dealing with this problem. Current approaches have all been to adopt specialized solutions for particular user groups or multimedia content. These approaches may well be able to resolve the 'satisfy their user group' problem. However, a new user who is not aware of the particular system or the language used in the system will have a problem in even beginning to search for data in that system.

A second problem with the current strategy is the 'islands of information' issue which, expressed in another way, is a problem of 'interoperability'. Over time we might have available, through computerized databases and web pages, unimaginable quantities of multimedia data. However, such multimedia data is likely to be 'available' only in that it can be accessed over the Internet: finding it is likely to be very 'hit and miss'. This is because, essentially, all of the separate databases, languages and so on form increasingly broad barriers to sharing and cooperation between the systems and their contents. This is the holy grail of interoperability but more than a simple technical interpretation, it is also interoperability of contents and meaning. Besser (2002) describes this as the 'Ideal Digital Library Model'.

Finally we have the problems of the content itself. This chapter has discussed technical solutions to the indexing and retrieval problem. However, many of the approaches do not move the problem on more than card indexes did. Data can be shared over the Internet but it is still the case that knowledge of the local practice, vocabulary, structure and so on is required. There is no single multimedia indexing (contents) standard yet, much less universal conformance to it.

Will these approaches ever deliver a single system that can access any multimedia data anywhere? It is unlikely: the approaches all promote specialist one-off solutions in the hope that others will agree but standards are almost never universally adopted in this fashion. It may be the case that such an objective is impossible to deliver and even irrelevant. Who, for example, could envisage someone asking for pictures of brain tumours and another of London buses from the same environment? Well, of course, any library or university has to support a very broad range of subjects and retrievals, many of which are difficult (or impossible) to predict in advance of them being made. There is a need to provide an effective 'universal' search engine for the internet (or its successor, whatever that may look like) because the ideal (universal access to all the freely available material) is worth achieving but just storing it on the net (as a web page or file) is not enough.

4 Using semiotics to analyse multimedia objects

INTRODUCTION

Underlying any indexing project lie certain assumptions regarding the philosophy of language and communication. The process of indexing, searching and finding information is only possible if language is considered to be a shared, social, communicative process. *Semiotics* provides a philosophical and analytical framework which allows us to think about language and other communicative practices as signs. This in turn allows us to think about meaning in a range of signifying practices, for example, pictures, film, text and library classification schemes. This chapter provides a basic introduction to some of the issues of semiotics and the politics of interpretation. The language of semiotics is used elsewhere in the book to discuss issues relating to determining meaning in and through a range of multimedia information objects.

There are a number of perspectives which may be used to analyse and discuss cultural artefacts within humanities scholarship. Some of these are concerned with introspective and intuitive subjective interpretation which in the past has sometimes crystallized into authority and canonicity. Such approaches are of little value to us in the domain of multimedia indexing. Semiotic approaches to analysing the operation of meaning in cultural artefacts differ in kind from such approaches because a semiotic approach always includes the identification of models within which individual instantiations may be analysed. The dialectic which operates in relation to the model or system with its rules and elements, and the individual object of perception or cultural artefact, is reminiscent of Saussure's 'langue'/'parole' distinction which, despite all the ambiguities surrounding the specific meanings of the terms in particular instances of use (Holdcroft, 1991), offers a useful framework for mapping out the relationship between the cultural store and particular instantiations.

In semiotics the relationship between 'langue' and 'parole' assumes that there are rules, codes and conventions which can be mapped out and which determine signifying practices in specific societies at specific historical moments. The 'langue'/'parole' relationship is particularly compatible with the philosophical underpinnings of library 'classification theory'. Traditional library classification theory is built on the assumption that objects and ideas in the world can be divided into 'classes' governed by sets of rules. In contemporary semiotics, systems mapping out 'langue' are reappraised and reconstituted if necessary after analysis of new instantiations at the level of individual artefacts or signs. To some degree, faceted classification shares something of this diachronic dynamism, although the methodologies are clearly quite different. We would suggest that a semiotic approach to discussing meaning is the most appropriate in the context of multimedia indexing because of the shared concern with models, systems, sets and individual instantiations at the level of objects of perception.

In recent years, scholars within information science and librarianship have become increasingly interested in using aspects of semiotics to explore the mechanics of meaning and interpretation, and the processes of scholarly communication and indexing. Rafferty, Cronin and Carson (1988) used aspects of semiotics to study the mechanics of meaning in information technology (IT) industry advertisements. More recently Cronin (2000; 2001) has used Peircean semiotics to map and model the practice of scholarly citation. Mai's PhD, and much of his recent writing, is concerned with using Peircean semiotics to explore the processes of subject indexing (for example, Mai, 2001). Material semiotics views communication as a process involving the producer of communication, the communication itself in the form of communication-as-thing, and the receiver(s) of communication operating within the codes and conventions of specific societies and cultures at specific historical moments. Such an approach offers fruitful ways of exploring the process of indexing.

Subsections in this chapter will explore the following topics:

● the founding fathers of semiotics (Ferdinand de Saussure and C.S. Peirce)
● analytical categories (paradigms, syntagms, denotation and connotation)
● social semiotics and modality
● communication models
● semiotics of film
● Goran Sonesson and visual semiotics
● semiotics of music.

THE 'FOUNDING FATHERS' OF SEMIOTICS

SAUSSURE AND SEMIOLOGY

In contemporary cultural theory semiotic analysis is used to explore the operation of meaning and communication in a variety of cultural artefacts including images, music and film, but much of semiotics as we know it today developed from the linguistic theory of Ferdinand de Saussure. The recording, interpretation and dissemination of Saussure's linguistic theory itself has an interesting history because the *Course in General Linguistics* (Saussure, 1974 [1915]) was compiled by Charles Bally and Albert Sechehaye after Saussure's death partly from lecture notes taken by his students and partly from Saussure's own personal notes. We always approach Saussure through second-hand interpretations.

Saussure's linguistics was in part a critique of the comparative and historical linguistic scholarship then in vogue. He took the view that language should not be viewed as referential but as conceptual and believed that language is arbitrary and conventional. This means that there is no necessary link between a word and the thing to which it refers (arbitrariness), and that language is a system of signs which has to be learnt (conventional). He distinguished between langue and parole. *Langue* referred to the structures and systems of language from which individual *parole*, or speech utterances, could be formed.

For both Saussure and Peirce, the sign was the basic unit of analysis. The Saussurean sign was composed of signifier and signified which together form the sign. In the *Course in General Linguistics*, the sign is represented in the form of the diagram in Figure 4.1.

In the classic Saussurean model, which was designed with spoken language as the object of analysis, the *signifier* is a sound-pattern which is not spoken but which is the hearer's psychological impression of the pattern, while the *signified* is a concept which again is psychological. This representation of the sign is fairly idealist. Daniel Chandler commented that contemporary models tend to materialize the Saussurean sign by turning the signifier into the material form that the sign takes, for example, that which can be heard, smelled, touched, seen,

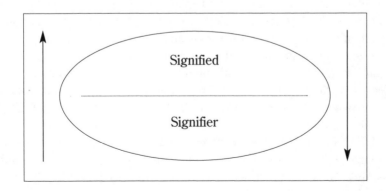

Figure 4.1   The Saussurean sign

while the signified is the concept to which the signifier refers. Holdcroft (1991, p. 27) makes the point that Saussure himself does not take a completely idealist view of language but sees language as a social product.

Although his semiotics was grounded in linguistics and particularly in the spoken word, Saussure himself suggested that the semiotic model could be developed and used to analyse other types of communication systems, for example, images, gestures and behavioural codes. Early in the *Course of General Linguistics* we find the following:

> Language is a system of sign that express ideas, and is therefore comparable to a system of writing, the alphabet of deaf-mutes, symbolic rites, polite formulas, military signals, etc. But it is the most important of all these systems.
>
> *A science that studies the life of signs within society* is conceivable; it would be a part of social psychology and consequently of general psychology; I shall call it *semiology* (from Greek sĕmeîon 'sign'). Semiology would show what constitutes signs and what governs them. Since the science does not yet exist, no one can say what it would be; but it has a right to existence, a place staked out in advance. Linguistics is only a part of the general science of semiology; the laws discovered by semiology will be applicable to linguistics, and the latter will circumscribe a well-defined area within the mass of anthropological facts. (Saussure, 1974 [1915], p. 16)

PEIRCE AND SEMIOTIC

In the later years of the nineteenth century and the early twentieth century the American philosopher Charles Peirce formulated his own semiotic theory relating to human signs, meaning and communication. For Charles Peirce, the sign was made up of:

- the *representamen*: the form which the sign takes (not necessarily material)
- an *interpretant*: *not* an interpreter but rather the sense made of the sign
- an *object*: to which the sign refers (Chandler, 2002, p. 32).

What is interesting about this triadic version of the sign is the inclusion of the interpretant which, although not strictly a reference to a material hearer, suggests that communication is of central significance in the sign system. For Peirce, human signs and signifying systems operate as communicative processes in which interpretation leads on to unlimited semiosis and uncertainty.

Where semiotic theory has been used in information science it has often been in the form of semiotic theory based on the Peircean tradition. Mai's PhD (2000), for example, was concerned with using a framework based on Peircean semiotics to model the information retrieval process. Mai's concern was with the limitations of traditional approaches to the issue of subject analysis core to the indexing process. He argued that the traditional approach to subject indexing typical of LIS literature 'lacks an understanding of what the central nature of the process is.

Indexing is not a neutral and objective representation of a document's subject matter but the representation of an interpretation of a document for future use'. The alternative subject indexing model that he proposed was one in which

> Semiotics, based on key ideas found in Charles Sanders Peirce, is offered here as a framework for understanding the 'interpretative' nature of the subject indexing process. Peirce's semiotics offers an especially valuable terminology for describing the different kinds of interpretation that takes place throughout the subject indexing process. By placing the subject indexing process within Peirce's semiotic framework of ideas and terminology, a more detailed description of the process is offered here than has been previously possible. This description shows that the uncertainty related to the subject indexing process is due to the fact that the indexer in steps through the indexing process creates the subject matter of the document and that this creation is itself based on the indexer's social and cultural context. While this attempt to show what occurs in the subject indexing process offers a more realistic view of what actually happens in the process, a result of great benefit to those who are teaching indexing, it also suggests strongly that there is no certainty to the result of the subject indexing process. (Mai, 2000)

Peirce's approach to the communicative operation of signs emphasized the process of semiosis through which meanings could be generated endlessly from signs. He was interested in mapping the types of signs which humans use to communicate and referred to 66 different types of signs. In contemporary semiotic literature reference is generally made to the three types of signs within the broader semiotic system to which Peirce referred most often:

- *Index*: a sign which is not arbitrary but in some way is connected with the signified/object, for example thunder, medical symptoms or hoofprints.
- *Icon*: where the sign is seen as resembling the signified/object, for example a portrait, a scale model.
- *Symbol*: where the sign is arbitrary or conventional so that the meaning of the sign must be learned, for example language, traffic lights (Chandler, 2002, p. 37).

A specific sign can operate as any or all of these functions at any given moment read from different perspectives by different readers, and the functions may be historically contingent. It can be difficult to distinguish between iconicity and indexicality. Hodge and Kress argued that indexicality is a matter of judgement, so that icons are the class of signs which has the highest modality, in other words, icons have a higher reality status than either indexes or symbols, where 'reality' refers to a relationship with the world (Hodge and Kress, 1988, p. 27). In his essay 'Encoding/decoding' Stuart Hall (2001) argued that even the seemingly iconic signs of television media are constructed and ideological, and are thus indexical. Indeed, he suggests that iconicity is itself an ideological position. These distinctions are of considerable interest in relation to interpretation of images and of moving images.

ANALYTICAL CATEGORIES

PARADIGMS AND SYNTAGMS

For the Saussurean linguists meaning in language is constructed through difference, so that signifiers only have meaning relative to other signifiers, present or absent. A sign needs other signs, both present and absent, which are different from it to give it definition and meaning, and systems of signs are relational. Saussure emphasized the negative or oppositional differences between signs. The construction of meaning is governed by operations on two planes, Saussure named these planes the *associative* and the *syntagmatic* planes, but the associative plane is now usually referred to by the term that Roman Jakobson used, the *paradigmatic* plane. For structuralist semiotics, these relationships are of great importance.

A *paradigm* is a set of associated signifiers or signifieds which are all members of some defining category, but is a set in which each is significantly different from the others (Chandler, 2002, p. 80). In linguistic signs, paradigms might be specific verbs or nouns. The choice of one word rather than another shapes the preferred meaning of the text. In a paradigmatic set of words which signify the female sex, choosing the signifier 'lady' rather than 'woman' can determine meanings and readings. In the nineteenth and early twentieth centuries, the distinction in some discursive formations was between 'lady' and 'person', a distinction which was class based and ideological. For semioticians working within critical theory frameworks the choice of specific signifiers always involves ideological implications, or at least points to the construction of a specific discursive formation.

Paradigmatic sets operate not only in linguistic signs, but also in other types of signs, for example, images. The choice of one type of female model rather than another in the construction of an advertisement determines the meaning of the advertisement and the ways in which viewers will interpret the advertisement, determining perhaps whether the advertisement is a representation of an appealing and aspirational lifestyle, or not. Contemporary codes and conventions relating to beauty, fashion and commodity-rich lifestyles provide the frameworks within which advertisers make paradigmatic choices. Dawson and Rafferty (2001) discussed the ways in which paradigmatic choice works as ideology in their paper '"Careless Talk Costs Lives": a case study examining the operation of information in British domestic posters of the Second World War'.

Syntagms are the combinations or 'chains' of elements which form a meaningful whole within a text (Chandler, 2002, p. 81). In text or speech, syntagm refers to the syntactical rules and conventions which govern language. In music and language, syntagms are sequential and temporal. Syntagms operating within visual sign systems such as images, photographs and drawings are spatial, relating to the positioning and combining of elements. In film, television, cinema and the World Wide Web, syntagmatic relationships are both temporal and spatial. Narrative forms depend on temporal and causal syntagmatic relationships, while argument and exposition depend on conceptual syntagmatic relationships, but this type of discourse also adheres to narrative structures (beginning, middle, ending) (Chandler, 2002, p. 82).

For many semioticians, syntagmatic relationships are also ideological. The placing of elements in relation to each other can signify hierarchical relationships. In *Reading Images: The Grammar of Visual Design* (1996) Kress and Van Leeuwen identified three spatial relationships in visual texts which have informational value: left/right; top/bottom; centre/margin. The distinction between left and right in Kress and Van Leeuwen's typology is the distinction between the Given and the New. Their examples were taken from layouts in women's magazines, advertisements and medieval art forms. In the context of these texts, to be Given is to be something which the viewer is already familiar with; to be New means that what is being presented is something which is not yet known or is not yet agreed upon by the viewer (by the dominant ideology). The New is 'problematic' and 'contestable', 'the information', while the Given is commonsensical and self-evident (ibid., p. 187).

The meanings of the top and the bottom of images in this typology are the Ideal and the Real. In advertisements, the elements at the top of the image represent the 'promise of the product' while the elements at the bottom of the image are more factual and informational. Kress and Van Leeuwen argued that the elements at the top of the image tend to make an emotive appeal, showing 'what might be', while the elements at the bottom of the image are more practical, showing the viewer 'what is' (ibid., p. 193). The Ideal in an image is that which is presented as the generalized idealization or essence of the information, while the Real is more concrete, specific and 'down-to-earth'. The third informational relationship is that between the Centre and the Margins. In images which make significant use of centre/margin relationships, the element in the Centre will be the nucleus of information to which all the marginal elements are in some way subservient. But structures can be more complex than this. Circular structures can create gradual, and graded, distinctions between the Centre and the Margins (ibid., p. 206). In triptych structures, the Centre is sometimes used as a space for the Mediator between the Given and the New. All of these structural meanings are ideologically coded.

DENOTATION AND CONNOTATION

Another important distinction in semiotic analysis is the distinction between *denotation* and *connotation*, although, as we shall see, these are disputed categories. These analytical terms as they are used in contemporary semiotics grew from the work of the French philosopher and literary critic, Roland Barthes, a significant figure in semiotic scholarship, whose work spanned the period from the early 1950s to the late 1970s. Between 1954 and 1956, Roland Barthes wrote a series of short essays for the left-wing magazine *Les Lettres nouvelles*, which marked an important turning point in the use of semiotics because of his insistence on focusing attention on the 'everyday' cultural artefacts that he found around him in post-war France.

These articles were written in a journalistic discourse which brought the semiotic project to a wide readership for the first time. The articles, which included short essays on the meanings of wrestling contests, the Hollywood film *Julius Caesar*, Greta Garbo's face on screen, steak and chips, electoral photography and Charlie Chaplin, were later collected together to form the first part of *Mythologies* (Barthes, 1973). The second part of *Mythologies* consists of a theoretical essay 'Myth today' in which Barthes explores his conception of 'mythology' as a system of representations through which the ruling class reproduce their economic dominance at the level of everyday culture. In 'Myth today', Barthes made the distinction between *denotation* or first-level signification, by which he meant the straightforward or common-sense meaning of the sign, and second-level signification or *connotation*, by which he meant the cultural meanings attached to the sign. An example which is often used to demonstrate the difference between denotation and connotation is that of the rose which is a flower, but also comes to signify 'passion' in western culture. Critiques of semiotics might argue that while the rose might signify 'passion', it could also signify other things as well. In contemporary Britain for example, the rose might signify the Labour Party. Semioticians are increasingly registering that context and communication frameworks play an important role in pinning down meaning.

For Barthes, where connotations have become naturalized or normal, they can be seen to have become hegemonic, and thus they become conceptual maps for us to make sense of the world. This level of signification Barthes described as third level signification, or *myth*. Myth then refers to cultural constructions which appear to contain common-sense universal truths within them. Myths are thus like ideology which works at the second level of signification.

Barthes's use of the term 'connotation' has been the source of contention: partly because in his model 'denotation' appears to be the primary and foundational meaning of the sign; partly because his use of the term differs from Hjemslev's use. Barthes's essays were explicitly concerned with ideology critique from a Marxist perspective and his use of the term 'connotation' emphasizes the conventional and social meanings of signs. These meanings can sometimes be affective meanings, but in *Mythologies*, the meanings are not personal meanings as much as cultural meanings.

In his essay, 'The photographic message' Roland Barthes (1977) distinguished between the denotative aspects of the photograph, its analogical and 'objective' quality, and the connotative aspects which are institutionalized (producing the advertisement, producing the electoral poster), and realized at the different levels of production of the photograph (choice, technical treatment, framing, layout), and of reception of the photograph which is read as one of the historical/cultural 'stock of signs' (ibid., pp. 19–20). Chandler made the point that the distinction between denotation and connotation is similar to Erwin Panofsky's distinction between primary or natural subject matter and secondary or conventional subject matter which is culturally determined (Panofsky, 1993, pp. 53–4).

However the phrase 'natural subject matter' is based on assumptions that everyone is able to recognize the image. 'One suspects,' wrote Chandler 'that this excludes very young children and those regarded as insane, for instance' (Chandler, 2002, p. 140). He reinterpreted primary recognition as 'culturally well-adjusted' viewing, which immediately turns the primary, or the denotative, into the cultural, or the connotative. Stuart Hall argued in 'Encoding/decoding' that distinguishing between denotation and connotation is useful for analytical purposes, but in the real world, the sign always bears with it its associative meaning (Hall, 2001, p. 171). For many critical theorists, the sign, even an iconic sign which seems to foreground denotation, such as the photograph, is always ideological.

INTERPRETATION AND INTERTEXTUALITY

Many linguists have been interested in the distinguishing between different discourses which are to be found in textual documents. Barthes distinguished between 'readerly' and 'writerly' texts and Eco distinguished between 'open' and 'closed' texts. Implicit in both of these distinctions is the acknowledgement that meaning does not reside entirely in the text but is a consequence of the interaction between author–text–reader. This emphasis on meaning as a communicative process was crucial for Mikhail Bahktin who in his work distinguished between 'monologic' and 'dialogic' utterance. Monologic texts are utterances which are closed and directed from an authoritative source to an audience. Monologic texts include sermons and speeches. The dialogic aspects of utterances relate to openness and interpretation, to the relationship which exists between the text and the audience. Some types of utterances are more dialogic in form and function than others, inviting interpretation and response from audiences.

These insights, although originally developed to describe and analyse textual documents, can be used to map the operation of meaning in non-textual information (in this context the term 'text' refers to the symbolic language of writing). There are some non-textual informational objects in which the semiotic encoding is tightly controlled, possibly more so in texts which are monologic in nature, while in other texts ambiguity is sought as part of the encoding process. It may be that the possibility of multiple interpretations is related to whether the author intentionally created a document which was monologic or dialogic, moreover, the modality of the object might determine whether multiple meanings are possible or not.

The underlying assumption in dialogical approaches to communication is that the sign communicates in a dynamic made up of addresser and addressee operating within the socio-political frameworks, or logonomic systems, that exist at any given historical moment within specific and concrete societies. There are issues about exactly what constitutes the 'given historical moment' and the 'specific and concrete society'; indeed, some technological-determinist orientated pro- and anti-globalization theorists might argue that electronic communication forms are catalysts ushering in a homogenous McCluhanite 'global village', increasingly operating within the philosophical and cultural norms of democratic neo-liberal political economy.

The concept of intertextuality is based on a viewpoint which sees all utterances as part of a dialogic process. Such a view of language focuses on the interaction and intersubjectivity of material speakers, and authors and audiences. Hodge and Kress's social semiotics explores dialogic communicative practices, and they, like other critical thinkers, explore the dialogic aspects of communication at work even in relation to monologic utterances, with particular interest in power struggles operating in and through communicative practices.

In *Social Semiotics* Hodge and Kress use the example of a billboard advertisement for Marlboro cigarettes which shows a cowboy riding a horse in the sunset under the textual anchorage 'New. Mild. And Marlboro'. Billboard messages are normally monologic texts, but this message has been changed by graffiti artists who added critical text to the image and changed the textual anchorage to 'New. Vile. And a bore' (Hodge and Kress, 1988, p. 8). Hodge and Kress are interested in identifying and exploring the networks of meanings and dialogic responses and transformations that even the most self-consciously controlled monologic communicative forms are subject to within society. Lagoze's (2001) event awareness approach to resource description might enable us to capture the dialogic elements inherent in the graffiti billboard reinterpretation in metadata form.

SOCIAL SEMIOTICS AND MODALITY

The social semiotics approach developed by Robert Hodge and Gunther Kress (1988) was an attempt to materialize and historicize the semiotic tradition. Their semiotic practice is based on the dialectic materialist language philosophy of V.N. Volosinov (1973). This reworking of semiotics follows Volosinov in reconstituting language as dialogue rather than as the 'abstract objectivism' that Volosinov read in Saussurean-influenced structuralists or as the generative monologue issuing from the 'individualistic subjectivity' of linguists following phenomenological traditions. Practitioners of social semiotics are interested in exploring the construction of meaning as a social activity, acknowledging the role of the reader, located in specific material logonomic systems, in 'making meaning'. Social semiotics with its focus on diachronic transformation, acknowledges that meaning of a text, formed from the interplay of polysemic signs and a range of reading positions, at the point of reception does not necessarily equate to the meaning of that text at the point of production. Meaning consists of specific interplays of a range of variables and is constituted by actualized, material reading subjects at different diachronic moments.

Social semiotics is concerned with questions of representation of the real and the acknowledgement that some representations of the real are more reliable than others. Hodge and Kress (1988, p. 121) explained that news coverage is considered a more reliable representation of reality than fiction or drama, and some fictional representations are considered more reliable than others. Representation is a site of struggle, with different groups seeking to ensure that their definitions of what counts as 'truth' and 'reality' will assume a dominant position in society. In social semiotics the term 'modality' is used to refer to the relationships between representation in multimedia objects and reality. For social semioticians there is an acceptance that knowledge systems are socially constructed, although, as Chandler points out, this constructionism does not take the extreme subjectivist position of arguing that there are many individual and unique realities (Chandler, 2002, p. 122). The social semiotic position is that society is made up of many groups who have different positions of power, and semiosis is a process of imposing and contesting ideologically coded representations of reality.

Modality judgements involve comparisons with models of the real world, and with models of the genre, so modality works on both mimetic and semiotics planes. For some viewers film and television might be considered to have high modality value, to closely represent reality, however, there are film theorists who would suggest that modality is the relationship between the perception-interpretation of the viewer and the codes and conventions of filmic versions of reality rather than reality itself. Filmic versions of reality have a historical dimension, so that early filmic representations which were interpreted as having high modality value and thus were reliably representative of reality, such as early 1930s gangster movies, would now be considered to have lower modality value and therefore to be less reliable in their representation of reality. The intervening time gap allows contemporary viewers to view these representations as constructions. Photographs are likely to be considered more real than drawings or cartoons, but we have already discussed the ideology of the iconic. Writing might be considered to have lower modality because it is a symbolic semiotic system. One of the issues which will be of some interest to us in relation to multimedia indexing is whether high modality signs are more likely to generate a closed range of meanings than low modality signs.

The issue of representing reality is of some interest to multimedia indexing. If we accept that the indexing of multimedia objects includes the analysis and representation of physical properties using retrieval tools such as have been developed in the AACR, and analysis and representation of subject content, then it is in the area of subject content that we face the greatest challenge.

We explained that for Hodge and Kress, modality judgements involve comparisons with models of the real world, and with models of the genre, so modality works on both mimetic and semiotic planes. The issue is more complex still because what is considered to closely represent reality at one historical moment within a specific material society may for future generation seem conventionalized and artificial. Judgements about the representation of the real depend on the codes and conventions within which and through which the viewer reads and interprets the multimedia informational object. When we think about meaning in multimedia, it may be helpful to consider both the content of the informational object, and the codes and conventions relating to specific historical and societal moment at which reception occurs, in other words, the meaning of information might 'change' over time. Moreover, following Hodge and Kress, it may be possible to speculate that some forms of multimedia information objects are more ambiguous than others and, so, open to multiple interpretations.

In some of the literature of image indexing, there is an assumption that meaning in images per se is problematic, but the insights of pragmatic communication theories might lead us to wonder whether the issue is more nuanced and specific than this generalization might suggest. We can explore this issue using visual communication as an example. Within the communicative domain of visual communication, images range from those which are extremely high in modality, for example spontaneous and 'unposed' photographic 'snaps', to images which have self-consciously low modality, for example abstract painting, with most images occupying a point within those two extremes along a continuum representing modality, or relationship with reality. The purpose and provenance of the image will be important in thinking about semiotic encoding and about whether the 'preferred' reception position has been determined and controlled by the encoder, or whether the meaning(s) might be more fluid, ambiguous and open to interpretation.

This issue leads us to questions about the interpretation and reception of signs. Contemporary semiotics acknowledges the post-structuralist interest in the role of the reader in making meaning. Roland Barthes for example, moved from a theoretical position in the early *Mythologies* essays which allowed the enlightened reader, Barthes, to 'decode' the false consciousness of a number of cultural artefacts, to a much more post-structuralist position which heralded the death of the author and the consequent freedom for a range of reception positions. In its most extreme form some types of post-structuralist thinking allow for unlimited opportunities for interpretation and reading, any of which might be deemed as legitimate as another. The historian Richard Evans, a witness for Deborah Lipstaddt in the case against David Irving, warned that such a position might allow radical misinterpretation and falsification to be legitimized in the absence of notions of truth, of respect for the author's construction of the text and, one might argue, in the absence of notions about the basic shared communicative properties of language (Evans, 1997).

Post-structuralist philosophers are interested in issues regarding determinism, structure and agency in relation to the construction of meaning. Text is encoded by the transmitter (author, painter, photographer, composer, song-writer or any other person or people responsible for the creation of the sign. Coded information relating to the creator(s) of a document is referred to in AACR2 as the 'statement of responsibility') and is disseminated to the consumer through some kind of publishing process, but the question is how much is it transformed and injected with meaning as it is consumed by the receiver (reader or viewer or listener), who may occupy any one (or maybe more) of a range of reading positions? Is it possible that a range of meanings can be derived from one material object (mechanically reproduced, which itself, as the philosopher-literary critic Walter Benjamin (2000 [1937], argued, can change the function and meaning of the media object)? Personal, private meanings attached to texts can transform the text from the 'preferred' meaning inscribed within it by the author (Hall, 2001), to a range of possible meanings. Does the meaning of a text, in its broadest sense, depend on the meaning attached by the author, and if so how can we know what that meaning is, or does the construction of meaning occur when the reader interprets the text? Is the text the sole source of meaning or does the reader '(re-)create' meaning in interpreting the text? Some extreme reader reception positions might locate the construction of meaning solely in the individual reader's interpretation.

On his website, John Lye discusses the:

general positions within the understanding that the 'meaning' of a text is what happens when the reader reads it. The positions presuppose various attitudes towards such considerations as:

- the question of in what sense a text, ink-marks on a page or electrons on a screen, exists,
- the extent to which knowledge is objective or subjective,
- the question of whether the world as we experience it is culturally constructed or has an essential existence,
- how the gap, historically, culturally and semiotically (as reading is a decoding of signs which have varying meanings) between the reader and the writer is bridged, and the extent to which it is bridged,
- the question of the extent to which interpretation is a public act, conditioned by the particular material and cultural circumstances of the reader, vs the extent to which reading is a private act governed by a response to the relatively independent codes of the text,
- the question of what the process of reading is like, what it entails,
- and so forth. (Lye, 1996)

Daniel Chandler (1995) provided a useful model which maps out the variety of positions which have been adopted by contributors to the 'location of meaning' debate from a range of disciplines including literary theory, cultural studies, communication studies and media studies. He identified a set of generic positions, Objectivist, Constructivist and Subjectivist, and located these positions within a continuum which represents the locus of meaning in the reading of texts (Figure 4.2).

Formalist literary critics have tended to adopt objectivist positions which view meaning as residing entirely in the text. Phenomenological approaches to the 'role of the reader' which stress the experience of the individual reader in 'realizing' the text have been generated by reader reception and reader response

Objectivist	*Constructivist*	*Subjectivist*
Meaning entirely in text - - - - - - - - - -	Meaning in interplay between text and reader - - - - - - - - - -	Meaning entirely in its interpretation by readers
'transmitted'	'negotiated'	're-created'
- - - - - - - - - -> reader as less 'passive', more 'active'		

Figure 4.2   Locus of meaning in the reading of texts

schools of literary criticism. In the institutionalized practice of Cultural Studies, empirically based research projects have examined the meanings constructed about specific material texts or cultural artefacts by sets of material readers (Ang, 1985; Morley, 1999; Radway, 1991), but these approaches bring with them their own methodological problems relating to the versions of 'ethnography' that they used and the construction of the 'group' of readers or viewers (Turner, 1996, pp. 122–55).

COMMUNICATION MODELS

We argued in Chapter 1 that the indexing process can be theorized as a communicative process. In the literature of semiotics, communication models are sometimes developed to represent the processes of human intersubjective communication. In the *Course of General Linguistics*, the diagram in Figure 4.3 is included to represent an individual act of language from within the speaking circuit. The act of language requires the presence of at least two people to 'complete the circuit' (Saussure, 1974 [1915], p. 11).

On the following page of the *Course*, this pictorial diagram gives way to an abstract model of the speech circuit (Figure 4.4). The model in Figure 4.4 is linear and two-dimensional, and assumes as a given that the two speakers are able to understand the same language and communicate with each other.

In 1949 Shannon and Weaver published *The Mathematical Theory of Communication* in which they developed a model to represent the elements and the process involved in communication. The model has become widely known and is to be found reproduced in many textbooks and websites concerned with communication, linguistics and media studies in the form shown in Figure 4.5.

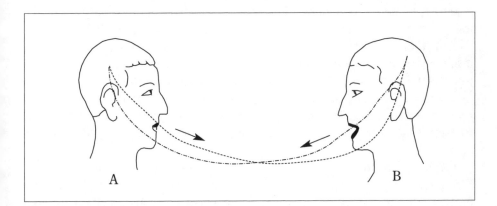

Figure 4.3   Saussure's model of the speech circuit 1

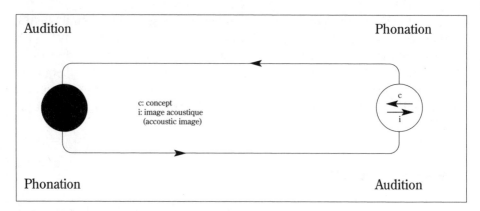

Figure 4.4   Saussure's model of the speech circuit 2

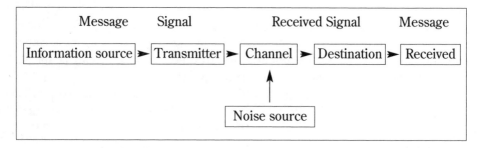

Figure 4.5   Representation of Shannon and Weaver's model of communication

Figure 4.5 is a diagram which attempts to represent communication, but it is very mechanistic in orientation and there is no reference at all to human communication. Since Shannon and Weaver's engineering model of communication was published many other communication theorists have tried to construct models of communication, some of which are more clearly orientated towards human communication than the Shannon and Weaver model.

Roman Jakobson's (1960) communication model (Figure 4.6) is an interesting if limited model. Communication proceeds from the addresser and is directed towards the addressee. The message is only understood if the addressee is able to contact the message through understanding the language or the lines represented on paper. The message requires a context to be referred to and is transmitted through a code, a language which is shared by both addresser and addressee.

Jakobson argued that each factor determines a different function of language. Writing which is orientated towards the addresser or writer has *expressive* purpose, that is, the writer expresses his or her feelings and opinions through journals, diaries, free writing and poetry; writing orientated towards the reader

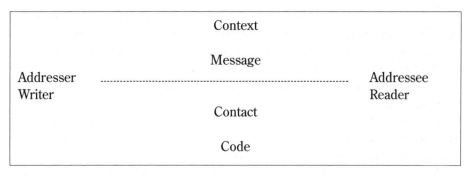

Figure 4.6 Jakobson's model of communication

has *conative* purpose, which means that the writer is attempting to affect or persuade the reader; context-orientated writing is *informative*, for example, maps or prose; message-orientated writing is *poetic* in function, focusing on the message itself, the language and structure and composition; contact-orientated writing is *phatic* in function, that is, it is primarily concerned with establishing and maintaining contact, for example, postcards and Christmas cards; and code-orientated writing is *metalinguistic*, that is, writing which comments on writing, for example, the preface to a book.

This model is good for exploring the function and purposes of writing. It may be that Jakobson's model could be adapted for use with other types of signs. A preliminary attempt to reconstitute the model to account for types of textual and non-textual information operating in British Second World War domestic posters was made by Dawson and Rafferty (2001). Such a model might offer useful foundations for a classification scheme based on function rather than subject terminology.

Among the most influential work done on reception positions and communication is Stuart Hall's work on encoding/decoding. Stuart Hall's model of audience reception offers an interesting framework through which texts might be read and suggests that within particular cultures at particular moments there may be an identifiable range of reception positions. The model was constructed to represent the moments of production and reception of mass media, specifically television news, nevertheless it offers some interesting starting points for a broader range of research programmes which examine issues of production and reception of multimedia objects.

In his essay 'Encoding/decoding' (2001) Hall used an Althusserian model of 'structure in dominance' to analyse specific moments in the production and reception of media texts. The moment of production is one in which institutional practices and discursive knowledge predominate. At the moment of the text, discursive forms predominate, and at the moment of decoding, reception and interpretation by the viewer dominates. Hall was attempting to construct a communication model within which reception becomes more active, so that the consumption of the text is also in itself a 'moment' which is the point of departure for the meaning of the text. It is important to acknowledge that unlike some other cultural theorists of the same historical juncture, Hall was not prepared to suggest that reception and creation of meaning is entirely constructed through the process of reading by individual readers. The encoded message forms parameters which contain expectations about meaning and set limits on reading practices although aberrant reading practices are always possible.

Within this framework Hall (2001) identifies three different reception positions that the individual viewer might adopt in relation to the text:

- Dominant-hegemonic position: when the viewer takes the connoted meaning from the text 'full and straight' and decodes the meaning within the terms of the code in which the text has been encoded. The viewer operates inside the dominant code (ibid., p. 174).
- Negotiated code or position: this position acknowledges the dominant code at the abstract level but reserves the right to make its own ground rules, and negotiated meaning, at local level – so it operates with exceptions to the rule (ibid., p. 175).
- Oppositional code: this position is one in which the viewer understands the literal and connotative inflection given by media discourse, but decodes the message in a globally contradictory way. This is the case of the viewer who listens to a debate on the need to limit wages but 'reads' every mention of 'national interest' as 'class interest' (ibid., p. 175).

Critics of Hall's model have argued that there is too much emphasis on ideology at the expense of questions relating to structure and control within the model. Some might find Hall's approach to signifying systems as outlined in 'Encoding/decoding' too structuralist, emphasizing structure, rules and regulations and discursive parameters at the expense of agency at the level of personal, individualized responses, but the significance of interpretation in this model is quite clear, indeed the reception positions are often cited in the literature with little or no reference to the other moments in the encoding/decoding model.

The big issue for multimedia indexing relates to the question of interpreting media objects. Is there any consensus about the meaning of media objects which can form the basis of a subject-orientated information retrieval system? Are there some types of media objects which through their structures and forms determine a fairly narrow range of meanings (acknowledging, even so, that aberrant meanings are always possible)? Are there multiple possible meanings to be derived from media objects, or one single 'truth'? Is it possible to model media types so that the indexer, in advance can determine the 'readerly-ness' or 'writerly-ness' of specific objects? Is it desirable, or possible, to index at many levels of meaning: denotative/connotative; pre-iconographic, iconographic, iconological; generic/specific/affective; 'hard' objective information and 'soft' subjective information? What are the specific semiotic issues relating to images and pictures, music and film?

The following sections provide brief overviews of some specific issues relating to the semiotics of film, pictures and music.

SEMIOTICS OF FILM

Writers have been exploring the issues of meaning and communication in film since films first began to be made in the late 1890s. The semiotic tradition of film theory and analysis owes much of its original impetus to the work of the Russian Formalists in the 1920s. These thinkers were concerned with the 'scientific' exploration of the 'imminent' features of film, its structures and systems (Stam, 2000, p. 48), and sought to avoid the subjectivity of aestheticism. Film for the Formalists was however to be considered in aesthetic terms. The study and the meaning of film was always 'filmic' and concerned with the 'artfulness of the object' (Shlovsky, quoted in Stam, 2000, p. 49). The Bakhtin circle, while approving aspects of Formalism relating to the acknowledgement of the constructedness of film and the rejection of subjective, romantic views of art, critiqued the Formalist 'imminent' rigidity which focused on the artwork to the exclusion of sociocultural concerns. The Bahtkin circle insisted on the social nature of art. The Formalist movement has influenced much of film theory since the 1920s both in the sense of providing working concepts, such as the notion of 'defamiliarization', which have been developed by other writers and indeed film-makers, and in the sense of providing foundational material for subsequent critique.

The issue of concrete spatio-temporal structures is of concern to film semioticians. The notion of the chronotope has been borrowed from Bahtkin in discussions of the cinematic chronotope. The chronotope, which Bahtkin originally conceived of in relation to fiction, is defined by Stam as:

> the constellation of distinctive temporal and spatial features within a genre defined as a 'relatively stable type of utterance.' The chronotope mediates between two orders of experience and discourse: the historical and the artistic, providing fictional environments where historically specific constellations of power are made visible ... The chronotope offers specific settings where stories can 'take place' (the atemporal other-worldly forest of romance, the 'nowhere' of fictional utopias, the roads and inns of the picaresque novel). In the cinema one thinks, for example, of the relations between character and environment, whether in synch (the cowboy ambling along the wide-open spaces), out-of-synch (Monica Vitti lost and disoriented against the

backdrops of Antonioni's Red Desert), or comically deterministic (characters commandeered by architecture in Tati's Play-time). (Stam, 2000, pp. 204–5)

The chronotope is appropriate to film because:

> Film is a medium where, at a particular place and a specific time, a visual representation of spatial reality unfolds at around twenty-four frames per second, projected onto a screen with definite spatial parameters. It presents spatial relationships with a tangibility that the novel, no matter how descriptive or imaginative, cannot approach; it can traverse temporal limits in a way that stage drama, despite its three-dimensionality, cannot match (for example, the manipulation of time in slow-motion or freeze-framing). (Flanagan, 1998)

The notion of the chronotope is related to the notion of genre and of narrative structures, so that, to use Flanagan's example, the Indiana Jones films of the 1980s used a 1940s chronotope which intertextually reflects the chronotopes used in Saturday morning serials. If it were possible to construct a classification scheme based on chronotopes, for example, chronotopes of the Hollywood filmic tradition or of the Bollywood filmic tradition, such a scheme might offer a way of relating films intertextually, complementing generic classifications, possibly facilitating indexing of chronotopes at the level of scenes.

Film unfolds in time and space. Clearly syntagmatic relationships are therefore of some importance in film semiotics. Christian Metz's 'grande sytagmatique' of cinema includes eight filmic syntagms based on ways of ordering narrative time and space:

- The *autonomous shot* (for example establishing shot, insert)
- The *parallel syntagm* (montage of motifs)
- The *bracketing syntagm* (montage of brief shots)
- The *descriptive syntagm* (sequence describing one moment)
- The *alternating syntagm* (two sequences alternating)
- The *scene* (shots implying temporal continuity)
- The *episodic sequence* (organized discontinuity of shots)
- The *ordinary sequence* (temporal with some compression) (Metz, quoted in Chandler, 2002, p. 98).

These syntagms for Metz are analogous to sentences in verbal language. This syntagmatique has since been critiqued as being difficult to apply to all films. Chandler refers to Hodge and Tripp's 1986 study of children in which they divided syntagms into four kinds based on syntagms existing at the same time (synchronic), different times (diachronic), same space (syntoptic) and different space (diatoptic):

- Synchronic/syntopic (one place, one time: one shot)
- Diachronic/syntopic (same place sequence over time)
- Synchronic/diatopic (different places at same time)
- Diachronic/diatopic (shots related only by theme)

> They add that whilst these are all continuous syntagms (single shots or successive shots), there are also discontinuous syntagms (related shots separated by others). (Chandler, 2002, p. 98)

The issue of continuous and discontinuous syntagms leads on to a discussion of narrative structures in film. Early films were often quite short in duration and took the form of the 'act' or event or action moment. There was some notion of an event unfolding over time but often little in the way of story or chains of causally connected narrative structures. Mainstream film since the early twentieth century has tended towards some narrative structure, so the issues relating to stories and the ways in which stories might be told are crucial. The Formalists distinguished between *fabula* and *szujet*. Fabula refers to chronological events, the 'what happened?' of the story, while szujet refers to how the story is told, or the representation of the story. There may be different filmic versions of one story which unfold in different ways. With increasing digitalization of cultural artefacts one of the questions is at what level indexing might possibly take place. If indexing is to take place at the level of syntagmatic structures within film, then the questions relating to fabula and szujet may well become important in the domain for multimedia information retrieval.

GORAN SONESSON AND VISUAL SEMIOTICS

Sonesson is concerned to establish traditions in pictorial semiotics. For Sonesson, Barthes's early work on photographs and adverts form the foundation for a critical 'visual semiotics' discipline which was born out of the efforts of many scholars to spell out what they thought was wrong in Barthes's early text. Visual semiotics takes issue with Barthes's reinterpretation of Hjelmslev's *connotation*.

Sonesson is interested in the distinction made between the 'expression' plane, or the signifier, and the 'content' plane, or the signified in visual signs by Groupe μ in their visual semiotic analysis. In visual semiotics the signifier relates to the marks on the page or the geometrical shapes and colours within photographs. Content is related to denotational meaning and to the Barthesian misunderstanding of connotational meaning. The emphasis on the expression plane in visual semiotics is of some interest in multimedia indexing because this recognition of the physical dimensions of shape, colour and space in visual 'language' is what underpins the content-based multimedia information retrieval systems currently researched by the AI and computing communities.

Content for Sonesson relates to iconicity which means that in pictures objects represented are recognizable from the 'ordinary perceptual Lifeworld' (Sonesson, 1999). Iconicity in pictures is a particular kind of iconicity which he calls 'pictorality'. The iconic level is not the only level in pictorial semiotics: there is also the 'plastic' level on which 'the expression is conveyed by simple qualities of the picture thing itself, which tends to correspond to increasingly abstract concepts' (Sonesson, 1999). The plastic layer can also contain content. In his analysis of the Girl-with-hat-and-watch advertisement, for example, Sonesson asserts that the plastic property 'beige', which is a colour at the expression plane (signifier), has the meaning 'calm, smooth colour' at the content plane. 'A few almost parallel lines' which is a plastic property at the expression plane has the meaning 'simple, calm, uncomplicated' at the content plane. Sonesson claims that there are elements of pictorial meaning which are not directly translatable into language.

Sonesson distinguishes a number of ways in which the sub-categories of pictures may be differentiated while still remaining pictorial signs:

- Pictorial kinds of signs may be differentiated from the point of view of their *construction*. A photograph differs from a painting or a cut-out.
- Pictorial kinds of signs may be distinguished according to the *effects* they are trying to produce. This is not the same as actual effects which may vary and cannot be known. Advertisements are intended to sell products and caricature is meant to ridicule the person depicted. Sonesson makes the point that the intended effects of fine art are much less well defined.
- Pictorial categories may be differentiated on the basis of the *channels* through which they circulate. The picture postcard follows a different trajectory than a television picture, a wall poster or an illustration in a newspaper.
- Sonesson claims that there is another way of distinguishing picture categories dependent on the 'nature of the configuration occupying the *expression plane* of the picture'. Once again the importance of the specific form and structure of the signifier in visual semiotics is being highlighted. But he says that 'ordinary language does not possess any terms for differentiating pictures in this way' (Sonesson, 1999).

The first three kinds of sub-categories can be expressed through language and might offer useful access points for information retrieval systems. The fourth sub-category might be explored using content-based information retrieval approaches.

The photograph has been of particular interest in semiotic writings after Barthes's essays 'The photographic message' and 'Rhetoric of the image' in *Image-Music-Text* (Barthes, 1977). Early writers on photography looked on photographs as icons, that is, as mirrors of reality. There then was a 'celebrated generation of iconoclasts' which included Eco, Metz and Barthes, who tried to demonstrate the conventionality of all signs including the photograph which was theorized as a coded version of reality. To them, the photograph was a symbol. Then there are writers who see the photograph as an index, that is, as a trace left behind by the referent itself. Sonesson (1999) differentiates the photograph from the Peircean index, an example of which would be the horse's hoofprint. The horse's hoofprint is a sign in which both content and expression (signified and signifier) are located at a particular time and place; in a photograph, only the content is bound with time and place. The essential meaning of the hoofprint is embodied in indexicality; it tells us the whereabouts of the animal. For Sonesson (1988) the dominant sign function of the photograph is icon, because before it can be interpreted indexically, the iconic relationship must have been identified. The photograph is an icon with indexical traits.

Of some concern to Sonesson is the question of the need for iconicity in order that a picture should to be a picture. Sonesson comments on the 'curious problem' of the existence of pictures containing no depictions. He comments that there have been attempts to conduct semiotic analysis on the abstract artworks of Paul Klee but that these efforts have met with limited success. We would agree with Sonesson in his contention that the approach to establishing meaning and communicative functions would be to analyse and read such works within a broader semiotics of culture, so that the work of Paul Klee could be read as constituting 'classic 1950s North American modernism'.

SEMIOTICS OF MUSIC

What drives Philip Tagg's approach to the semiotics of music is the idea that music is culturally specific as a communicative form. The semiotics of music is really a question of determining what sounds mean what to whom in which context (Tagg, 1999, p. 3). Such questions might form the basis of effective music retrieval systems. Semiosis is concerned with communication: Tagg includes an interesting 'basic communication model' in his introductory notes (Figure 4.7).

Tagg explains that:

> At the centre of the model you see the central process going from idea (intended message) through 'transmitter' and 'channel' to 'receiver' and 'response'. The transmitter is any individual or group of individuals producing the music – composer, arranger, musician, vocalist, recording engineer, DJ, etc. The channel or 'coded message' is the music as it sounds and the receiver is anyone hearing the music – the 'transmitters' themselves or other people. The 'intended message' is what the 'transmitters' want to get across – the right sounds at the right time in the right order creating the right 'feel'. (Tagg, 1999, p. 9)

Tagg assumes that the transmitter has a message which is to be transmitted through musical communication and that in a successful communicative act this message will be decoded in the intended fashion by the receiver. Musical

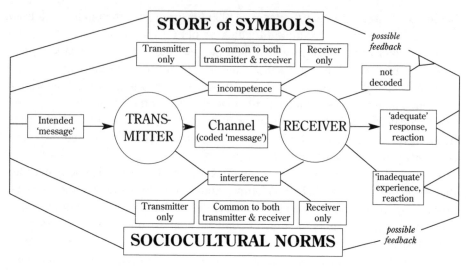

Figure 4.7   Tagg's musical communication model

communication can sometimes break down but there are always solid reasons which might include:

- coded incompetence: where the transmitter and receiver do not share the same vocabulary of musical symbols
- coded interference: where the transmitter and receiver do share the same basic store of musical symbols but different sociocultural norms and expectations.

Visual, narrative and social contexts of music can also interfere with its message. Television commercials can change the meanings of music, for example, Dvořák's New World Symphony is the Hovis bread music, as connotative arguably of a mythological North of England as of America or Czech and Slovak music. Sometimes 'interesting semiosis' (Tagg. 1999, p. 3) can arise from such confusion, for example, as when Nessun' Dorma ended up in the British pop charts in 1990 because of its association with the World Cup.

Tagg makes the point that the term 'music' is culturally specific and is not shared by all other cultures. His definition of music is as follows:

> Music is that form of interhuman communication which distinguishes itself from others in that individually and collectively experienced affective/gestural (bodily) states and processes are conceived and transmitted as humanly organised nonverbal sound structures to those creating these sounds themselves and/or to others who have acquired the mainly intuitive cultural skill of 'decoding the meaning' of these sounds in the form of adequate affective and/or gestural response. (Tagg, 1999, p. 16)

Moreover, music refers to itself; it is also related to society so that it can refer to other musical codes, reflect changes in technology or reflect changes in class structure or to other demographic change. There are relationships between music and the human body, which Tagg refers to as 'musical "universals"' (ibid., p. 17). This might mean that there is a relationship between musical tempo (pulse) and heartbeat (pulse). Music has a collective character and communication can take place between an individual and himself or herself, an individual and another individual, an individual and a group, a group and an individual, individuals within the same group, members of one group and another group.

Tagg explains the semiotics of musical structure in some detail and argues that in discussions of musical semiosis it is essential that no detail of musical structure is overlooked to which end he includes a 'checklist' of 'Parameters of Musical Expression'.

Tagg is aware that the model as described above takes an 'auteur-centric' view of what semiosis is about:

> However, the model and the terminology is there only as ONE way of understanding the communication process. My own, more holistic, view is that the proof of the semiotic pudding is in the eating, and that music's users are the final arbiters of its meaning[s], i.e. that the codal 'incompetence' and 'interference' are only one way (an auteur-centric way) of explaining the issue. I only ever intended the model as a starting point for problematising how musical meanings are created. After a while ... it becomes clear that 'incompetence' and 'interference' are part and parcel of everyday semiotic practices when it comes to music and really ought to be either labelled differently, or viewed from another angle (and labelled accordingly). (Tagg, 2003)

ICON, INDEX, SYMBOL REVISITED

The photographic sign can, depending on the provenance, purpose, form and content, range from the iconic to the symbolic. The iconic photograph might include informal 'snaps' taken without self-conscious posing and positioning by the subjects or of the subjects by the photographer. Some photo-journalistic images might be considered iconic. Coloured photographs might be considered more iconic than black and white photographs. Symbolic photographic signs might include photographs of signs which themselves are symbolic, for example, national flags, football club logos and political party emblems. To understand the meaning of such signs, the viewer would need a knowledge base which encompassed the codes and conventions of the society from which the symbolic sign derives and within which it has meaning.

Western art forms range from the representational to the abstract. From a contemporary viewpoint, paintings, even representational portrait paintings, would probably be considered more indexical than photographic representations which appear to capture reality through mechanical means, but it might be that, to a viewer of a portrait painted and viewed before photographic representation was possible, portraits could be considered iconic. However, the literature of art theory suggests that even within portraiture, symbolic codes and conventions operated within specific historical periods and specific societies.

Films also range from the iconic to the symbolic. Mike Leigh's films might be considered attempts at iconic filmic representation; while, for example, within the German cinematic tradition of the 1930s, films such as *Nosferatu* were much more symbolic, indeed symbolist. From the 1950s onwards, when the big screen had to fight off challenges for audience from the small screen, films have become spectacular, depicting special effects which could not have the same impact as the small screen. It may be that it is through the medium of television that the intimacy of iconic representation is fully established.

Fiction allows authors to explore alternative worlds or speculate about other possibilities, such as life after death, ghosts or Santa Claus. These speculative cultural information objects cannot be discussed within any knowledge-bound discourse, but fiction offers the space to explore imagination, faith and fantasy. Film, because it is able to conjoin two types of sign at opposite ends of the spectrum – the iconic, concrete human actors playing the roles of people or animals or robots and so on, and the symbolic, Santa Claus, Frodo and Bilbo Baggins and other fantastical human creations – is a particularly powerful and strong medium for the exploration of the fantastical in the guise of the real.

Music is always symbolic; music is perhaps the most symbolic of all the cultural art forms. Understanding music depends on understanding the specific codes and conventions within which the music has been composed. Musical forms can be quite rigid; even within Western traditions, there have been specific rules about what would constitute a concerto, a sonata and a symphony. Musical genres arguably form a knowledge base about this symbolic form, and these can be used to categorize specific musical works. Even in contemporary Western pop music, the genres and forms are relatively clear and transparent. The structural and formal properties of music can then be identified. More challenging is the identification of emotional and aesthetic appeals.

Understanding an emotional connection with a specific musical genre would seem to be enhanced if the listener already has a knowledge base which encompasses an understanding of the form. This might include a broader knowledge, an understanding of the codes and conventions, and of the time and the place from which the music emanates. This highly symbolic and historically contingent communicative form requires that potential listeners engage in a considerable level of education and enculturation to facilitate sympathy and understanding. This is as true for forms of 'pop' music, for example, rap and hip-hop, as it is for western 'classical' music, but there are differences because art forms such as contemporary pop music are specifically constructed for consumption by mass audiences within a culture which has commercialized mass art. In his *The Philosophy of Mass Art*, Noel Carroll (1997) asserted that the ontology of mass art relates to its function as having been produced for mass consumption, that is, for easy accessibility. Assertions about whether specific concrete examples of art are easily accessible or difficult are open to debate, but what is clear is that time plays a factor in determining levels of accessibility. It may well be that in 100 years time, the rap and urban music which is considered accessible by contemporary audiences will have to be learned by audiences for whom this form is no longer an everyday staple of the cultural diet.

Music is perhaps truly an acquired taste. This is true even of the human voice: there are many styles of singing, the style of the Senegalese Orchestra Baobab, the country blues style of Roy Orbison, the highly stylized singing of the operatic soprano – even here, knowledge of the genre is crucial to understanding the specific expression of the genre. Knowing where it comes from, why it has developed in this way, how it relates to other styles and how various exponents of the style relate to each other helps in understanding and interpreting. These things are not 'natural' but are highly cultural and constructed, and so too will be our responses and reactions to them.

TOWARDS THE IDEAL MULTIMEDIA RETRIEVAL SYSTEM: TAKE 2?

In this chapter we have explored a range of concepts and expressions which have been developed within the framework of cultural semiotics. This discussion will help us to form a view of the elements which come into operation in the communicative process and consider which of those elements might be incorporated into an ideal multimedia information retrieval system.

Ideally, a multimedia retrieval system might be a system which operates as a multiple decoder of meaning clearly situated within and reflecting the logonomic system inhabited by the searcher and capable of responding as meaning shifts and changes over time. This system would be one in which the understanding of meanings of media objects would not reside within the system, but would be the product of ongoing communication between users and the system. It would be an information retrieval system rooted in society rather than one which is built with the view that meaning is somehow abstract and absolute. This system would be able to:

● respond to a range of readings and encode a range of interpretations
● change over time
● code modality (objective/subjective)

- code 'readerly'/'writerly' media objects
- include syntagmatic information relating to spatial and temporal properties
- code specific elements within media objects.

The semiotic and interpretive framework outlined in this chapter formed the basis of an analytical approach in the discussion of media objects and information retrieval tools in Chapters 2 and 3. In the next chapter we will examine existing tools which have been designed with multimedia indexing in mind. It will be possible for us to examine these tools in relation to both the semiotic framework and the 'wish list' which derives from the framework. This in turn will enable us to evaluate the strengths and limitations of current solutions.

5 Using multimedia indexing tools

INTRODUCTION

In this chapter we describe a number of multimedia retrieval tools and use them to index some examples of multimedia objects. Aspects of semiotic analysis are used to explore the range of meanings which might be derived from the multimedia objects.

The identification of the 'level of meanings' that we make in this chapter will not be scientific or complete, and the question of 'shared-ness' still remains to be examined further. There may be a range of interpretations of multimedia objects, particularly those containing subjective information, available to any individual viewer within a particular society at a particular historical juncture.

The subsections in this chapter are concerned with the following topics:

- specialist multimedia retrieval tools
- semiotic readings of a range of multimedia objects
- interpretation and modality
- indexing multimedia objects using specialist multimedia retrieval tools.

SPECIALIST MULTIMEDIA INFORMATION RETRIEVAL TOOLS

A number of specialist information retrieval tools have been developed specifically for a variety of types of non-textual information.

ART AND ARCHITECTURE THESAURUS

The Art and Architecture Thesaurus is a structured vocabulary for the description of western art and architecture which contains around 125 000 terms and other information about concepts. It is not a classification scheme but is a vocabulary which can be used within database retrieval systems. The AAT can be used to describe art, architecture, decorative arts, material culture, and archival materials. According to the official Getty AAT site, the AAT, the Union List of Artists Names (ULAN) and the Thesaurus of Geographic Names (TGN) can be used in the following ways:

- They may be used as data value standards at the point of documentation or cataloguing. In this context, they may be used as a 'controlled vocabulary' or 'authority'. They provide 'preferred' terms (or 'descriptors') for concepts, as well as other synonyms that could be used by the cataloger or indexer. They also provide structure and classification schemes that can aid in documentation.
- They may be used as search assistants in database retrieval systems. They are 'knowledge bases' that include semantic networks that show links and paths between concepts, and these relationships can make retrieval more successful.
- They may be utilized as research tools, valuable because of the rich information and contextual knowledge that they contain (AAT Online Homepage, 2000).

The primary users of the Getty Vocabularies include museums, art libraries, archives, visual resource collection cataloguers, bibliographic projects concerned with art, researchers in art and art history, and art information specialists.

The AAT is structured around the notion of concepts. The focus of each AAT record is the concept which is identified by a unique numeric identification (ID). Each concept also includes links to terms, related concepts, a position in a hierarchy, sources for the data, and notes. One term for each concept is flagged as the 'descriptor' or preferred term, but other terms including plural forms, singular forms, spelling variants, natural order and inverted order, and various forms of speech and synonyms are also included in the record. Figure 5.1 is an example of an AAT record.

The AAT can be used to describe objects, textual materials, images, architecture and material culture from antiquity to the present. The official Getty site describes the terms as referring to

> objects of significance in the discussion and analysis of material culture, encompassing the natural and built environments, furnishings and equipment, and artifacts of visual and verbal communication.
>
> The AAT provides not only the terminology to generically name art objects and architecture, but the vocabulary necessary to describe them as well. This supporting terminology includes the materials and techniques relating to their construction and conservation (such as *deacidification*), their physical attributes (such as shape and color), terminology associated with their production and study (such as the roles of persons), vocabulary indicating their style or period, and concepts relating to their history, theory, criticism, and purpose. (AAT Online Homepage, 2000)

Descriptor: *information science*

Term ID: 54574

Hierarchy: *Disciplines* [KD]

Scope note – *use for the study of the nature, collection, and management of data and information in automated environments.*

Synonyms and spelling variants {UF}:

> *science, information*

You may also be interested in the following related concepts {RT}

> <u>information handling functions</u>

Sources:

> information science ... <u>LG5</u>
> information science ... <u>RHDEL2</u>
> information science ... <u>LCSH</u>
> information science ... <u>PG</u>
> science, information ... <u>AAT</u>

Figure 5.1   AAT record

The identification of relationships which link concepts and terms is crucial in the construction of a research-orientated thesaurus. The AAT contains equivalent, hierarchical and associative relationships. The relationship between terms which represent the same concept is called the Equivalence Relationship. Descriptors represent the used terms: other terms, such as synonyms or spelling variants can be used as access points.

The Hierarchical Relationship operates between broader and narrower concepts, or 'broader terms' and 'narrower terms'. The AAT has seven facets or categories which are subdivided into 33 sub-facets, or hierarchies. The conceptual framework of the facets and sub-facets is designed to allow a general classification of arts and architecture and is not subject specific, so that there is no portion of AAT specific to Renaissance painting. The facets and subfacets which make up the AAT are listed in Figure 5.2.

ASSOCIATED CONCEPTS FACET
Hierarchy: Associated Concepts
PHYSICAL ATTRIBUTES FACET
Hierarchies: Attributes and Properties, Conditions and Effects,
Design Elements, Color
STYLES AND PERIODS FACET
Hierarchy: Styles and Periods
AGENTS FACET
Hierarchies: People, Organizations
ACTIVITIES FACET
Hierarchies: Disciplines, Functions, Events, Physical Activities, Processes and
Techniques
MATERIALS FACET
Hierarchy: Materials
OBJECTS FACET
Hierarchies: Object Groupings and Systems, Object Genres,
Components
Built Environment: Settlements and Landscapes, Built Complexes and
Districts, Single Built Works, Open Spaces and Site Elements
Furnishings and Equipment: Furnishings, Costume, Tools and Equipment,
Weapons and Ammunition, Measuring Devices, Containers, Sound Devices,
Recreational Artifacts, Transportation Vehicles
Visual and Verbal Communication: Visual Works, Exchange Media

Figure 5.2   Facets and hierarchies in the AAT

The facets are conceptually organized to proceed from abstract to concrete, physical artefacts. Siblings within hierarchies are generally organized alphabetically, however, some are arranged by another logical order, for example, chronology. The AAT is conceptually 'polyhierarchical' which means that a concept can be placed in two different sections of the thesaurus.

The Associative Relationships are generally called 'related terms' in the language of thesaurus construction. These terms are similar to 'see also' references in the index of books. Figure 5.3 is an example of an AAT record which contains a related concept (RT).

The Getty Research Institute emphasizes that the AAT is a compiled resource which is not comprehensive. It grows through contributions from Getty projects and from other 'outside' organizations. Users of the AAT include the National Art Library which is the Victoria and Albert's curatorial department for the art, craft and design of the book (National Art Library, 2001), ADAM, the Art, Design,

Descriptor: *carnivals*

Term ID: 69042

Hierarchy: *Events* [KD]

Scope note – *Use for traveling or seasonal amusement enterprises, consisting of sideshows, games of chance, rides, and other similar entertainments. For the festive period of balls, masquerades, parades, and general revelry held in the pre-Lenten season, use 'Carnival (pre-Lenten festival)'.*

Alternate Forms of Speech {ALT}:

> *carnivals (entertainment events)*

You may also be interested in the following related concepts {RT}

> Carnival (pre-Lenten festival)

Sources:

> carnivals (entertainment events) … AAT
> carnivals … OED2
> carnivals … EB1591
> carnivals … CAND
> carnivals … LCSH
> carnivals … W
> carnivals (fairs) … BHA

Figure 5.3   AAT record containing a related concept

Architecture and Media Information Gateway, which is a searchable catalogue of Internet resources (ADAM, 2003), and the many contributor institutions including the National Gallery of Art, Washington, the Getty research institutions and the University of California, Berkeley.

ICONCLASS

Iconclass is an iconographic classification system devised by Henri van de Waal, the late professor of art history at Leiden University. It took 40 years for this system to be developed resulting in 17 printed volumes published between 1973 and 1985. Iconclass is a classifying thesaurus arranged using hierarchical principles and containing about 24 000 definitions of objects, persons, events, situations and abstract ideas (van den Berg). Van den Berg describes the system as a 'collection of *a priori* definitions that can be the possible subject matter of visual materials' (ibid.). It is a priori because these terms function as ready made abstract concepts which can be attached to works of art but do not describe specific works of art. Van den Berg cites the following as features of Iconclass:

- It has classification schedules showing the relationships of the definitions and concepts.
- It has alphanumeric notations forming the spine of the system and used as descriptors. This makes Iconclass to a large extent 'language independent' as translations of definitions from English into other languages would not affect the position of concepts in the hierarchy.
- It is the sum of iconographic knowledge of a large group of scholars.
- It offers about 5000 cross-references between associatively, thematically or iconographically related concepts.
- It offers access to concepts through about 16 000 controlled keywords and more than 50 000 references.
- It offers about 44 000 references to iconographic literature relating to many of the classified definitions and concepts (Van den Berg).

The classification system contains over 28 000 definitions, consisting of an alphanumeric classification code or notation, and its 'textual correlate' which can be used to index the iconographic content of works of art. This classification system is supported by an alphabetical index containing over 14 000 keywords used for locating the notation and/or the textual correlate needed to index an image. Iconclass is also an iconographic bibliography (Iconclass Official Homepage, 2002). The main divisions of the Iconclass system are represented by the digits 0–9 (Figure 5.4). The numbers 1–5 are 'general' topics, and divisions 6–9 are 'special' topics which are 'coherent subject matter of a narrative nature, with an emphasis on the Bible (7) and Classical Mythology (9)' (Iconclass Official Homepage, 2002). Class 0 was added in 1996, at the request of users, to accommodate abstract and non-representational art.

Subdivisions allow for increasing specificity. Main divisions are divided further to a maximum of nine using numbers 1–9. The third level of specificity is achieved by adding an upper case letter. The letter J is omitted from the scheme for reasons of legibility in the first printed edition. The Iconclass website documentation uses the example of 25: earth, world as a celestial body, as an example to show how the notation works (Figure 5.5).

The next levels of specificity are all achieved by the addition of numbers to the

0	Abstract, Non-representational Art
1	Religion and Magic
2	Nature
3	Human beings, Man in general
4	Society, Civilization and Culture
5	Abstract Ideas and Concepts
6	History
7	Bible
8	Literature
9	Classical Mythology and Ancient History.

Figure 5.4   Main classes of Iconclass

25A	maps atlases
25B	continents represented allegorically
25C	geological phenomena
25D	rock types; minerals and metals; soil types
25E	geological chronological division; historical geology
25F	animals
25G	plants; vegetation
25H	landscapes
25I	cityview, and landscape with manmade constructions
25K	landscapes in the non-temperate zone, exotic landscapes
25L	cities represented allegorically or symbolically
25M	the Seven Wonders of the World
25N	fictitious countries

Figure 5.5   Subdivisions of 25 earth, world as a celestial body

existing notation. For example, the subdivision 25F animals can be further subdivided as shown in Figures 5.6, 5.7, 5.8 and 5.9. The double lettered notation 25FF designates fabulous or fantastic animals. The notation 25GG is used in a similar way to denote fantastic plants and fabulous vegetation.

There are additional features available in Iconclass which have been developed in an attempt to increase the accuracy of meaning of a notation. These features are:

1. *Bracketed text*: which enables the user to break away from the hierarchy of alphanumeric notations. The user is invited to add a species name, a proper name, a number or combination of these in parenthesis to the end of the notation.

```
25F1   groups of animals
25F2   mammals
25F3   birds
25F4   reptiles
25F5   amphibians
25F6   fishes
25F7   lower animals
25F8   extinct animals
25F9   misshapen animals; monsters
25 FF  fabulous animals; sometimes wrongly called 'grotesques'); 'Mostri'
       (Ripa)
```

Figure 5.6   Subdivisions of 25F animals

```
25FF1  groups of fabulous animals
25FF2  fabulous animals ~ mammals
25FF3  fabulous animals ~ birds
etc
```

Figure 5.7   The class 25FF can be further divided

```
25FF21  fabulous animals ~ domestic animals
25FF22  fabulous animals ~ monkeys
25FF23  fabulous aniamls ~ predatory animals
25FF24  fabulous animals ~ hoofed animals
```

Figure 5.8   The class 25FF2 can be further divided

```
25FF241  unicorn
25FF242  'hippogriffe' (horse/eagle)
25FF243  'antalops'    (fabulous reindeer)
25FF244  'leucrota'
```

Figure 5.9   And the class 25FF24 can be further divided

2. *Keys* are 'elements of the Iconclass that are declared in lists' (Iconclass Official Homepage, 2002). These keys, which are made up of strings of digits and are preceded by the plus '+' sign, add 'shades of meaning' to the meaning of the notation proper. The notation for lion is 25F23 (LION). Keys which are valid for use with notations beginning 25F include:

+ 1 animals used symbolically
+11 bestiaries, 'Physiologus'
+12 heraldic animals.

The notation for a heraldic lion would read: 25F23 (LION)(+12).

3. *Doubling of letter:* the duplication of letters such as we saw in use with letters 25FF and 25GG modifies the meaning of notation. Doubling of letters is context specific. Often some kind of opposition is intended.

4. *Structural digits* are guidelines for structuring information concerning large groups of characters such as Greek gods, persons from classical history or saints. Important episodes in a character's lifetime can be numbered consecutively using structural digits, as, for example, in Figure 5.10. The notation for the story of Apollo reads 92B3. The notation for stories of the love affairs of Apollo would read: 92B32, where the final 2 is a structural digit signifying love affairs. The meanings of structural digits are valid only for a particular part of Iconclass, but, unlike keys which are contained within brackets, there are no rules for explicitly flagging a structural digit.

The philosophy underlying Iconclass is that, for the purposes of iconographic research, descriptions have to be detailed and systematic. To search on motifs such as angels with or without wings, the images must be described in detail. An image depicting 'the church symbolized by a sailing vessel' should be classified by using the notations 11C (the Church) and 46C24 (sailing ship). Van de Waal suggested combining these notations using a colon (11C: 46C24). Van de Waal also suggested that notations which were used to classify a detail of an 'iconographic unit' should be placed within square brackets, for example [71A42] would signify 'Eve offering Adam the apple as detail of an image' (Iconclass Official Homepage, 2002)). The use of such signs is optional, and determined by local practice. Several notations can be used to describe complex subjects. Van de

---

Classical gods:
1   early life
2   love affairs
3   most important deeds

Figure 5.10   Structural digits relating to the classical gods

Waal seemed to think that establishing that a specific image means 'the church symbolized by a sailing vessel' is not an issue. This view derives from the fact that the function of Iconclass is to be used by experts in art history as an academically orientated iconographic classification system. There are many assumptions about user groups, indexers' knowledge base and the subject domain built into the system which was never intended as a universal image retrieval classification scheme.

Institutional users of Iconclass include the Courtauld Institute (Courtauld, 2003), the Bodleian Library (Bodleian, 2003), the Corbis Corporation (Corbis, 2003), Fogg Art Museum, Harvard University (Fogg, 2003), Rijksmuseum, Amsterdam (Rijksmuseum, 2003) and the Kunst Indeks Danmark, the National Database of Art in Danish Museums (Kunst Indeks, 2003).

LIBRARY OF CONGRESS THESAURUS FOR GRAPHIC MATERIALS I: SUBJECT TERMS (TGM I)

This thesaurus which was developed by the Library of Congress Prints and Photography division was constructed to provide indexing terms for a broad range of pictorial materials, and was designed primarily for use in automated cataloguing and indexing systems being authorized for use with MARC. The vocabulary can also be used in manual indexing systems. The TGM I can be used to index subjects represented in a variety of media and formats including prints, photographs, drawings, posters, cartoons and architectural drawings. The thesaurus provides a controlled vocabulary describing a broad range of subjects including activities, objects, and types of people, events and places. The TGM I adheres to the American National Standards Institute's guidelines for thesaurus construction.

The TGM I grew out of the subject matter found in materials held by the Library of Congress Prints and Photography division which means that terms are added only as the topic is encountered in the course of cataloguing and indexing. The developers of the TGM I do not claim universality of coverage but specificity of coverage, however, the Prints and Photography division is a large one, and the TGM I includes over 5000 authorized, or postable, indexing terms, and over 4000 cross-reference or non-postable terms. The TGM I includes facet indicators for national, geographic and chronological subdivisions.

Many of the topics covered by the TGM are no different from those occurring in other media, but there are some terms which refer to more visual concepts such as 'Children playing in Sand' or 'Hammer and Sickle' which are more frequent as subjects for images than for non-pictorial materials. The most frequent source of terminology for the TGM I is the Library of Congress Subject Headings, and terms are incorporated without alteration wherever possible. The

Legislative Indexing Vocabulary (LIV) is consulted for vocabulary useful for indexing images relating to social and political issues. The Art and Architecture Thesaurus is another source of terminology used by the TGM I. Whereas the scope of the AAT is to provide terminology for art and architecture in the western world, the TGM I's scope is broader and includes a range of people, events and activities which are not within the remit of the AAT.

The thesaurus is organized in an alphabetical format and postable and non-postable terms are interfiled. The reference structure includes unauthorized terms (UF), broader terms (BT), narrower terms (NT) and related terms (RT). Compound terms are included when deemed necessary:

- when a single concept is expressed by multiple words in natural language
- when it would be difficult or unnecessary for an indexer to differentiate between two closely related concepts, and
- when splitting them into single terms to be placed in separate fields would lead to retrieval of irrelevant material (Library of Congress Thesaurus for Graphic Materials I: Subject Terms [TGM I], 1995).

The second section of the introduction to the 1995 printed edition, reproduced on the Internet, is concerned with the principles of indexing images. The editors make the point that whereas subject indexing of textual materials can often be aided by the availability of a range of sources of information, such sources are frequently not available to picture indexers. The cataloguer has to identify the 'who, what, when and where' of the material's creation and purpose and beyond these issues the cataloguer has to ask further questions:

- How historically significant is the subject matter of the images?
- Is the subject matter widely depicted, or are there aspects which are not widely represented and included in collections?
- Is the depiction of a specific subject clear or can that subject be represented better through another image?
- How does the material relate to other material within the collection?
- Can any such relationships be highlighted through consistent indexing across collections?
- Does a group of images show that the creator had a certain point of view or a particular message? (Library of Congress Thesaurus for Graphic Materials I: Subject Terms [TGM I], 1995)

The editors also refer to the 'ofness' and 'aboutness' issue of images discussed by Shatford Lane. Most images are 'of' something, that is, they depict a signified. Abstract images, as we have already noted in this chapter, are not clearly 'of' a signified and may well depict different things to different viewers. Images can also be 'about' something, that is, there may be a discernible intent or theme. The editors of the TGM I believe that subject indexing must take both of these aspects into account to satisfy as many queries as possible, but they distinguish between an 'aboutness' which is objective and an 'aboutness' which is subjective, arguing that subject cataloguers should limit their indexing and avoid the inclusion of subjective interpretation. However, making such distinctions could be quite difficult.

As an example, a political cartoon depicting a basketball game in which the players are dribbling a globe is discussed. This image is 'of' basketball and 'about' international relations. The editors also discuss the Dorothea Lange photograph known as 'Migrant Mother' which depicts a migrant worker and her children. In this case, the editors claim that the photograph is 'of' Mothers and Children and Migrant Labourers. They claim that in this case it would be overly subjective to assign terms for 'aboutness' since there is no caption to tell us whether the photographer's focus was poverty, despair, hardship, survival or other abstract concepts. The example of the basketball image is metaphorical and allusive. The Lange photograph has rich but less clearly encoded connotations. The image is more readerly than the example of the cartoon in which the cartoonist self-consciously directs the reader to a specific set of meanings. Arguably the TGM editors limit the indexing potential by constraining the range of interpretation.

The editors suggest that it can be useful to index the subject at the most specific level, so that an image of a rose would be indexed under 'roses' but not under 'flowers' and not under both terms. When an image is indexed under a proper name heading however, the editors suggest that both the name heading and a generic subject term can be applied, so that a photograph of Lillie Langtry would be indexed under her name and under the generic term 'Actresses'. The editors recognize that this practice can become highly impractical in some institutions, particularly where the catalogue record needs many subject headings or when the establishment of the headings for proper names needs considerable authority work.

The TGM I's terms can be used for post-coordinate indexing. Terms from the thesaurus may be listed separately to cover all aspects of the subjects represented in the image without indicating any relationships which may exist among the subjects, and searchers may combine terms at the searching stage. The TGM I's terms can also be used as elements in subject headings 'strings' in order to bring out relationships among topics, for example Women-Sports. The editors argue that subject strings are still valuable even in an age of automated Boolean and keyword searching because the explicit linking of subjects can help searchers to search more quickly and avoid 'false drops', or retrieval results where the relationship between the subjects is not what the searcher intended. Combining the terms Women and Sports might result in the retrieved set containing images of women watching sports. In a well-managed database, the subject string

Women-Sports could ensure that the searcher retrieves only those images which show women doing sports.

The TGM II is concerned with terms relating to genre and physical characteristics. It is a thesaurus of more than 600 terms developed by the Library of Congress Prints and Photographs Division with input from other archival image repositories. It is the second edition of *Descriptive Terms for Graphic Materials: Genre and Physical Characteristic Headings* (1986). The TGM II's terms are intended to be applied to two-dimensional, chiefly pictorial, graphic materials (among them, prints, photographs, drawings and ephemera) whether they are part of a book, or in a manuscript, graphic, or other collection; some non-pictorial and three-dimensional material commonly found in graphic collections, such as visiting cards and photograph cases; and materials commonly found in general graphic collections of research libraries and historical societies. There are more terms for photographs and historical prints than for fine prints, drawings and paintings. The TGM II does not claim to be exhaustive: it was designed to provide terms for access to categories of media and formats rather than to index every possible aspect of graphic materials. The editors claim that the degree of specificity permits reasonably direct searches to locate commonly requested examples of graphic materials. Terms describing art movements or styles, and terms requiring 'subjective judgement' such as 'propaganda' and 'primitive painting' are beyond the scope of the TGM II.

Terms that combine broad subject categories and forms are included. A searcher can search for DANCE POSTERS rather than having to search a database for the topical term DANCE and the form term POSTERS. The editors explain that this practice reflects typical categories for filing posters, listing them in auction catalogues or writing about them in books. The phrases also draw together posters which may have many different subject headings that cannot easily be retrieved together, for example, WAR POSTERS indexed under the names of many different wars and POLITICAL POSTERS indexed under presidential elections, protest movements and other subjects.

The TGM II is constructed within the Library of Congress's practical philosophical framework. The editors insist that it is not a 'theoretical list' but a 'practical representation' of the categories of materials encountered at the Library of Congress and other major American historical collections. The terms included are chosen on the principle of literary warrant. In a MARC record, terms from the TGM II are to be entered in sub-field 'a' of field 655 (Figure 5.11).

There are many institutions worldwide which use TGM I and II because they are authorized for use in MARC records, including large general libraries such as New York Public Library (NYPL, 2003) which have collections of historical images, and special collections such as the Chicago Historical Society (CHS, 2001).

100	Bimrose, Art, 1912– artist.
245	It's spring again [grahic]/Art Bimrose.
260	1953 April 11.
300	1 drawing.
520	Cartoon shows boy and girl (labeled AFL and CIO) carving overlapping hearts (labeled merger talks) on a tree. Refer to renewed efforts to combine the American Federation of Labor and the Congress of Industrial Organizations in 1953.
581	Published in The Oregonian.
610	American Federation of Labor—1950–1960.
610	Congress of Industrial Organizations (U.S.)—1950–1960.
650	Labor unions—1950–1960.
650	Courtship—1950–1960.
655	*Periodical illustrations*—1950–1960.
655	Editorial cartoons—1950–1960.
655	Drawings—American—1950–1960.

Figure 5.11   MARC record for a cartoon taken from a periodical

READING NON-TEXTUAL INFORMATION OBJECTS

In this section, we will use the semiotic communicative approaches outlined in Chapter 4 to read an exemplary selection of non-textual information objects. These examples will include images ranging from the iconic to the symbolic, music, speech and film.

To ensure that our reading is systematic and transparent, the following reading template will be used to read and interpret all the examples:

- Bibliographic information: information relating to author or creator of the item, title, publishing details, information relating to the materiality of the object.
- Knowledge-based information: provenance, purpose if known, people, places, times, objects if known. This level of information is denotative in semiotic terms and conventional in Panofsky's terminology.
- Interpretative information: connotative information in semiotic terms and iconological in Panofsky's terminology.

Semiotic aspects which will be analysed are:

- type of sign: iconic, indexical, symbolic
- modality markers

- denotation and connotation
- paradigmatic and syntagmatic planes.

READING IMAGES: REPRESENTATIONAL BUT NOT ICONOLOGICAL

Images might be representational but not necessarily iconological. This type of image, such as might be found in cartoon art or in the art of Lichtenstein, is more properly considered indexical, and is often highly stylized and historically contingent. The example here is a representational image which was submitted as part of an A level portfolio (Figure 5.12).

At the level of knowledge-based information it is possible to identify the artist, currently a student at Coventry University's Department of Art, Design and Media, and the title of the image, 'In the car' (Voisey, 2001). It is also possible to identify the provenance and purpose of this image. It comes from an A level portfolio and has been constructed to comply with the demands of a specific assignment task. The image was created in 2001.

Within the image there are two motivated representational signs denoting a man and a woman. These signs are represented in a cartoon style. They seem to be in a moving car and the man appears to be at the steering wheel. The cartoon

Figure 5.12 'In the car', Kristen Voisey, June 2001

113

woman has yellow hair and is wearing a yellow outer garment which would appear to be some kind of fur. The man is depicted with blue-black hair and his face has an intense expression, signified through his eyes, eyebrows and mouth. He leans forward towards the steering wheel while the woman leans back. Paradigmatic choice in this image is significant: the woman is blonde which in western culture traditionally connotes the feminine, specifically the pure and 'marriageable' feminine, while the dark hair and pale skin tone of the male is connotative of traditional western Heathcliffian images of the male. The paradigmatic choice then is very traditional although the form of the image is relatively contemporary. This image, unlike the paintings of Lichtenstein, has been computer-generated.

At the connotational level, this image is highly reminiscent of the cartoon images of Lichtenstein. At a knowledge-based level, the author knows this to have been the case because the artist had to complete the task in the style of a chosen artist or art movement and chose to focus on Pop Art, and in this image, specifically on Lichtenstein. What the authors know at knowledge-based level, but viewers cannot know from looking at the image in isolation, is that this image is part of a 'work in progress' which resulted in the construction of an original image linking the styles of Lichtenstein and Andy Warhol. What we *can* tell from looking at the image in isolation is that unlike the Lichtenstein posters on which it was based, this image does not have any anchoring text, so that at a connotational level, there is considerable opportunity for interpretation.

In Chapter 1 we discussed transparency and opacity of meaning in different discourses and referred to Roland Barthes's distinction between 'readerly' and 'writerly' texts, where readerly texts are those in which the author keeps tight rein on the range of possible interpretations and writerly texts are those which invite the user's involvement in interpreting meaning. It was suggested that images might also be discussed in relation to transparent and opaque meanings. This image is an interesting mixture. It is a representational image of a single moment which might or might not be part of a narrative, in which some cues structure meaning, for example, the black lines which run across the woman's face are symbolic cues representing speed to viewers attuned to cartoon symbolism, while other aspects are left open to the reader's interpretation, so that it is not clear whether there has been an interaction between the man and woman, what that interaction might have been and what emotions are being represented. In summary, this image is representational and indexical rather than iconological. It can be read at a denotational level by viewers who share the same cultural codes as representative of a man and woman in a moving car. If the viewer shares the broader cultural knowledge base of the artist, then the relationships between this image and Lichtenstein's Pop Art images will be obvious.

PHOTOGRAPHIC IMAGES: HIGH MODALITY

The first photographic image in this section (Figure 5.13) is one which was taken in Paris outside the Shakespeare and Company bookshop on the left Bank, and which has relatively high modality and iconicity. This photograph is not self-consciously posed or staged, although it would be possible to argue that there is some element of staging in almost every photographic image.

This image denotes a scene outside Shakespeare and Company in Paris. We (because of our privileged knowledge base in relation to this holiday snapshot) know that this photograph was taken in May 2002. In this photograph are a man and two women. The man sits on a stool outside the shop. The women browse through the bookshelves which are outside the shop. The photograph has a high modal value because there is a clear relationship between the represented image and the signified represented thing. The three people are syntagmatically linked, making a neat chain of people outside the shop. Although this photograph was not posed, it would be reasonable to suggest that this particular shot was taken because of the slightly 'bohemian' grouping of the people, particularly the inclusion of the seated man. On the paradigmatic plane, that the bookshop

Figure 5.13   'Shakespeare and Company', Martyn Voisey, Paris, May 2002

photographed is Shakespeare and Company as opposed to any of the many bookshops in Paris is absolutely crucial to the construction of the meaning of this photograph.

At a connotational level, Shakespeare and Company is a culturally significant bookshop in relation to British cultural codes, conventions and history. In Shakespeare and Company from the 1920s, Sylvia Beach was able to sell a number of avant-garde books which were banned in Britain. It was Shakespeare and Company who first sold James Joyce's *Ulysses*. This particular bookshop has cultural value and signifies bohemian chic, the avant-garde, and the modern in literature and culture. This level of signification would be possible only to those who shared the same cultural codes as the photographer.

PHOTOGRAPHIC IMAGES: READING THE HISTORICAL GAP

A photographic image with relatively high modality interpreted at a different (later) historical moment might only be meaningful for the viewer who has external historical and cultural knowledge with which to decode and interpret all the elements. The straight-backed stillness of the traditional British Edwardian family photograph, posed and serious, is at least partially a consequence of the photographic technology of the period. At what point denotational meaning (technological necessity in this case) merges with and emerges as connotational meaning (the straight-backed British Edwardian photograph as a metaphor for straight-backed Edwardian Britain) is perhaps easier for the viewer with cultural knowledge to determine.

The ideological and connotative aspects of an historical image might also be interpreted quite differently from the way in which the encoder intended if the image is decoded at a later historical moment, although it might be possible for the viewer to identify the 'preferred' meaning while still opposing it. A photograph taken in the late nineteenth century depicting British hunters posing with the dead tiger which is the trophy of their tiger shoot might be summarized as the memorial recording of a happy and successful activity by members of the British imperialist upper classes who were unselfconscious about both imperialism and tiger shoots. It would be possible for a twenty-first century viewer with strong historical and cultural awareness and knowledge to decode the intended meaning of a photograph of a nineteenth-century tiger shoot, the preferred encoded meaning at the moment of production, but at the same time to construct a contemporary anti-imperialist, anti-hunting interpretation. In other words, a viewer decoding an image at a later historical moment might well have access to a range of interpretations, contemporary and historical.

Figure 5.14 denotes a man in an old-fashioned car. It is a black and white photograph, and would appear, by the quality of the photographic process, the

Figure 5.14 '1926 Morris Cowley', Margaret Reavey, 1926/27

man's hair and dress, and the car itself, to be an amateur photograph which was taken in the 1920s. We (the authors) know that this photograph was taken in 1926. This knowledge is possible because of text written by the subject of the photograph on the back of the photograph. This text also informs us that the car is a Morris Cowley. Strictly speaking, this knowledge is merely second-hand testimony and depends on the subject having been correct and truthful in writing the text to really count as 'knowledge' rather than 'belief'. Experts on early cars would be able to add more generalized technical knowledge to the limited statement made here, using their cultural, historical knowledge base. The photograph has high modal value because there is a clear relationship between the represented image and the signified thing. Although it is iconic, this is a posed shot. One of the authors has the personal familial knowledge base which can allow for identification of the subject (maternal grandfather), and enough knowledge to know that the photograph would have been taken in Scotland.

At the level of connotation, the meanings that can be derived from this photograph are historically determined. At the time of production, this photograph was a proud recording of the subject's first car. The car was modern and up to date, and the subject was delighted by his acquisition. This car, and the recording of this photograph, signified that the subject was becoming a successful young man with enviable possessions and the possibility of independent travel and opportunity ahead of him.

Read now, at the beginning of the twenty-first century, this photograph is of particular and personal interest to the subject's family. For a more general audience, this photograph is of interest because it records an early 1920s Morris Cowley. The company has long disappeared, as has most car manufacture industry in Great Britain, so these types of recorded documents which are not professionally shot, but are records of real people interacting with their cars have some historical and cultural value.

ABSTRACT IMAGES: CULTURAL NOT NATURAL

In our examples so far, the purpose and function of the creators have been to create images which are representational. This is not always the case. There is a tradition of abstract art in western art which goes back to the mid-nineteenth century. For artists working within this tradition, representation of the real was and is not a necessary part of creating art. Artists working within this tradition are very often self-consciously rebelling against assumptions about representation of the real, and adopting a philosophy of art for art's sake. These artists would sometimes construct their own private 'languages' of colour, forms and symbolism.

Wassily Kandinsky was one of the most important figures in the development of abstract art in the early part of the twentieth century. Influenced by the Impressionists, his work became increasingly abstract. He experimented with non-representational art forms, and was influential in the development of both the Blue Rider group, of which Paul Klee was a member, and the Bauhaus. Examples of his paintings can be found at the Paris Webmuseum (Webmuseum, 2002). For the purposes of this section of the chapter, we will focus on the painting *Black and Violet*. At the level of bibliographical information this specific copy of the original painting has two levels of information relating to it. First, there is the bibliographical information relating to the painting itself, which we know was painted by Wassily Kandinsky in 1923 and is entitled *Black and Violet*. The copy of this painting to which you have been directed is to be found on a website which is entitled WebMuseum, Paris, created and maintained by Nicolas Pioch, Ecole Nationale Supérieure des Télécommunications, Paris.

At a denotational level, the painting is composed of a number of geometrical shapes and forms of different colours against a mustard background. There are two major discernable 'shape domains' in the painting, one of which is dominated by a round-ish or oval-ish black shape, and the other of which is dominated by a violet square. Other geometric shapes for example triangles and circles, in various colours are attached to these dominant forms. At the connotational level, it is difficult to attach any specific subject analysis to this painting because it is not representational, nor does the title offer any clue as to whether any specific meaning was intended by the painter. It is an object in its own right rather than a representation of a signified. At a broader connotational level or ideological level, we might read this painting as meaning 'high modernism' and the 'avant-garde'. At the time that it was first displayed, Kandinsky's work, indeed abstract art in general, often elicited outrage in a public which was not used to non-representational art forms. Since that time, early abstract painters and paintings have become much more widely known and accepted, this example even comes from a website. In our contemporary culture it is not unusual for paintings to be reproduced in the form of posters, so that it is not unusual for many famous works of art, including the abstract art of Kandinsky, to be found on the walls of people's houses in reproduced print form. One might argue that its cultural meaning has thus shifted from avant-garde to canonical.

RECORDED MUSIC: SYMBOLIC AND CULTURAL

Music is a highly symbolic communicative signifying practice. There is a tradition in western classical music of representing signified through musical forms. In relation to our reading template, we can identify the bibliographic elements of a specific recording of Beethoven's Sixth Symphony, the 'Pastoral' symphony, quite easily, and using an information retrieval tool such as AACR2 would ensure that we identified and recorded all the essential physical elements relating to the compact disc (CD) format. The recording referred to in this book is a recording by the Berliner Philharmoniker conducted by Herbert von Karajan. This recording is produced by an orchestra of human musicians conducted by a specific musical conductor. It would be possible to identify and to record the names of all the players within the orchestra. Conventionally, music library catalogues tend to limit this level of recording to soloists, orchestral leaders and possibly principals. This Deutsche Grammaphon recording was first released, on vinyl, in 1984.

In his Sixth Symphony, the Pastoral, Beethoven explicitly anchored the symbolic musical signs through the subtitles he gave to the various elements within the symphony, for example, the adagio section was subtitled 'Scene by the Brook'. This symphony often comes complete in recorded format with an expert's notes about the connotations of the symbolic signs, the denotation being the musical notes which the listener hears while listening to the recording. Stefan Kunze, writing an essay entitled 'Beethoven's symbolic language' for the Deutsche Grammaphon's recordings of the Berliner Philharmoniker, wrote that:

> the aim of the new symphony, whose 'pastoral' F major tonality followed a long tradition, – [was] to give form to nature's 'echoing' of a human sensibility. Beethoven

was anxious to forestall any possible misunderstanding, any supposition that he was simply concerned with 'depicting' natural scenes; he therefore enlarged the title of the work to 'Pastoral Symphony or Memories of Country Life (Expression of feeling rather than illustration). Not that illustration was altogether excluded: there is plenty of it in the storm scene and it is both ingenious and effective, but always subservient to the transposition into emotional terms of an ideal picture of the natural world. ... The dancing countryfolk's experience of nature is of a blindly threatening power that spreads destruction. In the 'Shepherd's Song' we hear their grateful thanksgiving for their deliverance from catastrophe, together with the blissful Arcadian harmony between Man and Nature. (Kunze, 1998, [1984], p. 58)

There are two levels of anchorage then relating to this recording of the Pastoral symphony. At one level the creator of the work, Beethoven, explicitly anchored the meaning of the music through his use of subtitles. At another level, the expert critic, Kunze, uses the secondary literature to further anchor meaning through his subjective comments on both the connotative meaning of the music, and through his comments about the effectiveness of the message. The reception of this symphony might well depend on the listener's cultural knowledge. Clearly, the subtitles of the symphonic movements encode the composer's preferred meaning, and the secondary literature underlines this meaning, but for the listener of the recorded music who does not have this information there may be other connotational meanings available. What is interesting about the production of this music, both by Beethoven and through the subsequent production is that the symbolic form does not 'stand alone' for personal interpretation but is highly disciplined by using the signifying symbols of language.

RECORDED SOUND: THE SPOKEN WORD

Recordings need not necessarily be of musical works. There are many recordings of the spoken word. There are many different types of spoken word recordings including recordings of particularly important political and historical speeches, for example recordings of Winston Churchill's wartime speeches; recordings of interviews; recordings of radio programmes, for example the *Goon Show* tapes; recordings of radio plays which have been written especially for the medium; recordings of the readings of novels, sometimes complete, sometimes abridged, either by one person or by a cast; and the recordings of the readings of poetry.

In relation to our reading template, we can identify bibliographic elements of a classic recording of Dylan Thomas's *Under Milk Wood* (1998 [1954]) delivered by Richard Burton and 'an all Welsh cast'. This recording is made from the original British Broadcasting Corporation (BBC) recording of the play which was broadcast in 1954. The CD was released by Polygram, as part of their spoken word series, Speaking Volumes, in 1998. The CD sleeve notes include a cast list.

The CD of the original radio broadcast contains an interpretation, by the cast, of Dylan Thomas's written script which was originally written as a radio 'play for voices'. At a denotational level the recording of the play consists of the script spoken by the actors. Syntagmatic and paradigmatic choices of specific cast members are clearly important in this recording, so there is great emphasis on the Welsh origins of the cast. The choir of children comes from Laugharne School. Laugharne, a village on the Carmarthenshire coast, was where Dylan Thomas lived when he wrote the play, and it is generally supposed to be the village on which Llareggub was based. It is generally believed that the original impulse for the play came from a conversation between Dylan Thomas and Richard Hughes, the author of *A High Wind in Jamaica*, who leased a house in Laugharne before Thomas moved there, and who initially introduced Thomas to the village. The original radio broadcast was made in January 1954 after Dylan Thomas had died in New York on 9 November 1953. This information is cultural and knowledge based, and would not be known from listening to the recording.

The recording of a radio script is a symbolic sign, based on the language of the script. Arguably the language of poetry is a particularly highly symbolic discursive form as it tends towards non-representational content, allusion and metaphor. Even within the discursive bounds of poetry, Dylan Thomas's use of language is particularly interesting, being extremely metaphorical and lyrical. The richness of Thomas's language might be the locus of interest for listeners, and for searchers hunting within an information retrieval system for examples of a particular type of discourse in spoken form, because the metaphorical content is so much greater than in most types of discourse. Possible connotational interpretations might focus on the ways in which Dylan Thomas evokes Wales and Welshness through his use of English, or alternatively, how he constructs mythological representations of Wales through metaphor. Possible connotational interpretations might also focus on the cultural meaning and significance of Richard Burton, whose own life, we know now, mirrored that of the poet-author in its intensity and alcohol misuse. That juxtaposition of Richard Burton and Dylan Thomas, signifying Welsh poetry, creativity and drunkenness, is so strong now that the CD cover emphasizes Burton as much as Thomas. At the top of the cover the text reads 'Under Milk Wood by Dylan Thomas'. Under the photograph of Richard Burton which occupies most of the cover, the text reads 'Richard Burton and an all Welsh cast'. The words 'Richard Burton' are in the largest font. This Burton-Thomas-Welshness mythology is perhaps clearer to early twenty-first century listeners than it would have been in the first broadcast in 1954, when it might have been only the recently dead Thomas who was the subject of myth.

FILM: SYMBOLIC ICONOLOGY

Film is interesting in semiotic terms because it can be highly modal, in that the

121

representation can have a strong relationship with the thing signified, yet it can also be possible to create highly symbolic signs using film because of technological advances. Film theorists are interested in the relationship between the narrative and the ways in which the narrative can be represented on film, the differences between *szuject* and *fabula* in the terms of the Russian formalists (see 'Semiotics of film' in Chapter 4). There are also theorists who are interested in the whole learned language of film that over the years audiences have become accustomed to. It is difficult perhaps at this historical juncture for us to recollect that when the early film of *The Great Train Robbery* was first shown in 1903, audiences were afraid that the train shown travelling head on was somehow going to leave the screen and plough through the cinema seats (Harvey, 2000).

Film and television involves the use of visual and aural codes, even in the case of silent film. Cinematic and televisual codes include: genre; camerawork (shot size, focus, lens movement, camera movement, angle, lens choice, composition); editing (cuts and fades, cutting rate and rhythm); manipulation of time (compression, flashbacks, flash forwards, slow motion); lighting; colour; sound (soundtrack, music); graphics; and narrative style (Chandler, 2002, p. 165). Cinematic editing code is learned at a very early age, and we absorb it so that we do not consciously notice the conventions. Film theorists argue that it has become to seem so 'natural' to us that we find it hard to accept as a code at all, so that we think of some 'realistic' film and televisual codes as uncoded representations of reality. Choices made about specific codes determine the meaning of the film.

The example which will be used in this section is the film *Diary of a Lost Girl* (Tagebuch einer Verlorenen) which is a silent film directed by G.W. Pabst, starring Louise Brooks, originally released by the Pabst-Film company in Berlin in 1929. This film was released in video format in 2001 by Kino Video and was also released in digital versatile disc (DVD) format in the same year. This version has new music composed and played by Joseph Turrin.

A denotational-level discussion of the film would result in a frame-by-frame, scene-by-scene description of the film which would include a description of all the elements within each frame. Paradigmatically, the casting of Louise Brooks as leading lady is crucial. Louise Brooks was at the time the film was made known as a beautiful and enigmatic 'good-time girl', a film actress, dancer and 'pin-up'. She had already appeared in *Pandora's Box*, also directed by Pabst, and was known from photographs in magazines, and from her pictures which could be seen on cigarette postcards. The choice of hairstyle is also paradigmatically significant. Louise Brooks is now considered one of the major screen icons of the 1920s, and the 'black helmet' bobbed haircut has much to do with the construction of the myth.

Syntagmatically, the film's structure follows the pattern of the narrative. The story is about the fall and rise of Thymian (Louise Brooks), the daughter of a philandering pharmacist, who bears an illegitimate child, is placed in a sadistic reformatory only to escape to a brothel where she makes money by selling dance lessons (as Brooks herself did after her film career collapsed). She marries a poor young earl who commits suicide after hearing that Thymian has given her inheritance away to her manipulative stepmother. Thymian meets the rich uncle of her deceased husband who looks after her. The basic goodness of the victim Thymian assures her of a reasonably happy ending in this highly melodramatic silent film.

This film has many of the codes and conventions typical of its time. It is a silent film shot in black and white. Textual captions containing explanatory text or dialogue are included between scenes. There are aspects of the acting style which are typical of early silent film acting. In one scene, Brooks signifies fear by bringing her elbow to her face in a melodramatic fashion. The dress code is that of Germany in 1929. The reformatory girls wear plain dresses, black stockings and severe hairstyles. Dress styles for the women working in the brothel are quite different: the dresses are 'jazz age' spangled shifts, the stocking are silk, the shoes are satin and high-heeled, and the fashion is for elaborate hair adornment. The men wear conventional evening dress, and the melodramatic narrative is typical of its time.

The connotations we may draw from this film when we view it in the early twenty-first century will be different from the range of connotations possible in 1929, although the film (object) is the same in each case. Following Noel Carroll's (1997) model of mass art both the audiences of 1929 and of the early twenty-first century will be able to view the film and broadly understand the narrative and the moral code, whether they agree with it, partially agree with it or reject it. Carroll would argue that this is because mass art such as silent film is designed to be accessible to the largest audience possible. At a denotational level, we can understand and interpret the film as it has been constructed by the director. At a connotational level, the meanings that we make from interacting with the film include social and individual meanings that we draw from the whole, or from parts of the film (the mythological 'meaning' of Louise Brooks as screen 'icon', the subsequent historical development of the 'talkies'), and these twenty-first century meanings will be different from those which could be drawn by the 1929 audiences. Even at the level of production, we have become accustomed to a range of production codes which were not in existence at the time that the film was first released. We now have colour, recorded sound and a range of technical and editorial techniques which have developed since 1929.

The social and moral codes of Western Europe have changed considerably since 1929, and so have the narrative codes we expect to find in films. It may be that at the time of release, the acting styles appeared realistic, and that this was considered a hard-hitting social commentary exposing the hypocritical sexual immorality in Weimar Germany. It was certainly heavily censored at the time of release. Viewed now, the acting styles, production and the narrative are extremely melodramatic, more nineteenth century than twentieth century. We can now read the film as a cultural product of the Weimar Republic at a particular historical moment, just before Hitler became Chancellor of Germany in 1933. Much of this kind of information relating to the film is knowledge based and could not be derived from watching the film without external cultural and historical information.

For many viewers in the early twenty-first century, Louise Brooks has an iconic status as a film star that she did not have in 1929. *Diary of a Lost Girl* was her last big starring role. She left Germany and went to America where she took smaller parts in smaller productions. Louise Brooks was 're-discovered' by Kenneth Tynan in the 1960s as she was struggling to make a living in Rochester, New York. From the 1960s onwards Brooks has become a cult figure, mysterious and beautiful. She has come to signify the 'flapper' generation, and posters of Brooks are still bought and hung on walls.

In 1929 G.W. Pabst was known as a left-wing auteur who directed realist psychological and sociological films including *The Joyless Street* in 1925 with Greta Garbo. He is still considered one of the great silent film directors, but interpreting Pabst is more difficult and confusing for twenty-first century audiences. Although he did escape Germany when Hitler took over, first exiled in France and then moving to America, he ended up back in Hitler's Germany at the start of the Second World War and made two films for Goebbel's Reichsfilmkammer. These films were 'entertainment' rather than explicitly 'propagandist', nevertheless, he was working knowingly for Goebbels. After the war Pabst made *The Trial*, which attacked anti-Semitism, but his reputation suffered because of his return to Germany. The intervening history has made a difference to the connotations attached to G.W. Pabst, to Louise Brooks and to *Diary of a Lost Girl*, and the film, watched in the twenty-first century, carries a whole range of connotational meanings which were not available to audiences watching in 1929.

INTERPRETATION AND MODALITY

What becomes clear through our reading of many of the texts which were discussed in the previous section is that texts are not necessarily decoded at the same moment in time as they were encoded, and the interpretation of the text may change as a result of the historical 'gap'. Even if encoding/decoding occurs at the same moment in time, interpretation is dependent on a shared understanding of codes and conventions. There are some tentative suggestions about the decoding and interpretation process that might be made in relation to these issues:

- A *non-textual information object* of *high modality* decoded at the same historical moment, and within the same culture and logonomic system as the encoding moment, would be expected to evoke a limited range of denotational meanings.
- There may be a broader range of connotational level interpretations.
- Textual anchorage could help fix the intended encoded meaning, but decoding might evoke negotiated or oppositional interpretations.
- Interpretation within a different cultural and logonomic system would potentially evoke a broader range of connotational and denotational meanings.

- A *non-textual information object* of *low modality* decoded at the same historical moment and within the same cultural and logonomic system as the encoding moment will evoke a larger range of subjective interpretation than a high-modality non-textual information object, and will be dependent on textual anchorage supplied by the producer to fix meaning.
- The range of interpretation will be dependent on interpretations possible within the logonomic systems shared by encoder/decoder.
- Non-textual information objects can be self-consciously constructed as 'abstract' or ambiguous by the producer to encourage 'subjectivity' and a 'readerly' or 'userly' response.

- A *non-textual information object* of *high modality* decoded at a different historical moment might depend on the viewer having external historical and cultural knowledge to interpret and decode all the elements.
- The ideological, connotative aspects might also be interpreted in quite a different way than that which the encoder intended, although it might be possible for the viewer to identify the 'preferred' meaning while still opposing it. A viewer decoding an information object at a later historical moment might well have access to a range of interpretations, contemporary and historical.

- A *non-textual information object* of *low modality* decoded at a later historical moment might, ironically, lead to a narrower range of connotative interpretations, as the 'avant-garde' becomes 'establishment' over time.
- Principles governing the encoding of low-modality information objects, particularly those belonging to specific cultural movements, might become more generally known and 'readable', so that a greater amount of external 'anchoring' information is known than was available at the moment of encoding.

The specialist information retrieval tools that we have reviewed in this chapter are all subject based, as one might expect, but it occurs to us, based on our reading of semiotics, that questions of structure, form, creation and the historical moment of reception might offer alternative approaches to 'classifying' multimedia objects. In this book we intend to make only tentative suggestions about modality and multimedia objects which are recorded in the meaning and interpretation model above, but we hope to develop these ideas and this approach to constructing an analytical framework within which to place multimedia objects. Such approaches could work well in conjunction with more traditional 'subject'-based information retrieval tools.

INDEXING THE MULTIMEDIA OBJECTS USING MMIR TOOLS

The four still images and one moving film described in the preceding sections were indexed using AAT, Iconclass and the Library of Congress Thesaurus for Graphic Materials. We do not claim that our choice of indexing terms are the only possible ones or that they are necessarily the best possible ones. In earlier chapters in this book we have already discussed questions of interpretation and reading, but what is interesting about the results is that they show how constrained and specific indexing must become when a particular controlled vocabulary is adhered to. The results also demonstrate the different 'flavours' that each indexing tool has. Indexing tools can often work better for one type of document than another.

The method adopted for this activity was to identify terms to search for from the semiotic description/analysis. In practice, the initial set of terms was modified in the light of the specific terminology of each indexing tool. Each of the specialist tools offered a direct search option, but browsing remains a useful way becoming familiar with the specific approach of IR tools.

The initial set of terms drawn from the semiotic description/analysis were as follows:

- *In the car* – Cartoon, Man, Woman, Car, Pop Art
- *1926 Morris Cowley* – Man, Car (Old Car preferably)
- *Shakespeare and Company* – Photograph, Bookshop, Paris
- *Kandinsky* – Modernist Art, Shapes – Geometric Shapes, Ovals, Squares, Avant Garde
- *Diary of a Lost Girl* – Silent Film, Black and White Film, Actress, Melodrama, 1920s Dresses – Shifts.

The terms which were finally used are far from exhaustive and do not embody the richness of the semiotic description, but they do offer a broad range of vocabulary. The individual records of terms which have been selected from specialist multimedia retrieval tools to index the non-textual information objects chosen for the indexing exercise are listed below. The records are presented in the following order:

1. 'In the car'
2. 'Shakespeare and Company'
3. 1926 Morris Cowley
4. Kandinsky *Black and Violet*
5. G.W. Pabst/Louise Brooks *Diary of a Lost Girl*.

The Beethoven Sixth Symphony and Dylan Thomas/Richard Burton *Under Milk Wood* cannot be indexed using the multimedia retrieval tools in this exercise but they are discussed in the section entitled 'Multimedia examples 6–7: Beethoven's Sixth Symphony and *Under Milk Wood*.

For each multimedia object the records are organized in the following order:

1. AAT
2. Iconclass
3. Library of Congress TGM I and II

Browsing though narrower terms relating to 'automobile', leads the indexer to the record in Figure 5.24. This record is particularly appropriate for the 'In the car' image. Iconclass does include records for the terms 'man' and 'woman', and these are recorded in this section for information.

INDEXING 'IN THE CAR'

AAT: the AAT vocabulary included terms for 'men' and 'women' in the plural form and also a term for 'car' in its preferred form, 'automobile'. The term 'Pop Art' is included with a useful scope note explaining that Pop Art refers to 'the international art and cultural movement that flourished in Britain and America in the 1950s and 1960s. Influenced by the Dada, the movement advocated the use of everyday imagery, such as advertisements, signs, and comic strips, executed in the techniques and graphic styles of mass media'.

'Cartoon' as a separate search term is limited to humorous or animated cartoons. Lichtenstein's use of comic strip cartoons often depicts scenes which relate to difficulties in human relationships rather than humorous events, not unlike the ways in which teenage girls' magazines use comic strip. It is interesting that the use of comic strip as a Pop Art medium is acknowledged, but then the 'form' word assumes specific generic attributes.

Iconclass: Iconclass is a specialist classification scheme. Indexers are not necessarily confined to one class mark but can combine appropriate class marks using a colon to separate them. Iconclass offers a class mark which represents

MULTIMEDIA EXAMPLE 1: 'IN THE CAR'

ID: 300025928
Record Type: concept
men (male humans) (<people by gender>, people, People)
Note: Refers to male human beings from young adulthood through old age.

Terms:
men (male humans) (preferred, C,U,D,English, American-P)
man (C,U,AD,English, American)
man's (C,U,AD,English, American)
men's (C,U,AD,English, American)
human males (C,U,UF,English, American)
males, human (C,U,UF,English, American)

Facet/Hierarchy Code: H.HG
Hierarchical Position:
Agents Facet
.... People
.... people
.... <people by gender>
.... men (male humans)

Related concepts:
 related to .... male
 .... (sex, <biological concepts>, ... Associated Concepts) [300189559]
Sources and Contributors:
human males........ [VP]
.... CDMARC Subjects: LCSH (1988–)
males, human........ [VP]
.... CDMARC Subjects: LCSH (1988–)
man........ [VP]
.... Getty Vocabulary Program
man's........ [VP]
.... Getty Vocabulary Program
men (male humans)........ [VP Preferred]
.... BHA Subject Headings [unpublished] (1992–)
.... CDMARC Subjects: LCSH (1988–)
.... RILA, Subject headings, unpub. (1975–1990)
.... Webster's 3rd New Int'l Dictionary (1961)
.... Worcester Art Museum Library, List of subject headings,
unpub. (1976)
men's........ [VP]
.... Getty Vocabulary Program
Subject: ..... [VP]
Note: .... [VP]

Figure 5.15   AAT: term 1: Man

ID: 300025943
Record Type: concept
women (<people by gender>, people, People)

Note: Refers to female human beings from young adulthood through old age.
Terms:
women (preferred, C,U,D,English, American-P)
woman (C,U,AD,English, American)
woman's (C,U,AD,English, American)
women's (C,U,AD,English, American)
females, human (C,U,UF,English, American)
human females (C,U,UF,English, American)

Facet/Hierarchy Code: H.HG
Hierarchical Position:
Agents Facet
.... People
.... people
.... <people by gender>
.... women

Related concepts:
related to .... female
.... (sex, <biological concepts>, ... Associated Concepts) [300189557]

Sources and Contributors:
females, human........ [VP]
.... CDMARC Subjects: LCSH (1988–)
human females........ [VP]
.... CDMARC Subjects: LCSH (1988–)
woman........ [VP]
.... Getty Vocabulary Program
woman's........ [VP]
.... Getty Vocabulary Program
women........ [VP Preferred]
.... BHA Subject Headings [unpublished] (1992–)
.... CDMARC Subjects: LCSH (1988–)
.... RILA, Subject headings, unpub. (1975–1990)
.... Webster's 3rd New Int'l Dictionary (1961)
women's........ [VP]
.... Getty Vocabulary Program

Subject: ..... [VP]
.... CDMARC Subjects: LCSH (1988–) precoord.; women alcoholics
Note: .... [VP]
.... <people by gender>
.... boys
.... girls
.... men (male humans)
.... women

Figure 5.16   AAT: term 2: Woman

ID: 300178739
Record Type: concept
automobiles (passenger vehicles, <freewheeled vehicles by form or function>, ... Furnishings and Equipment)
Note: Use for self-propelled vehicles designed primarily to transport passengers over ordinary roads.

Terms:
automobiles (preferred, C,U,D,English, American-P)
automobile (C,U,AD,English, American)
autocars (C,U,UF,English, American)
automobiles, gasoline (C,U,UF,English, American)
carriages, horseless (C,U,UF,English, American)
cars (automobiles) (C,U,UF,English, American)
cars, passenger (C,U,UF,English, American)
gasoline automobiles (C,U,UF,English, American)
horseless carriages (C,U,UF,English, American)
motor-cars (C,U,UF,English, American)
motorcars (C,U,UF,English, American)
passenger cars (automobiles) (C,U,UF,English, American)

Facet/Hierarchy Code: V.TX
Hierarchical Position:
Objects Facet
.... Furnishings and Equipment
.... Transportation Vehicles
.... <transportation vehicles>
.... vehicles
.... <land vehicles>
.... <land vehicles by form>
.... <freewheeled vehicles>
.... <freewheeled vehicles by form or function>
.... passenger vehicles
.... automobiles
Sources and Contributors:
autocars........ [VP]
.... Goodsell, Dictionary of Automotive Engineering (1989)
automobile........ [VP]
.... Chenhall, Revised Nomenclature (1988)
automobiles........ [VP Preferred]
.... Automobile Quarterly, American Car since 1775 (1971) 10
.... Avery Index (1963–)
.... CDMARC Subjects: LCSH (1988–)
.... Goodsell, Dictionary of Automotive Engineering (1989)
.... HUD Research Thesaurus (1980)
.... McGraw-Hill Encyclopedia of Science and Technology, 6th ed. (1987) Vol. 2, 256

.... Random House Dictionary of the English Language, 2d ed. (1987)
.... RIBA, Architectural Keywords (1982)
.... RILA, Subject headings, unpub. (1975–1990)
.... ROOT Thesaurus (1981)
.... Standard Industrial Classification Manual (1987)
automobiles, gasoline........ [VP]
.... Getty Vocabulary Program
carriages, horseless........ [VP]
.... Getty Vocabulary Program
cars (automobiles)........ [VP]
.... CDMARC Subjects: LCSH (1988–)
.... HUD Research Thesaurus (1980) cars
.... RILA, Subject headings, unpub. (1975–1990)
.... ROOT Thesaurus (1981) cars
cars, passenger........ [VP]
.... Getty Vocabulary Program
gasoline automobiles........ [VP]
.... CDMARC Subjects: LCSH (1988–)
horseless carriages........ [VP]
.... Automobile Quarterly, American Car since 1775 (1971) 47
motor-cars........ [VP]
.... CDMARC Subjects: LCSH (1988–)
motorcars........ [VP]
.... Random House Dictionary of the English Language, 2d ed. (1987)
passenger cars (automobiles)........ [VP]
.... Getty Vocabulary Program
.... Goodsell, Dictionary of Automotive Engineering (1989) passenger cars
.... HUD Research Thesaurus (1980) passenger cars

Subject: ..... [VP]
.... Automobile Quarterly, American Car since 1775 (1971) 500; automotive museums
.... Avery Index (1963–) precoor.; Factories—Automobiles
.... Brownell, ed., Vintage Auto Almanac (1976) 203; car museums
.... Car and Driver (1955–) Vol. 3, No. 1, 76; car museums
.... CDMARC Subjects: LCSH (1988–) precoor.; Automobiles — museums
.... Chenhall, Revised Nomenclature (1988) car
.... Getty Vocabulary Program museums, automotive; museums, car
.... RIBA, Architectural Keywords (1982) motor vehicles

Note: .... [VP]

Figure 5.17   AAT: term 3: Car

ID: 300022205
Record Type: concept
Pop (<post-1945 fine arts styles and movements>, <international post-1945 styles and movements>, ... Styles and Periods)

Note: Refers to the international art and cultural movement that flourished in Britain and America in the 1950s and 1960s. Influenced by the Dada, the movement advocated the use of everyday imagery, such as advertisements, signs, and comic strips, executed in the techniques and graphic styles of mass media. The movement represented a move toward a more objective, immediate art form after the dominance of Abstract Expressionism.
Terms:
Pop (preferred, C,U,D,English, American-P)
Pop art (C,U,UF)
Art, Pop (C,U,UF)
Art, Commodity (C,U,UF,English, American)
Art, Factualist (C,U,UF,English, American)
Art, Gag (C,U,UF,English, American)
Art, OK (C,U,UF,English, American)
Commodity Art (C,U,UF,English, American)
Commonism (C,U,UF,English, American)
Commonist (C,U,UF,English, American)
Consumerist Realism (C,U,UF,English, American)
Consumerist Realist (C,U,UF,English, American)
Consumer Style (C,U,UF,English, American)
Factualist Art (C,U,UF,English, American)
Gag Art (C,U,UF,English, American)
Industrial Art (C,U,UF,English, American)
New Sign Painting (C,U,UF,English, American)
New Super Realism (C,U,UF,English, American)
New Super Realist (C,U,UF,English, American)
OK Art (C,U,UF,English, American)
Painting, New Sign (C,U,UF,English, American)
Reactionary Realism (C,U,UF,English, American)
Reactionary Realist (C,U,UF,English, American)
Realism, Consumerist (C,U,UF,English, American)
Realism, New Super (C,U,UF,English, American)
Realism, Reactionary (C,U,UF,English, American)
Sign Painting, New (C,U,UF,English, American)
Style, Consumer (C,U,UF,English, American)
Super Realism, New (C,U,UF,English, American)

Facet/Hierarchy Code: F.FL
Hierarchical Position:
    Styles and Periods Facet
.... Styles and Periods
.... <styles and periods by region>

.... \<international post-1945 styles and movements>
.... \<post-1945 fine arts styles and movements>
.... Pop
Related concepts:
related to .... Neo-Dada
.... (\<post-1945 fine arts styles and movements>, \<international post-1945 styles and movements>, ... Styles and Periods) [300022187]
Sources and Contributors:
Art, Pop........ [VP]
.... Getty Vocabulary Program
Commodity Art........ [VP]
.... Walker, Glossary of Art (1992) 518
Commonism........ [VP]
.... Walker, Glossary of Art (1992) 518
Consumerist Realism........ [VP]
.... Walker, Glossary of Art (1992) 518
Consumer Style........ [VP]
.... Walker, Glossary of Art (1992) 518; 518
Factualist Art........ [VP]
.... Walker, Glossary of Art (1992) 518
Gag Art........ [VP]
.... Walker, Glossary of Art (1992) 518
Industrial Art........ [VP]
.... Walker, Glossary of Art (1992) 518
New Sign Painting........ [VP]
.... Walker, Glossary of Art (1992) 518
New Super Realism........ [VP]
.... Walker, Glossary of Art (1992) 518
OK Art........ [VP]
.... Walker, Glossary of Art (1992) 518
Pop........ [VP Preferred]
.... Arnason, History of Modern Art (1977) 618
.... Avery Index (1963–) (source AAT) Subhead.
.... De la Croix and Tansey, Gardner's Art Through the Ages (1986) 951
.... Lucie-Smith, Late Modern (1975) 131
.... Oxford English Dictionary (1989)
.... Random House Unabridged Dictionary (1993)
Pop art........ [VP]
.... Grove Dictionary of Art online (1998-2002) 'Pop art.' Accessed 06/03/2002.
Reactionary Realism........ [VP]
.... Walker, Glossary of Art (1992) 518
Subject: ..... [VP]
.... CDMARC Subjects: LCSH (1988–) Pop art
.... Osborne, Oxford Companion to 20th C. Art (1981) Pop art; 442; Pop art
.... Oxford English Dictionary (1989) Pop art

.... Random House Unabridged Dictionary (1993) Pop art
.... RIBA, Architectural Keywords (1982) Pop architecture; Fantastic architecture
.................RILA, Subject headings, unpub. (1975–1990) Pop art; Pop architecture
.... Walker, Glossary of Art (1992) 518; Pop art
 Note: .... [VP]

Figure 5.18   AAT: term 4: Pop art

Context of: 31A71
3   Human Being, Man in General
31   man in a general biological sense
31A   the (nude) human figure; 'Corpo humano' (Ripa)
31A7   the sexes (human being)
31A71   male sex; man

Figure 5.19   Iconclass: term 1: Man (1)

Context of: 31D14
3   Human Being, Man in General
31   man in a general biological sense
31D   human life and its ages (young, adult, old, etc.)
31D1   the ages of man
31D14   adult man

Figure 5.20   Iconclass: term 1: Man (2)

Context of: 31D15
3   Human Being, Man in General
31   man in a general biological sense
31D   human life and its ages (young, adult, old, etc.)
31D1   the ages of man
31D15   adult woman

Figure 5.21   Iconclass: term 2: Woman (1)

Context of: 31A72
3   Human Being, Man in General
31   man in a general biological sense
31A   the (nude) human figure; 'Corpo humano' (Ripa)
31A7 the sexes (human being)
31A72 female sex; woman

Figure 5.22 Iconclass: term 2: Woman (2)

Context of: 46C161
4   Society, Civilization, Culture
46   social and economic life, transport and communication
46C   traffic and transport
46C1 traffic on land
46C16 traffic by road or path with motor-vehicle
46C161 automobile

Figure 5.23 Iconclass: term 3: Car

Context of: 46C161 (+22)
4   Society, Civilization, Culture
46   social and economic life, transport and communication
46C   traffic and transport
46C1   traffic on land
46C16   traffic by road or path with motor-vehicle
46C161   Automobile
46C161(+) KEY
46c161 (+2) number of persons ~ traffic and transport
46C161 (+22) two persons ~ traffic and transport

Figure 5.24 Iconclass: term 4: Two persons: traffic + transport

Men	
— *[country or state]* — *[city]*	
Public Note	This heading may be further subdivided by the subdivisions used for classes of persons (Appendix A). Search also under the subdivision – MEN used with names of ethnic, racial, and regional groups (Appendix A).
Catalogers	As appropriate, subdivide by the subdivisions used for classes of persons
Note	(Appendix A).
Used For	Males
Broader Term	People
Narrower Term	Bachelors
	Cowboys
	Dandies
	Emperors
	Gay men
	Kings
	Monks
	Princes
	Shepherds
	Strong men
	Waiters
	Widowers
Related Term	Actors
	Boys
	Children & adults
	Fathers & children
	Grandparents
	Machismo
	Spouses

Figure 5.25   TGM I (and II): term 1: Man

Women
— *[country or state]* — *[city]*

Public Note	This heading may be further subdivided by the subdivisions used for classes of persons (Appendix A). Search also under other headings beginning with WOMEN or WOMEN's. Search also under the subdivision – WOMEN used with names of ethnic, racial, and regional groups (Appendix A) and with names of wars (Appendix C).
Catalogers	As appropriate, subdivide by the subdivisions for classes of persons
Note	(Appendix A).
Broader Term	People
Narrower Term	Abused women
	Actresses
	Ballerinas
	Bathing beauties
	Beauty contestants
	Chorus girls
	Clubwomen
	Cowgirls
	Debutantes
	Divorced women
	Empresses
	Flappers
	Geishas
	Gibson girls
	Governesses
	Housewives
	Lesbians
	Mothers
	Nuns
	Policewomen
	Pregnant women
	Princesses
	Queens
	Rural women
	Shepherdesses
	Single women
	Waitresses
	Women domestics

Related Term	Birth control
	Children & adults
	Girls
	Grandparents
	Harems
	Sexual harassment
	Sibyls
	Spouses
	Suffragists
	Women's prisons
	Women's rights

Figure 5.26   TGM I (and II): term 2: Woman

Automobiles
— *[nationality]* — *[country or state]* — *[city]*

Used For	Cars
Broader Term	Vehicles
Narrower Term	Convertible automobiles
	Electric automobiles
	Experimental automobiles
	Hot rods
	Limousines
	Racing automobiles
	Sports cars
	Station wagons
	Steam automobiles
	Three wheel automobiles
Related Term	Automobile breakdowns
	Automobile dealerships
	Automobile driving
	Automobile equipment & supplies
	Automobile industry
	Automobile inspections
	Automobile racing

Automobile service stations
Automobile theft
Car washes
Chauffeurs
Convertiplanes
Driver education
Drive-in restaurants
Drive-in theaters
Garages
Hearses
Jeep automobiles
Model cars
Motorcades
Traffic accidents
Trailers

Figure 5.27   TGM I (and II): term 3: Car

Cartoons (Commentary)
Catalogers Note   TGM II term.
Used For   Cartoons
    Comic pictures

Figure 5.28   TGM I (and II): term 4: Cartoons

the phrase 'two persons ~ traffic and transport' as a more specific term than automobile which is higher up in the same hierarchy. This would appear to be the most appropriate class mark.

Searching the term 'cartoon' in Iconclass offers the choice of class marks representing (revolutionary action with the help of) libels, broadsides, cartoons and so on; making animated cartoons; animated cartoons; or cartoon, satire, caricature of historical event. 'Pop Art' is not included in the class scheme. Iconclass is designed as a classification scheme which is concerned with *description* of images rather than organizing images by school or style.

TGM I and II: the TGM I allows for the terms 'cartoons', 'women', 'men' and 'automobiles' in preference to 'car'. The complete records are included because the narrower and related terms for 'men' and 'women' make interesting reading. These juxtapositions are the result of the Library of Congress's (LC's) policy of literary warrant and listing in alphabetical order. Terms which are included in the list are derived from the multimedia objects which are dealt with by the Library of Congress Prints and Photography division. The basis of inclusion is pragmatic rather than rational or necessarily logical. The ordering system chosen to list the terms is based on alphabetical order which means that there are terms unrelated by subject which are brought together through the accident of alphabetical order. The contingent and accidental quality of the list is reminiscent of Borges' fabulous classification of animals in 'a certain Chinese encylopaedia which formed the impetus for Foucault's "The Order of Things"'.

In this monstrous classification animals are divided into:

'(a) belonging to the Emperor, (b) embalmed, (c) tame, (d) sucking pigs, (e) sirens, (f) fabulous, (g) stray dogs, (h) included in the present classification, (i) frenzied, (j) innumerable, (k) drawn with a very fine camelhair brush, (l) et cetera, (m) having just broken the water pitcher, (n) that from a long way off look like flies.' In the wonderment of this taxonomy, the thing we apprehend in one great leap, the thing that, by means of the fable, is demonstrated as the exotic charm of another system of thought, is the limitation of our own, the stark impossibility of thinking *that*. (Foucault, 1970, p. xv)

MULTIMEDIA EXAMPLE 2: '1926 MORRIS COWLEY'

ID: 300025928
Record Type: concept
men (male humans) (<people by gender>, people, People)
Note: Refers to male human beings from young adulthood through old age.

Terms:
men (male humans) (preferred, C,U,D,English, American-P)
man (C,U,AD,English, American)
man's (C,U,AD,English, American)
men's (C,U,AD,English, American)
human males (C,U,UF,English, American)
males, human (C,U,UF,English, American)

Facet/Hierarchy Code: H.HG
Hierarchical Position:
Agents Facet
.... People
.... people
.... <people by gender>
.... men (male humans)

Related concepts:
related to .... male
.... (sex, <biological concepts>, ... Associated Concepts) [300189559]

Sources and Contributors:
human males........ [VP]
.... CDMARC Subjects: LCSH (1988–)
males, human........ [VP]
.... CDMARC Subjects: LCSH (1988–)
man........ [VP]
.... Getty Vocabulary Program
man's........ [VP]
.... Getty Vocabulary Program
men (male humans)........ [VP Preferred]
.... BHA Subject Headings [unpublished] (1992–)
.... CDMARC Subjects: LCSH (1988–)
.... RILA, Subject headings, unpub. (1975–1990)
.... Webster's 3rd New Int'l Dictionary (1961)
.... Worcester Art Museum Library, List of subject headings,
unpub. (1976)
men's........ [VP]
.... Getty Vocabulary Program
Subject: ..... [VP]
Note: .... [VP]

Figure 5.29   AAT: term 1: Man

ID: 300178739
Record Type: concept
automobiles (passenger vehicles, <freewheeled vehicles by form or function>,
... Furnishings and Equipment)
Note: Use for self-propelled vehicles designed primarily to transport
passengers over ordinary roads.

Terms:
automobiles (preferred, C,U,D,English, American-P)
automobile (C,U,AD,English, American)
autocars (C,U,UF,English, American)
automobiles, gasoline (C,U,UF,English, American)
carriages, horseless (C,U,UF,English, American)
cars (automobiles) (C,U,UF,English, American)
cars, passenger (C,U,UF,English, American)
gasoline automobiles (C,U,UF,English, American)
horseless carriages (C,U,UF,English, American)
motor-cars (C,U,UF,English, American)
motorcars (C,U,UF,English, American)
passenger cars (automobiles) (C,U,UF,English, American)

Facet/Hierarchy Code: V.TX
Hierarchical Position:

Objects Facet
.... Furnishings and Equipment
.... Transportation Vehicles
.... <transportation vehicles>
.... vehicles
.... <land vehicles>
.... <land vehicles by form>
.... <freewheeled vehicles>
.... <freewheeled vehicles by form or function>
.... passenger vehicles
.... automobiles
Sources and Contributors:
autocars........ [VP]
.... Goodsell, Dictionary of Automotive Engineering (1989)
automobile........ [VP]
.... Chenhall, Revised Nomenclature (1988)
automobiles........ [VP Preferred]
.... Automobile Quarterly, American Car since 1775 (1971) 10
.... Avery Index (1963–)
.... CDMARC Subjects: LCSH (1988–)
.... Goodsell, Dictionary of Automotive Engineering (1989)
.... HUD Research Thesaurus (1980)
.... McGraw-Hill Encyclopedia of Science and Technology, 6th ed. (1987) Vol. 2, 256
.... Random House Dictionary of the English Language, 2d ed. (1987)
.... RIBA, Architectural Keywords (1982)
.... RILA, Subject headings, unpub. (1975–1990)
.... ROOT Thesaurus (1981)
.... Standard Industrial Classification Manual (1987)
automobiles, gasoline........ [VP]
.... Getty Vocabulary Program
carriages, horseless........ [VP]
.... Getty Vocabulary Program
cars (automobiles)........ [VP]
.... CDMARC Subjects: LCSH (1988–)
.... HUD Research Thesaurus (1980) cars
.... RILA, Subject headings, unpub. (1975–1990)
.... ROOT Thesaurus (1981) cars
cars, passenger........ [VP]
.... Getty Vocabulary Program
gasoline automobiles........ [VP]
.... CDMARC Subjects: LCSH (1988–)
horseless carriages........ [VP]
.... Automobile Quarterly, American Car since 1775 (1971) 47
motor-cars........ [VP]

.... CDMARC Subjects: LCSH (1988–)
motorcars........ [VP]
.... Random House Dictionary of the English Language, 2d ed. (1987)
passenger cars (automobiles)........ [VP]
.... Getty Vocabulary Program
.... Goodsell, Dictionary of Automotive Engineering (1989) passenger cars
.... HUD Research Thesaurus (1980) passenger cars

Subject: ..... [VP]
.... Automobile Quarterly, American Car since 1775 (1971) 500; automotive museums
.... Avery Index (1963–) precoor.; Factories—Automobiles
.... Brownell, ed., Vintage Auto Almanac (1976) 203; car museums
.... Car and Driver (1955–) Vol. 3, No. 1, 76; car museums
.... CDMARC Subjects: LCSH (1988–) precoor.; Automobiles — museums
.... Chenhall, Revised Nomenclature (1988) car
.... Getty Vocabulary Program museums, automotive; museums, car
.... RIBA, Architectural Keywords (1982) motor vehicles

Note: .... [VP]

Figure 5.30   AAT: term 2: Car

ID: 300128349
Record Type: concept
black-and-white prints (photographs) (<photographic prints by color>, photographic prints, ... Visual and Verbal Communication)
Note: Use for photographic prints whose images are composed of gray tones, black, and white; may include one hue as a result of process, toning, discoloration, or the use of a colored support.

Terms:
black-and-white prints (photographs) (preferred, C,U,D,English, American-P)
black-and-white print (photograph) (C,U,AD,English, American)
black-and-white photoprints (C,U,UF,English, American)
black and white photoprints (C,U,UF,English, American)
black and white prints (C,U,UF,English, American)
photoprints, black-and-white (C,U,UF,English, American)
prints, black-and-white (C,U,UF,English, American)

Facet/Hierarchy Code: V.VC
Hierarchical Position:
    Objects Facet
.... Visual and Verbal Communication
.... Visual Works
.... <visual works>
.... <visual works by medium or technique>
.... photographs
.... <photographs by form>
.... positives
.... photographic prints
.... <photographic prints by color>
.... black-and-white prints (photographs)

Sources and Contributors:
black-and-white photoprints........ [VP]
.... Getty Vocabulary Program
black and white photoprints........ [VP]
.... Zinkham and Parker, Descriptive Terms for
Graphic Materials (1986)
black-and-white print (photograph)........ [VP]
.... Getty Vocabulary Program
black-and-white prints (photographs)........ [VP Preferred]
.... Getty Vocabulary Program
.... International Center of
Photography Encyclopedia of Photography (1984) 414, subhead; Black-and-
white prints
black and white prints........ [VP]
.... Getty Vocabulary Program
photoprints, black-and-white........ [VP]
.... Getty Vocabulary Program
prints, black-and-white........ [VP]
.... Getty Vocabulary Program
Subject: ..... [VP]
Note: .... [VP]

Figure 5.31   AAT: term 3: Black and white photograph

```
Context of: 46C161 (+21)
4                Society, Civilization, Culture
46               social and economic life, transport and communication
46C              traffic and transport
46C1             traffic on land
46C16            traffic by road or path with motor-vehicle
46C161           Automobile
46C161(+)        KEY
46c161 (+2)      number of persons ~ traffic and transport
46C161 (+21)     one person ~ traffic and transport
```

Figure 5.32   Iconclass: term 1: Man (in car)

We learned from using Iconclass to index the image 'In the car' that this information retrieval tool includes terms which describe people or a person in a car. This classmark is particularly appropriate to index the image '1926 Morris Cowley'. The record relating to 'car' is included here for information (Figure 5.33).

```
Context of: 46C161
4                Society, Civilization, Culture
46               social and economic life, transport and communication
46C              traffic and transport
46C1             traffic on land
46C16            traffic by road or path with motor-vehicle
46C161           automobile
```

Figure 5.33   Iconclass: term 2: Car

```
Men
— [country or state] — [city]
Public Note      This heading may be further subdivided by the subdivisions
                 used for classes of persons (Appendix A). Search also under
                 the subdivision – MEN used with names of ethnic, racial, and
                 regional groups (Appendix A).
Catalogers       As appropriate, subdivide by the subdivisions used for classes
                 of persons
Note             (Appendix A).
Used For         Males
```

145

Broader Term	People
Narrower Term	Bachelors
	Cowboys
	Dandies
	Emperors
	Gay men
	Kings
	Monks
	Princes
	Shepherds
	Strong men
	Waiters
	Widowers
Related Term	Actors
	Boys
	Children & adults
	Fathers & children
	Grandparents
	Machismo
	Spouses

Figure 5.34   TGM I (and II): term 1: Man

Convertible automobiles	
— [nationality] — [country or state] — [city]	
Used For	Convertibles (Automobies)
Broader Term	Automobiles

Figure 5.35   TGM I (and II): term 2: Car

INDEXING '1926 MORRIS COWLEY'

- *AAT*: the AAT includes permitted terms for 'man', 'woman', 'automobiles' and 'black and white photograph'.
- *Iconclass*: Iconclass includes a specific class mark for the concept 'one person ~ traffic and transport'.
- *TGM I and II*: the TGM includes permitted terms for the concepts 'man' and 'automobile'.

MULTIMEDIA EXAMPLE 3: SHAKESPEARE AND COMPANY

ID: 300005297
Record Type: concept
bookstores (<stores by commodity sold>, stores, ... Built Environment)
Note: Use for stores in which books are the primary items sold.

Terms:
bookstores (preferred, C,U,D,English, American-P)
bookstore (C,U,AD,English, American)
bookshops (C,U,D,English, British-P)
bookshop (C,U,AD,English, British)
book-shops (C,U,UF,English, British)
book stores (C,U,UF,English, American)
book-stores (C,U,UF,English, American)
stores, book (C,U,UF,English, American)

Facet/Hierarchy Code: V.RK
Hierarchical Position:
   Objects Facet
.... Built Environment
.... Single Built Works
.... <single built works>
.... <single built works by specific type>
.... <single built works by function>
.... commercial buildings
.... mercantile buildings
.... stores
.... <stores by commodity sold>
.... bookstores

Related concepts:
activity/event taking place .... bookselling
.... (selling, business, ... Functions) [300264557]

Sources and Contributors:
bookshop........ [VP]
.... Getty Vocabulary Program
bookshops........ [VP]
.... Candidate term Comment – NALLON – 6/94

.... Random House Dictionary of the English Language, 2d ed. (1987)

.... RCHME, Revised Thesaurus of Architectural Terms (1989)

.... RIBA, Architectural Keywords (1982)

.... ROOT Thesaurus (1981)

book-shops........ [VP]

.... Oxford English Dictionary (1989)

bookstore........ [VP]

.... Getty Vocabulary Program

bookstores........ [VP Preferred]

.... Avery Index (1963–)

.... Random House Dictionary of the English Language, 2d ed. (1987)

.... Sturgis, Dictionary of Architecture and Building (1902)

book stores........ [VP]

.... Avery Index (1963–)

.... Canadian Thesaurus of Construction Science and Technology (1978)

book-stores........ [VP]

.... Oxford English Dictionary (1989)

stores, book........ [VP]

.... Getty Vocabulary Program

Subject: ..... [VP]

.... CDMARC Subjects: LCSH (1988–) precoord.; use women's, ALT of women + bookstores; women's bookstores

.... RIBA, Architectural Keywords (1982) Shops: book

Note: .... [VP]

Figure 5.36   AAT: term 1: Bookshop

ID: 300128359

Record Type: concept

color photographs (<photographs by form: color>, <photographs by form>, ... Visual and Verbal Communication)

Note: The broad class of photographs whose images are composed of more than one hue, plus the neutral tones. For photographs having a range of tones within one hue, see 'black-and-white photographs.'

Terms:
color photographs (preferred, C,U,D,English, American-P)
color photograph (C,U,AD,English, American)
colour photographs (C,U,D,English, British-P)
colour photograph (C,U,AD,English, British)
photographs, color (C,U,UF,English, American)
photographs, colour (C,U,UF,English, British)

Facet/Hierarchy Code: V.VC
Hierarchical Position:
    Objects Facet
.... Visual and Verbal Communication
.... Visual Works
.... <visual works>
.... <visual works by medium or technique>
.... photographs
.... <photographs by form>
.... <photographs by form: color>
.... color photographs
Sources and Contributors:
color photograph........ [VP]
.... Getty Vocabulary Program
color photographs........ [VP Preferred]
.... Museum Prototype Project, Medium of objects, unpub.
(1985)
.... O'Connor, Draft photographic thesaurus, unpub. (1987)
.... Swedlund Photography (1974) 34
colour photograph........ [VP]
.... Getty Vocabulary Program
colour photographs........ [VP]
.... Getty Vocabulary Program
photographs, color........ [VP]
.... Getty Vocabulary Program
photographs, colour........ [VP]
.... Getty Vocabulary Program
Subject: ..... [VP]
Note: .... [VP]

Figure 5.37   AAT: term 2: Photograph

ID: 300111188
Record Type: concept
French (<European regions>, European, ... Styles and Periods)
Note: Refers to the culture of the modern nation of France, or in general to cultures that have occupied the area of the modern nation in western Europe.

Terms:
French (preferred, C,U,D,English, American-P)

Facet/Hierarchy Code: F.FL
Hierarchical Position:
 Styles and Periods Facet
.... Styles and Periods
.... <styles and periods by region>
.... European
.... <European regions>
.... French

Sources and Contributors:
French........ [VP Preferred]
.... Oxford English Dictionary (1989)
.... Random House Dictionary of the English Language, 2d ed. (1987)
.... Worcester Art Museum Library, List of subject headings, unpub. (1976)
Subject: ..... [VP]
.... CDMARC Subjects: LCSH (1988–) precoor.; French...
.... RIBA, Architectural Keywords (1982) precoor.; French...
.... RILA, Subject headings, unpub. (1975–1990) precoor.; French...
Note: .... [VP]

Figure 5.38 AAT: term 3: French

Context of: 49M7

4   Society, Civilization, Culture
49   education, science and learning
49M production of printed matter, book-production
49M7 book-shop, bookseller

Figure 5.39 Iconclass: term 1: Bookshop

Context of: 48C614

<u>4</u>	Society, Civilization, Culture
<u>48</u>	art
<u>48C</u>	the arts; artists
<u>48C6</u>	photography, cinematography
<u>48C61</u>	photography
48C614	photograph

Figure 5.40 Iconclass: term 2: Photograph

Keyword Query result for: Paris (city) (4 found)

<u>11H(DENIS)41</u>	St. Denis preaching in Paris
<u>11H(LOUIS IX)43</u>	St. Louis IX carrying relics (crown of thorns and three nails) towards the Sainte-Chapelle in Paris
<u>11HH(GENEVIEVE)111</u>	St. Genevieve as patroness of Paris, watching over the population
<u>46B2211</u>	'cris de Paris', cries of London, etc.

Figure 5.41 Iconclass: term 3: Paris

Bookstores

— *[country or state]—[city]*

Public Note	Includes activities and structures.
Broader Term	<u>Stores & shops</u>
Narrower Term	<u>Secondhand bookstores</u>
Related Term	<u>Books</u>
	<u>Bookselling</u>

Figure 5.42 TGM I (and II): term 1: Bookshop

Secondhand bookstores	
Used For	Used bookstores
Broader Term	<u>Bookstores</u>
Related Term	<u>Books</u>
	<u>Bookselling</u>

Figure 5.43   TGM I (and II): term 1: Bookshop

Photographs	
Catalogers Note	TGM II term.

Figure 5.44   TGM I (and II): term 2: Photograph

INDEXING 'SHAKESPEARE AND COMPANY'

- *AAT*: AAT includes permitted terms for the concepts 'bookstore' in preference to 'bookshop' and 'colour photographs'. It was not possible to find a permitted term to represent the city 'Paris'. It was possible to find a permitted term for 'French' but this term relates to art, furniture and architectural style.
- *Iconclass*: it was possible to find class marks for the concepts 'book-shop' and 'photograph'. A search for 'Paris' returned four possible class marks. Three of these relate to images representing specific saints, while the fourth relates to 'cris de Paris'. None of these class marks are appropriate for this image.
- *TGM I and II*: it was possible to find permitted terms for both 'book stores' and 'second hand bookstores' as a more specific term. The term 'photograph' is also a permitted term.

MULTIMEDIA EXAMPLE 4: KANDINSKY

ID: 300021474

Record Type: concept

Modernist (<modern European styles and movements>, <European styles and periods>, ... Styles and Periods)

Note: Refers to the succession of 20th-century avant-garde art and architectural movements formed in a reaction to social modernity. Modernism was eclipsed by the Post-Modernism movement, which began in the 1970s.

   Terms:

Modernist (preferred, C,U,D,English, American-P)

Modernism (C,U,AD,English, American)

Facet/Hierarchy Code: F.FL

Hierarchical Position:

  Styles and Periods Facet

.... Styles and Periods

.... <styles and periods by region>

.... European

.... <European styles and periods>

.... <modern European styles and movements>

.... Modernist

Sources and Contributors:

  Modernism........ [VP]

.... CDMARC Subjects: LCSH (1988–) Modernism (Art)

.... Lucie-Smith, Thames & Hudson Dictionary of Art Terms (1986)

.... RILA, Subject headings, unpub. (1975–1990)

.... Turner, ed., , Grove Dictionary of Art (1996) Vol. 21, 775

Modernist........ [VP Preferred]

.... Candidate term Candidate term – AVERY – 10/88

.... Lewis and Darley, Dictionary of Ornament (1986)

.... Walker, Glossary of Art (1977)

Subject: ..... [VP]

.... CDMARC Subjects: LCSH (1988–) Modernist art

.... RIBA, Architectural Keywords (1982) Architecture: history: c1910–1940

.... RILA, Subject headings, unpub. (1975–1990) Modernist...

Note: .... [VP]

Figure 5.45   AAT: term 1: Modernist

ID: 300263819
Record Type: guide term
<shape: geometric> (shape, <form attributes>, ... Attributes and Properties)
Terms:
   shape: geometric (preferred, C,U,D,English, American-P)

Facet/Hierarchy Code: D.DC
Hierarchical Position:
   Physical Attributes Facet
 .... Attributes and Properties
 .... <attributes and properties>
 .... <attributes and properties by specific type>
 .... <form attributes>
 .... shape
 .... <shape: geometric>
Sources and Contributors:
Subject: ..... [VP]
Note: .... [VP]

Figure 5.46   AAT: term 2: Shapes

ID: 300263817
Record Type: concept
oval (shape) (<shape: geometric>, shape, ... Attributes and Properties)
Note: Having more or less the form or outline of an elongated circle.
Terms:
   oval (shape) (preferred, C,U,D,English, American-P)

Facet/Hierarchy Code: D.DC
Hierarchical Position:
Physical Attributes Facet
.... Attributes and Properties
.... <attributes and properties>
.... <attributes and properties by specific type>
.... <form attributes>
.... shape
.... <shape: geometric>
.... oval (shape)

Sources and Contributors:
   oval (shape)........ [VP Preferred]

.... Getty Vocabulary Program
.... Oxford English Dictionary (1989) oval
.... Webster's 3rd New Int'l Dictionary (1961) oval; oval
Subject: ..... [VP]
Note: .... [VP]

Figure 5.47   AAT: term 3: Oval

ID: 300263832
Record Type: concept
square (shape) (rectangular, quadrilateral (shape), ... Attributes and Properties)
Note: Having the form or outline of a square, a four-sided plane figure with four equal sides and four right angles.
Terms:
  square (shape) (preferred, C,U,D,English, American-P)

Facet/Hierarchy Code: D.DC
Hierarchical Position:
Physical Attributes Facet
.... Attributes and Properties
.... <attributes and properties>
.... <attributes and properties by specific type>
.... <form attributes>
.... shape
.... <shape: geometric>
.... polygonal
.... quadrilateral (shape)
.... rectangular
.... square (shape)
Sources and Contributors:
    square (shape)........ [VP Preferred]
.... Getty Vocabulary Program
.... Oxford English Dictionary (1989) square
.... Random House Unabridged Dictionary (1993) illustration;
square
.... Webster's 3rd New Int'l Dictionary (1961) square
Subject: ..... [VP]
Note: .... [VP]

Figure 5.48   AAT: term 4: Square

ID: 300055775
Record Type: concept
avant-garde (<cultural movements and attitudes>, <culture-related concepts>, ... Associated Concepts)
Note: Use to describe attitudes, ideas, or works of art or architecture, especially from the late 19th to the mid-20th century, that depart from the existing norm in an original and experimental way.
  Terms:
avant-garde (preferred, C,U,D,English, American-P)
avant garde (C,U,UF,English, American)

Facet/Hierarchy Code: B.BM
Hierarchical Position:
  Associated Concepts Facet
.... Associated Concepts
.... <culture and related concepts>
.... <culture-related concepts>
.... <cultural movements and attitudes>
.... avant-garde

Sources and Contributors:
avant-garde........ [VP Preferred]
.... CDMARC Subjects: LCSH (1988–) Avant-garde (Aesthetics)
.... RILA, Subject headings, unpub. (1975–1990)
.... Webster's 3rd New Int'l Dictionary (1961)
avant garde........ [VP]
.... Ehresmann, Pocket Dictionary of Art Terms (1979)
Subject: ..... [VP]
Note: .... [VP]

Figure 5.49 AAT: term 5: Avant garde

Context of: 48A98(+112)

<u>4</u>	Society, Civilization, Culture
<u>48</u>	art
<u>48A</u>	art and the public; styles and ornaments
<u>48A9</u>	stylistic and formal differentiation of art
<u>48A98</u>	ornaments ~ art
<u>48A98(+)</u>	KEY
<u>48A98(+1)</u>	surface pattern ~ ornaments
<u>48A98(+11)</u>	limited surface pattern ~ ornaments
<u>48A98(+112)</u>	main form circular or oval ~ limited surface pattern of ornament

Figure 5.50   Iconclass: term 1: Oval

of: 49D342 (SQUARE)

<u>4</u>	Society, Civilization, Culture
<u>49</u>	education, science and learning
<u>49D</u>	mathematics
<u>49D3</u>	planimetry, geometry
<u>49D34</u>	quadrilateral (~ planimetry, geometry)
<u>49D342</u>	regular quadrilateral
<u>49D342 (...)</u>	regular quadrilateral (with NAME)
49D342 (SQUARE)	regular quadrilateral (with NAME)

Figure 5.51   Iconclass: term 2: Square

INDEXING 'KANDINSKY'

- *AAT*: the AAT includes terms for 'shapes', 'oval' and 'square', 'Modernist' and 'Avant Garde'. This is a thesaurus which has been constructed for art scholarship and it provides many useful terms for describing the contents of fine art even when that art is abstract in style.
- *Iconclass*: Iconclass includes permitted terms to cover the concepts 'oval' and 'square', but it may be that a class mark consisting of the codes for these concepts conjoined would be of limited use in describing the Kandinsky image or facilitating retrieval.
- *TGM I and II*: the TGM I and II was not able to provide any of the terms that were chosen to describe the Kandinsky image.

157

MULTIMEDIA EXAMPLE 5: *DIARY OF A LOST GIRL*

ID: 300127344
Record Type: concept
black-and-white film (photographic film, photographic materials, ... Materials)

Terms:
black-and-white film (preferred, C,U,D,English, American-P)
black and white film (C,U,UF,English, American)
film, black-and-white (C,U,UF,English, American)

Facet/Hierarchy Code: M.MT
Hierarchical Position:
Materials Facet
.... Materials
.... materials
.... <materials by function>
.... photographic materials
.... photographic film
.... black-and-white film
Related concepts:
objects using/producing .... black-and-white negatives
.... (<negatives by color>, negatives, ... Visual and
Verbal Communication) [300128343]
Sources and Contributors:
black-and-white film........ [VP Preferred]
.... Swedlund Photography (1974) 158
.... Upton, Photography (1975) IND
black and white film........ [VP]
.... Rosenblum, World History of Photography (1981) 606
film, black-and-white........ [VP]
.... Getty Vocabulary Program
Subject: ..... [VP]
.... Random House Dictionary of the English Language, 2d ed. (1987)
Black-and-white
.... Webster's 3rd New Int'l Dictionary (1961) Black-and-white
Note: .... [VP]

Figure 5.52   AAT: term 1: Black and white film

ID: 300252071
Record Type: concept
silent films (motion pictures (visual works), <visual works by medium or technique>, ... Visual and Verbal Communication)
Note: Motion pictures made without a photographic or magnetic sound track carried on the physical medium of the film itself.

Terms:
silent films (preferred, C,U,D,English, American-P)
silent film (C,U,AD,English, American)
feature films, silent (C,U,UF,English, American)
films, silent (C,U,UF,English, American)
films, silent feature (C,U,UF,English, American)
motion pictures, silent (C,U,UF,English, American)
movies, silent (C,U,UF,English, American)
moving pictures, silent (C,U,UF,English, American)
pictures, silent motion (C,U,UF,English, American)
pictures, silent moving (C,U,UF,English, American)
silent feature films (C,U,UF,English, American)
silent motion pictures (C,U,UF,English, American)
silent movies (C,U,UF,English, American)
silent moving pictures (C,U,UF,English, American)

Facet/Hierarchy Code: V.VC
Hierarchical Position:
Objects Facet
.... Visual and Verbal Communication
.... Visual Works
.... <visual works>
.... <visual works by medium or technique>
.... motion pictures (visual works)
.... silent films
Sources and Contributors:
feature films, silent........ [VP]
.... Getty Vocabulary Program
films, silent........ [VP]
.... Getty Vocabulary Program
films, silent feature........ [VP]
.... Getty Vocabulary Program
motion pictures, silent........ [VP]

.... CDMARC Subjects: LCSH (1988–)
movies, silent........ [VP]
.... Getty Vocabulary Program
moving pictures, silent........ [VP]
.... CDMARC Subjects: LCSH (1988–)
pictures, silent motion........ [VP]
.... Getty Vocabulary Program
pictures, silent moving........ [VP]
.... Getty Vocabulary Program
silent feature films........ [VP]
.... Encyclopaedia Britannica, 15th ed. (1991) IND
.... Motion Picture Guide (1985–1987) Vol. 1, used in
introduction
silent film........ [VP]
.... Getty Vocabulary Program
silent films...... [VP Preferred]
.... Candidate term Candidate term – BA – 10/01/03
.... CDMARC Subjects: LCSH (1988–)
.... Lopez, Films by Genre (1993)
.... Motion Picture Guide (1985–1987) Vol. 1, TITL
.... Nadeau, Encyclopedia of Printing, Photographic (1989) Vol. 2,
IND
.... Oxford English Dictionary (1989)
.... Thesaurus of ERIC Descriptors, 12th ed. (1990) Use films
silent motion pictures......[VP]
................................CDMARC Subjects: LCSH (1988–)
silent movies......[VP]
...................Encylopaedia Britannica, 15th ed. (1991) IND
silent moving pictures......[VP]
...............................Getty Vocabulary Program
Subject: ......[VP]
Note: ......[VP]

Figure 5.53   AAT: term 2: Silent film

There are the movies genres which have been recorded in AAT:

Top of the AAT hierarchies
... Associated Concepts Facet
...... Associated Concepts
.........<concepts in the arts>
...........<genres in the arts>
..............<motion picture genres>
.................actuality (genre)
....................film noir
.......................screwball comedy
.........................swashbuckler

ID: 300025658
Record Type: concept
  ❏ *actors* (performing artists, <people in the performing arts>, ... People)
Note: Persons who use movement, gesture, facial expressions, speaking, and intonation to create a fictional character for the stage, motion pictures, or television.

  Terms:
actors (preferred, C,U,D, English, American -P)
actor (C,U,AD,English, American)
actor's (C,U,AD,English, American)
actors' (C,U,AD,English, American)
actors and actresses (C,U,UF,English, American)
actresses (C,U,UF,English, American)
players (actors) (C,U,UF,English, American)

Facet/Hierarchy Code: H.HG
Hierarchical Position:
          Agents Facet
  ....   People
  .... people
  ....   <people by occupation>
  .... <people in the humanities>
  .... <people in the arts and related occupations>
  ....   <people in the arts>
  .... <people in the performing arts>
  ....   performing artists
  ....   actors

Related concepts:
user/creator .... <u>acting</u>
.... (performing arts, arts, ... Disciplines) [300264355]

Sources and Contributors:
actor........ [<u>VP</u>]
.... Getty Vocabulary Program
actors........ [VP Preferred]
.... CDMARC Subjects: LCSH (1988–)
.... RILA Verification manual, unpub. (1987) 73
.... U.S. Employment Service, Dictionary of Occupational Titles (1977)
.... USMARC Code List for Relators (1988) 3, relator code: act.
actor's........[VP]
.... Getty Vocabulary Program
actors'........   [VP]
.... Getty Vocabulary Program
actors and actresses........   [VP]
.... RILA, Subject headings, unpub. (1975–1990)
.... Worcester Art Museum Library, List of subject headings, unpub. (1976)
actresses........   [VP]
.... Random House Dictionary of the English Language, 2d ed. (1987)
.... Webster's 3rd New Int'l Dictionary (1961)
players (actors)........   [VP]
.... Getty Vocabulary Program
.... Oxford English Dictionary (1989) players
.... Random House Dictionary of the English Language, 2d ed. (1987) players
.... Webster's 3rd New Int'l Dictionary (1961) players
Subject: .....[VP]
Note: ....[VP]
.... U.S. Employment Service, Dictionary of Occupational Titles (1977)

Figure 5.54   AAT: term 3: Actress

ID: 300214100
Record Type: concept
chemise dresses (<dresses by form>, dresses, ... Furnishings and Equipment)

Note: Dresses which hang straight from the shoulders, sometimes tapering slightly at hips.

Terms:
chemise dresses (preferred, C,U,D,English, American-P)
chemise dress (C,U,AD,English, American)
chemise frocks (C,U,UF,English, American)
chemise gowns (C,U,UF,English, American)
chemises (dresses) (C,U,UF,English, American)
dresses, chemise (C,U,UF,English, American)
frocks (C,U,UF,English, American)
frocks, chemise (C,U,UF,English, American)
gowns, chemise (C,U,UF,English, American)

Facet/Hierarchy Code: V.TE
Hierarchical Position:
   Objects Facet
.... Furnishings and Equipment
.... Costume
.... costume
.... <costume by form>
.... main garments
.... dresses
.... <dresses by form>
.... chemise dresses

Sources and Contributors:
   chemise dress........ [VP]
.... Getty Vocabulary Program
chemise dresses........ [VP Preferred]
.... LACMA, Elegant Art (1983) GLOS
.... Picken, Fashion Dictionary (1957) 59
.... Rose, Children's Clothes (1989) illustration, 38
.... Waugh, Corsets and Crinolines (1954) 91
chemise frocks........ [VP]
.... Waugh, Corsets and Crinolines (1954) 91

chemise gowns........ [VP]
.... Rose, Children's Clothes (1989) illustration, GLOS
.... Waugh, Corsets and Crinolines (1954) 117
chemises (dresses)........ [VP]
.... Getty Vocabulary Program
.... Random House Dictionary of the English Language,
2d ed. (1987) chemises
.... Webster's 3rd New Int'l Dictionary (1961) chemises
dresses, chemise........ [VP]
.... Getty Vocabulary Program
frocks........ [VP]
.... Picken, Fashion Dictionary (1957)
.... Random House Dictionary of the English Language, 2d ed. (1987)
.... Webster's 3rd New Int'l Dictionary (1961)
frocks, chemise........ [VP]
.... Getty Vocabulary Program
gowns, chemise........ [VP]
.... Getty Vocabulary Program
Subject: ..... [VP]
.... Chenhall, Revised Nomenclature (1988) dress; chemise
Note: .... [VP]

Figure 5.55   AAT: term 4: Chemise dresses

ID: 300216052
Record Type: concept
tuxedoes (suits, main garments, ... Furnishings and Equipment)
   Note: Semiformal evening suits consisting of a dinner jacket and trousers,
the trousers having a stripe of material, such as silk or faille, down the outside
of the legs. May also include a bow tie, cummerbund and a shirt.

Terms:
tuxedoes (preferred, C,U,D,English, American-P)
tuxedo (C,U,AD,English, American)
tuxedos (C,U,UF,English, American)

Facet/Hierarchy Code: V.TE
Hierarchical Position:
     Objects Facet

.... Furnishings and Equipment
.... Costume
.... costume
.... <costume by form>
.... main garments
.... suits
.... tuxedoes

Related concepts:
related to .... dinner jackets
.... (coats, main garments, ... Furnishings and Equipment)
[300217691]

Sources and Contributors:
tuxedo........ [VP]
.... Chenhall, Revised Nomenclature (1988)
tuxedoes........ [VP Preferred]
.... Kidwella and Steele, eds., Men and Women (1989) illustration, 40
.... Livandi, Thesaurus of Clothing and Textile Terms, Pt. 1, Personal
Artifacts (1990)
.... NMAH, Dictionary of costume, unpub., n.d.
.... Picken, Fashion Dictionary (1957) 360
.... Webster's 3rd New Int'l Dictionary (1961)
tuxedos........ [VP]
.... Random House Dictionary of the English Language, 2d ed. (1987)
Subject: ..... [VP]
.... Chenhall, Revised Nomenclature (1988) jacket, dinner
.... Random House Dictionary of the English Language, 2d ed. (1987)
dinner jackets
.... Webster's 3rd New Int'l Dictionary (1961) tuxedo coats; tuxedo
jackets
Note: .... [VP]

Figure 5.56   AAT: term 5: Tuxedoes

Context of: 48C8731

<u>4</u>	Society, Civilization, Culture
<u>48</u>	Art
<u>48C</u>	the arts; artists
<u>48C8</u>	the arts of the stage: ballet, theatre, musical drama, motion picture
<u>48C87</u>	motion picture, film show
<u>48C873</u>	genres ~ film
48C8731	feature movie

Figure 5.57   Iconclass: term 1: Black and white film, silent film

Context of: 48C8712

<u>4</u>	Society, Civilization, Culture
<u>48</u>	art
<u>48C</u>	the arts; artists
<u>48C8</u>	the arts of the stage: ballet, theatre, musical drama, motion picture
<u>48C87</u>	motion picture, film show
<u>48C871</u>	actors on the screen
48C8712	film actress (on the screen)

Figure 5.58   Iconclass: term 2: Film actress

Context of: 41D1

<u>4</u>	Society, Civilization, Culture
<u>41</u>	material aspects of daily life
<u>41D</u>	fashion, clothing
41D1	fashion

Figure 5.59   Iconclass: term 3: Dress, flapper dress, shift dress

Motion pictures

Used For	Cinema
	Films
	Movies
	Moving pictures
Broader Term	Audiovisual materials
Narrower Term	Educational/cultural films & video
	Erotic films
	Short films
Related Term	Action & adventure dramas
	Animation
	Comedies
	Entertainment
	Historical dramas
	Horror dramas
	Melodramas
	Motion picture audiences
	Motion picture devices
	Motion picture industry
	Motion picture premieres
	Motion picture producers & directors
	Motion picture production & direction
	Motion picure theaters
	Romances
	Sociological dramas
	Tragedies
	Westerns

Figure 5.60   TGM I (and II): term 1: Motion pictures

Melodramas

Public Note   For images representing dramatic productions or scenes (theatrical, film, radio, or television) which feature passive protagonists who are victimized by situations related to society, family, or sexuality, frequently characterized by extreme emotion.

Related Term   <u>Motion pictures</u>
                     <u>Radio broadcasting</u>
                     <u>Television programs</u>
                     <u>Theatrical productions</u>

Figure 5.61   TGM I (and II): term 2: Melodrama

Actresses

Public Note   For female actresses. For groups of males and females use ACTORS. Search also under the subdivision — PERFORMANCES used with names of persons (Appendix B).

Catalogers   Used in a note under COSTUMES and ACTORS.
Note

Used For   Movie stars

Broader Term   <u>Entertainers</u>
                     <u>Women</u>

Related Term   <u>Actors</u>
                     <u>Auditions</u>
                     <u>Motion picture industry</u>
                     <u>Opera singers</u>
                     <u>Television industry</u>
                     <u>Theatrical productions</u>

Figure 5.62   TGM I (and II): term 3: Actress

Clothing & dress

—[country or state]—[city]

Public Note   Search also under groups of people associated with particular types of clothing, e.g., FLAPPERS and COWBOYS. Search also under the subdivision—CLOTHING & DRESS used with names of ethnic, racial, and regional groups, and with classes of persons (Appendix A).

Used For   Accessories
             Apparel
             Costume
             Dress
             Fashion
             Garments

Figure 5.63   TGM I (and II): term 4: Dress, flapper dress, shift dress

Dresses

—[country or state]—[city]

Broader Term Clothing & dress

Related Term Ball dresses
               Dress forms
               Evening gowns

Figure 5.64   TGM I (and II): term 2: Dresses

Tuxedoes

Broader Term <u>Clothing & dress</u>

Figure 5.65   TGM I (and II): term 5: Tuxedoes

Flappers

Catalogers Note Used in a note under CLOTHING & DRESS.

Broader Term   <u>Women</u>

Figure 5.66   TGM I (and II): term 6: Flapper

Hairstyles

—[country or state]—[city]

Used For   Coiffures
                 Hair styles
                 Hairdos

Narrow Term   <u>Braids (Hairdressing)</u>

Related Term   <u>Baldness</u>
                 <u>Barbers</u>
                 <u>Beards</u>
                 <u>Clothing & dress</u>
                 <u>Hairdressing</u>
                 <u>Hairpieces</u>
                 <u>Mustaches</u>
                 <u>Wigs</u>

Figure 5.67   TGM I (and II): term 7: Bobbed haircut

INDEXING *DIARY OF A LOST GIRL*

- *AAT*: the AAT was able to provide terms for the concepts 'black and white films' and 'silent films'. The AAT also includes terms relating to costume and clothing. It is possible to find terms for 'dresses' and 'tuxedoes'. A specific term is available to describe 'chemise dresses' and this might be appropriate to describe the 1920s flapper dresses worn in the brothel scenes. The AAT provides terms for certain film genres which are: actuality, film noir, screwball comedy and swashbuckler. The criteria for choosing these genre and no others are not made explicit. It was not possible to use the term 'melodrama'.

- *Iconclass*: it was possible to find terms for 'feature movie' and 'fashion' but not possible to be more specific. The specific name of the actress, Louise Brooks, could be attached to the term 'film actress', for example, film actress – Louise Brooks.
- *TGM I and II*: the TGM I and II includes terms for 'motion pictures' and for 'melodrama' as a related term to 'motion pictures'. There are terms for 'tuxedoes' and various types of dresses, but TGM also includes a term for the concept 'flapper'. The public note suggests searching under groups of people associated with specific types of clothing for example, cowboys and flappers.

MULTIMEDIA EXAMPLES 6–7: BEETHOVEN'S SIXTH SYMPHONY AND *UNDER MILK WOOD*

The subject-specific tools used to describe the contents of still and moving images have been created to describe visual documents. There are specialist music indexing languages, for example, Musaurus which is available in print copy but was last published in 1991 and is now dated. The recorded music and recorded speech that have been described in the section above are currently in CD format. In traditional library information management environments we would expect these objects to be catalogued using AACR2. A classification mark possibly from a general classification scheme such as DDC or LC would be assigned. These schemes deal with aesthetic subjects from an academic viewpoint and, so, the class mark attached to the Beethoven symphony would represent concepts relating to musical form (symphony, concerto and oratorio), performance (orchestral, chamber music, opera) and, possibly, geographical place of origin and date of composition. Subject terms relating to form, performance, geography and history might be assigned from an in-house controlled vocabulary or from a published list such as SLOSH or LCSH. The sound recording of the radio play *Under Milk Wood* on CD format would also be catalogued using AACR2 rules relating to the CD format. This object would probably be classified using a class mark related to 'radio plays' or possibly relating to post-1945 poetry. Subject indexing terms would focus on discursive form.

It is conceivable that the content of both multimedia objects could be stored in digitized format and be accessible via the Internet. In such a case, we might expect metadata information to adhere to the codes and conventions of Dublin Core. The advice relating to the Subject element of Dublin Core is that 'best practice' would be to select from a 'controlled vocabulary or formal classification scheme' (Figure 5.68).

This advice directs us back to the types of resources we would have used to index the conventional CD-based resource (music CD or spoken word CD) within the traditional library information management environment. The Description element of Dublin Core does allow the indexer to add more content-based information including a free-text account of the content (Figure 5.69).

Subject element of Dublin Core metadata:
Definition: A topic of the content of the resource.
Comment: Typically, Subject will be expressed as keywords, key phrases or classification codes that describe a topic of the resource. Recommended best practice is to select a value from a controlled vocabulary or formal classification scheme.

Figure 5.68   Definition and scope of the subject element of Dublin Core metadata

Description element of Dublin Core metadata:
Definition: An account of the content of the resource.
Comment: Examples of Description include, but is not limited to: an abstract, table of contents, reference to a graphical representation of content or a free-text account of the content.

Figure 5.69   Description element of Dublin Core metadata

Each MMIR tool that we have examined has been constructed with a particular agenda, particular users and particular range of multimedia objects in mind, and this will affect the structure, form and terminology. We can see even from our limited exercise that some MMIR tools will be more successful in describing certain multimedia objects than others. The AAT was the most successful tool with which to describe the Kandinsky. The TGM I and II actually includes the term 'flapper' but none of the others really offered that level of specificity or that kind of popular culture terminology.

The tools are constructed to describe the content of objects but they are all organized in an ahistorical fashion and it is difficult to capture historicity using these tools. This is important when dealing with multimedia objects such as the photograph of the 1926 Morris Cowley. The indexer can attach dates and indeed specific makes of car to the subject description (automobiles: 1900–1945 – Morris Cowley), but while this describes the car in denotational terms, it does not capture the connotational meanings attached to possession of such a car at that particular historical moment. We have commented on the fact that the term 'flapper' is used in TGM I and II but not in any other indexing tool. Popular culture terms such as 'flapper', 'sweater-girl', 'teddy-boy' are very historically specific and, while arguably capturing the 'spirit of the times' because they represent vernacular language of particular historical moments, they tend to disappear from popular vocabulary and possibly never even enter the restricted language of academic use. Yet these are terms which may well be the best ones to use to describe the contents of photographs, often taken by amateur photographers of everyday cultural practices, and film, both commercial mass market films and amateur home films.

None of the subject terms chosen from the MMIR tools has the richness of the free description undertaken in the semiotic description/analysis section. Rich description is always lost in adhering to controlled vocabularies and classification schemes, but such systems are possibly more cost-effective. The Dublin Core model does offer the indexer the opportunity to include more content-based text but it is unlikely that this in practice would include much in the way of the affective dimension or connotational description. As a result there are meanings which can be read from the multimedia objects which are completely lost in the translation from interpretation to encoding in controlled vocabularies, for example, the entrepreneurial satisfaction which might be read on the face of the young man in the Morris Cowley.

Post-structuralist communication theory makes us wary of imposing meanings onto documents and assigning specific interpretations authoritative status, but it may be worth speculating about whether it is likely that interpretation of any particular object can go beyond the bounds of what is known and what is believed in a particular society at a particular historical moment. In other words, is it the case that individual interpretation sits within a spectrum of possible interpretations? Could it be possible to describe what lies within that spectrum (including aberrant and eccentric interpretation) at any given moment and use interpretation as a foundation for indexing?

In the final chapter we examine a philosophical approach to MMIR which attempts to retain some of the richness of free description and association which semiotic analysis permits us and controlled vocabulary curtails.

6   Research issues

INTRODUCTION

Two themes are discussed in this final chapter. In the first part content-based image retrieval (CBIR) will be briefly reviewed from the perspective of content/meaning indexing. In the second part the authors discuss some of their own research about content/meaning indexing called 'Democratic Indexing'.

CONTENT-BASED IMAGE RETRIEVAL

Eakins and Graham (1999) in their report to the Joint Information Systems Committee (JISC) describe CBIR thus:

> The term has since been widely used to describe the process of retrieving desired images from a large collection on the basis of features (such as colour, texture and shape) that can be automatically extracted from the images themselves. The features used for retrieval can be either primitive or semantic, but the extraction process must be predominantly automatic. Retrieval of images by manually-assigned keywords is definitely not CBIR as the term is generally understood – even if the keywords describe image content.
>
> CBIR differs from classical information retrieval in that image databases are essentially unstructured, since digitized images consist purely of arrays of pixel intensities, with no inherent meaning.
>
> ... While there are grey areas (such as object recognition by feature analysis), the distinction between mainstream image analysis and CBIR is usually fairly clear-cut. An example may make this clear. Many police forces now use automatic face recognition systems. Such systems may be used in one of two ways. Firstly, the image in front of the camera may be compared with a single individual's database record to verify his or her identity. In this case, only two images are matched, a process few observers would call CBIR. Secondly, the entire database may be searched to find the most closely matching images. This is a genuine example of CBIR. (Eakins and Graham, 1999, s. 2.5)

This view of 'content' illustrates a different perspective than that adopted earlier in this book. Eakins and Graham (1999) acknowledge this difference in their analysis of characteristics of user queries:

Level 1 comprises retrieval by *primitive* features such as colour, texture, shape or the spatial location of image elements. Examples of such queries might include 'find pictures with long thin dark objects in the top left-hand corner', 'find images containing yellow stars arranged in a ring' – or most commonly 'find me more pictures that look like this'. This level of retrieval uses features (such as a given shade of yellow) which are both objective, and directly derivable from the images themselves, without the need to refer to any external knowledge base. Its use is largely limited to specialist applications such as trademark registration, identification of drawings in a design archive, or colour matching of fashion accessories.

Level 2 comprises retrieval by *derived* (sometimes known as *logical*) features, involving some degree of logical inference about the identity of the objects depicted in the image. It can usefully be divided further into:

1. retrieval of objects of a given type (for example 'find pictures of a double-decker bus');
2. retrieval of individual objects or persons ('find a picture of the Eiffel tower').

To answer queries at this level, reference to some outside store of knowledge is normally required – particularly for the more specific queries at level 2(b). In the first example above, some prior understanding is necessary to identify an object as a bus rather than a lorry; in the second example, one needs the knowledge that a given individual structure has been given the name 'the Eiffel tower'. Search criteria at this level, particularly at level 2(b), are usually still reasonably objective. This level of query is more generally encountered than level 1 – for example, most queries received by newspaper picture libraries appear to fall into this overall category [Enser, 1995b].

Level 3 comprises retrieval by *abstract* attributes, involving a significant amount of high-level reasoning about the meaning and purpose of the objects or scenes depicted. Again, this level of retrieval can usefully be subdivided into:

1. retrieval of named events or types of activity (for example 'find pictures of Scottish folk dancing');
2. retrieval of pictures with emotional or religious significance ('find a picture depicting suffering').

Success in answering queries at this level can require some sophistication on the part of the searcher. Complex reasoning, and often subjective judgement, can be required to make the link between image content and the abstract concepts it is required to illustrate. Queries at this level, though perhaps less common than level 2, are often encountered in both newspaper and art libraries. (Eakins and Graham, 1999, s. 2.3)

It is level 2 and level 3 queries, which correspond to our view of 'content and meaning', that we are most concerned with. As Eakins and Graham point out there are a variety of applications that are suitable for the 'vision' approach (level 1, above) but equally there are a range for which such an approach is, at best, peripheral and needs supplementing with human indexing knowledge (level 2 and 3).

176

DEMOCRATIC INDEXING: AN ALTERNATIVE APPROACH TO CONCEPT-BASED RETRIEVAL

The Democratic Indexing project grew out of an interest in the challenges of designing and implementing image retrieval systems. Initial reviews of the literature suggested that the subject indexing of images is considered particularly difficult and the problems relate to establishing the meaning of images that do not necessarily have text to anchor meaning. Researchers in the field seemed to agree that Erwin Panofsky's (1993) approach to analysing levels of meaning in Renaissance artworks offered a foundation for a 'levels of meaning' approach to identifying subject content of images in general.

The prototype design was based on a theoretical foundation that owed much to the work of Panofsky and Roland Barthes, however the project is now more clearly situated within a pictorial semiotics framework. The Democratic approach is a response to the issues of connotation, specifically to the issue of whether a 'spectrum of connotation' based on the range of possible meanings available in society at a particular moment might exist. The design of the database allows changes in meaning over time to be captured. Thus the database addresses synchronic issues about the structure of meaning at any one time, and diachronic issues about the changes in the system over time.

By focusing on user interpretation, Democratic Indexing differs from traditional IR models that assume that retrieval mechanisms are constructed by the librarian/indexer. In contrast to conventional 'authoritarian' approaches to indexing whereby an item is indexed by an 'expert' using an information retrieval framework very likely to have been designed and constructed by yet another 'expert' or committee of 'experts', the Democratic approach considers that 'readers' of the images play active roles in constructing their own meanings and that a collection of meanings constructed by 'readers' should be used to create a subject-based index. The Democratic approach determines 'authority' from the agreement of its users rather than from some predetermined 'expert' view: its warrant comes from the constructive interpretation of its users.

The Democratic approach does not cover all image contents, for example, information such as photographer, date of creation and title that are not subject to variation. However the Democratic approach is applied to all forms of interpreted information that might be summarized as 'what does this mean?' or 'what is important here?' A 'levels of meanings' table has been developed and is being used as an 'indexing template' for retrieval purposes. The principle of Democratic Indexing is that individuals will have their own, potentially different, interpretation(s) of an image. The differences may be manifested as different focus on parts of the image and different use of vocabulary to describe the image. This concept could be extended and used in many types of information retrieval, particularly with information media in which meaning is subjective and interpretative.

Democratic or user-based indexing is intended for use in a dynamic retrieval system which would allow users to contribute to the indexing and retrieval process. Our primary interests in the area of information media are to analyse and define 'meaning' in relation to interpretative media and subsequently to design and develop retrieval systems that exploit 'levels of meaning' as generators of access points. This approach to information retrieval has incorporated a number of novel features:

- The information which is to be recorded for each information item includes descriptive cataloguing and subject indexing based on user perceptions of the item (Brown and Hidderley, 1995).
- The collection of user-generated indexes will be used to compile a 'public' index through a process which we have called 'reconciliation'.
- The ability of individual users to record their private indexes offers a 'democratic' approach to indexing.

If Democratic Indexing proves to be practical and effective then it promises to revolutionize the retrieval of 'subjective' information items and to enrich the knowledge that information professionals are able to gather about their users and their approaches to the retrieval of subjective information items. Democratic indexing may be able to facilitate the practical delivery of multimedia collections to a wide audience without the significant overhead of trained librarians being compelled to participate in large volumes of indexing, while the information gathered about users as a by-product of the indexing activity offers the possibility of tailoring services and information to that individual based on their previous demands.

Democratic Indexing began as a method of indexing still images but its theoretical application has been considered in relation to film, poetry and fiction (Hidderley and Rafferty, 1997a; 1997b). We believe that the principle could also work in the domain of music retrieval. Prototype information retrieval templates dealing with still images, moving images and poetry have been developed to begin the assessment of the practical use of Democratic Indexing for users. Capturing information, particularly the interpretation and response to information items, will provide evidence about the range of meaning that an item provokes and the agreement that a user population exhibits when those items are viewed. A long-term objective for the system is to enable the interpretations to be examined over time so that any changes in the ways items are perceived may be identified and studied.

DEMOCRATIC INDEXING AND LEVELS OF MEANING

Central to the project has been the construction of 'levels of meaning' indexing templates, initially to capture a range of information relating to images, but subsequently developed to capture information relating to film and fiction. The image-based levels of meaning template is shown in Table 6.1.

The purpose of the levels of meaning indexing template is to provide active 'readers-as-indexers' with a structure to prompt their free-text interpretations. This template has been used by postgraduate Information Studies students and it was discovered that it produces very rich description, however, the reading, interpretation and indexing process can take a considerable amount of time to complete. This issue of indexing time is one which indexers and librarians face when using any kind of rich indexing template, for example the Bookhouse

Table 6.1   Levels of meaning for still images

Level and category	Description	Some examples
1.1 Biographical	Information about the image as a document	Photographer/artist, date and time of creation, colour/B&W, Size, Title
1.2 Structural contents	Significant objects and their physical relationship within the picture	Object types, position of object in the frame, relative size (or importance?) within the picture. for example person bottom left, car top right ...
2.1 Overall content	Overall classification of the image	Type of image, 'landscape', 'portrait', ...
2.2 Object content	Classification of each object defined in 1.2	Precise name and details of each object (if known), for example Person object is Margaret Thatcher, Car object is Ford Orion ...
3.1 Interpretation of whole image	Overall mood	Words or phrases to summarize the image, for example 'happy', 'shocking', ...
3.2 Interpretation of objects	Mood of individual objects (when relevant)	For example, Margaret Thatcher triumphant, defeated ...

indexing template. The results may well be impressive in terms of scope and detail, but the economics might render the approach impractical. Omissi's (1998) MSc dissertation on the indexing of detective fiction applied various indexing tools including conventional general classification schemes (Library of Congress and DDC) and Bookhouse to the indexing of a range of detective novels, and concluded that the Bookhouse indexing template produced the richest indexing but was prohibitively time-consuming.

The approach adopted in the levels of meaning indexing template is based on some assumptions that still require verification. First, it is assumed that, at least for the higher levels of meaning (3.1, 3.2), there is no single 'correct' interpretation of an image. Secondly, that there will be common terms used by viewers to index images (Brown and Hidderley, 1995). Thirdly, that the natural way to describe images is through words and phrases rather than more specialized 'picture languages' (for example, Benson and Zick, 1992; Gary and Mehotra, 1992) which have been developed.

PRIVATE AND PUBLIC VIEWS AND THEIR USE IN THE RETRIEVAL OF IMAGES

Individual users are encouraged to record their own views that will then be 'reconciled' to produce a 'public' or general index of terms supported by a thesaurus. A view corresponds to a mapping between an image and a set of terms associated with that image. An image may have any number of terms associated with it. The private view corresponds to the set of terms used by an individual and the images associated with each term. The terms may exist in the system thesaurus or they may only exist in the private user's view. In both cases only the individual user may see their terms and the associated images. The public view is a set of terms, all of which exist in the system thesaurus, and the associated images of each term. A term may have many images associated with it and an image may have many terms associated with it.

MOVING IMAGE AND MODELS OF MEANINGS

Underpinning the level of meanings tables are theoretical models of meaning in pictures, images and moving image. Like still image, the production of moving image documents encompasses a broad range of structures, forms and content. Moving images, fictional or factual, or combinations of both are and have been produced by commercial film-makers and by amateur film-makers. Moving images can be shot by anyone who has had access to the necessary technology. Theorists of the narratology and semiotics of film such as Genette, Bordwell and Metz have generally been concerned with the analysis of constructed cinematic film, mainly fictional, produced for commercial purposes (commercial in this sense would include specialist art-house cinematic films). In this context the consensus is that constructed cinematic film is based on narrative form. This is true for a straightforward story such as Keaton's *The General* (1927) and for the more arcane convolutions of Bunuel's *Le Chien Andelou* (1928).

For Stam (1992) narrative is the recounting of two or more events (or a situation and an event) logically connected, occurring over time and linked by a consistent subject into a whole. Giannetti (1993) identified four classes of narrative: the Classic Paradigm or plot structure which describe a narrative model based on conflict, between a protagonist and an antagonist, and its resolution; the Realistic Narrative or 'slice-of-life' narrative which is often cyclical in structure; the Formalistic Narrative which, like Bunuel or the musicals of Astaire and Rodgers, are clearly artificial; the Non-fictional Narrative into which category Giannetti fits documentaries and avant-garde films.

For Genette (1980), the distinction between story and plot was not enough and he identified three elements which together create narrative: the recit, the histoire and the narration. The recit is the signifier or the narrative text itself, the actual shot patterning in a film. The histoire is the signified, or the narrative content of the film while the narration relates to the act of recounting the narrative and becomes apparent as the narrative unfolds.

Bordwell's (1989) identified four types of meaning made by viewers and critics when they are making sense of a film. His first type of meaning is referential meaning, which refers to the construction of a concrete world in the film. The second type of meaning is the explicit meaning, which moves meaning up a level of abstraction to assign a conceptual meaning or 'point' to the fabula. The third level of meaning, implicit meaning, refers to the covert or symbolic meaning. Units of implicit meaning can be called 'themes' or identified as 'problems', 'issues' or 'questions'. The fourth level, repressed or symptomatic meaning, is at odds with referential, explicit or implicit meaning, for example, Hitchcock's *Psycho* may be interpreted as male fear of women's sexuality. Levels two to four in Bordwell's model relate to Genette's histoire and narration and are increasingly subjective and user inferred.

The level of meanings table for moving images (Table 6.2) is based on an earlier model developed for still images. Table 6.3 plots the relationship between the models of analysis derived from Bordwell, Genette and Gunning and our level of meanings table (Table 6.1).

LEVELS 1.2 AND 1.3: EVENTS IN A FILM

The purpose of these levels within the framework is to enable a film to be indexed according to its narrative structure. The narrative structure may not be identical to the sequential order of frames within the film and so the two levels are required

Table 6.2   Levels of meaning for moving images

Level and category	Description	Some examples
1.1 Biographical	Information about the film as a document	Director, writer(s), technical personnel, colour (type of process for example Technicolour/ B&W, title, and so on
1.2 Events	A subdivision of a film defined by a start and end point, the smallest part being an individual frame (corresponding to a still image)	<u>Scene</u> – an editorial division of a film where subject matter and contents change from the previous sequence <u>Viewpoint</u> – camera's eye, a subdivision of a scene, a filmic device <u>Time-based narrative event</u>, determined by an interpretation of a sequence of frames
1.3 Linked events	An identified set of events defined in 1.2 which have a defined sequence, possibly independent of the film sequence	A character's interactions, linking the events which the character directly participates in A sequence of interactions between associated objects
1.4 Structural contents	Significant objects and their physical relationship within the event defined in 1.2	Object types, position of object in the frame, relative size (or importance?) within the picture. For example, person bottom left, car top right …
2.1 Overall content	Overall classification of the image including references to 'external' objects	Type of film, possibly generic categories: for example Western, Musical, Melodrama, Film Noire

2.2 Object content	Classification of each object defined in 1.2 including references to 'external sources'	Precise name and details of each object (if known), for example Person object is Margaret Thatcher, Car object is Ford Orion ...
3.1 Interpretation of whole 'film', event or sequence, defined in 1.2, 1.3 and 1.4	Overall mood	Words of phrases to summarize the film, for example 'happy', 'shocking' ...
3.2 Interpretation of objects	Mood of individual objects (when relevant)	for example Margaret Thatcher triumphant, defeated ...

Table 6.3   Level of meanings table and models of meaning in film theory

Genette	Gunning	Bordwell
Recit 1.1, 1.2, 1.4, 2.1, 2.2	Pro-filmic 1.1, 1.2, 2.2	Referential 1.1, 1.2, 1.4, 2.2
Histoire 1.3, 3.2	Enframed 1.2, 1.4	Explicit 2.1, 3.1
Narration 3.1	Editing 1.3, 2.1, 3.1, 3.2	Implicit 1.3, 3.1, 3.2
		Symptomatic 3.1, 3.2

to facilitate the division of the film into 'interpreted sequences' (a reinterpretation of the syuzet).

Level 1.2 identifies a meaningful 'chunk' of the film, defined by starting and finishing frames. This sequence of frames is chosen by an indexer and is treated as a unit. An event 'Objects', such as characters, places or things may be identified within an event, this information being recorded in levels 1.4, 2.2 and 3.2. Events defined in this level may be 'stand alone'. There is no compulsion to link them to other events which have been defined.

Level 1.3 collects together two or more events defined in 1.2. This level enables a series of events to be related together and indexed as a whole sequence. The events in the set are ordered but the order does not have to follow the sequence of events as they appear in the film (see Figure 6.1). This facility would enable indexers to identify the occurrence of characters or the interaction of characters within a film.

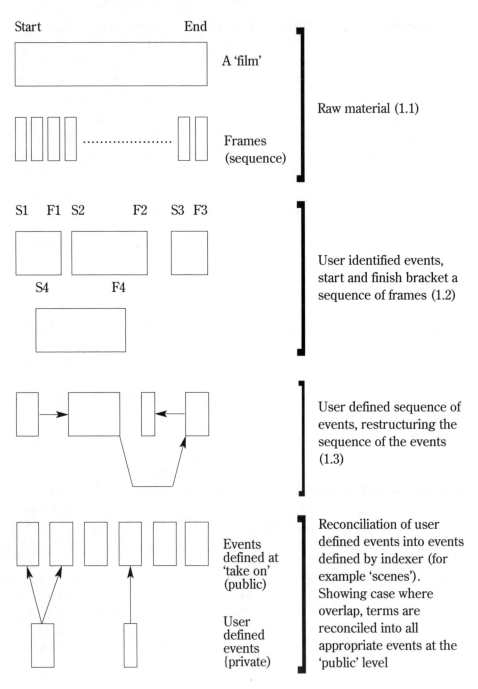

Figure 6.1 A film, events and sequences defined within the framework

DEMOCRATIC INDEXING AND LEVEL 1.2

The opportunities for an indexer to identify events determined by start and end frames means that the likelihood of two indexers agreeing on a division of a film into events is small. The question of equivalence (which events are the same?) would not produce much agreement based on the need for a perfect match between events. This would then have a knock-on effect. If the number of events multiplied, then each event would have to be considered to be unique with its own set of indexing terms. This approach, albeit completely free from the indexers' perspective, is therefore likely to be unproductive. The analogy with still images (Brown and Hidderley, 1995) is that there is no agreement between the indexers and, although the film might be indexed at the 'private' level, it would be virtually impossible to produce a 'public' index.

At least two approaches to resolve this problem are being considered. The first approach surrenders the opportunity for indexers to identify events. The events are determined by a 'mechanical' (human or automated) analysis of the film that identify scene and viewpoint changes. Thus the 'event' unit will be fixed and then an event could be considered to be equivalent to a still image. This has some attractions, mainly because this process could be automated. However, in practice the analysis may deliver events of too small a size to be useful to an indexer.

The second approach would look for overlap between events. Thus if two indexers had each identified an event but the precise start and stop frames were different the events could be considered to be equivalent if they overlapped. The degree of overlap is an issue here but if a satisfactory measure can be identified this may be a valid approach. The last section of Figure 6.2 illustrates this concept.

DEMOCRATIC INDEXING AND LEVEL 1.3

The collection of level 1.3 information will resemble a hypertext. Each indexer may identify (with a set of terms) a sequence of 1.2 events (indexers are not restricted to just one set of linked events, but might identify any number of such sets). Thus a link will be defined from one event to another. The first reconciliation step would be to identify corresponding links between pairs of events. The second step would be to examine the terms used to describe the link: from that point on the standard reconciliation method would apply (see above). Only those terms above the 'threshold' would apply to the link (it may therefore be possible to identify a link but not find agreement on what to name it in the public index). Figure 6.2 illustrates this activity.

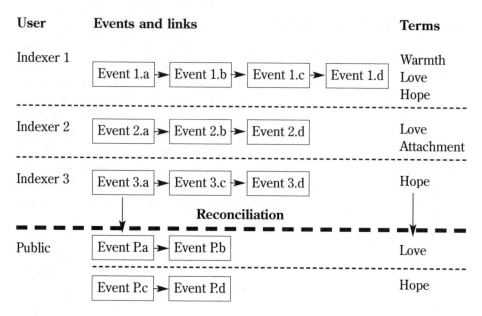

Notes:
1. a, b, c and d are equivalent events identified in 1.2.
2. The linked sequence are identified by the arrows, the terms apply to a whole sequence identified in the 1.3 level. Reconciliation for links and terms is +50 per cent for this illustration, therefore only a to b and c to d are reconciled.

Figure 6.2 Reconciliation of event sequences and associated terms

A 'DEMOCRATIC HYPERTEXT'?

The application of Democratic Indexing to film, in particular levels 1.2 and 1.3 discussed above, produces many new opportunities and problems. Key areas which are still to be evaluated include the practical process of indexing films and the usefulness of the resulting index. Detailed work is still to be undertaken regarding the reconciliation process.

If, and it is still to be investigated, the system is able to produce a public index based on events, links and terms, then there is no reason why this approach could not be applied to general hypermedia systems. The key question is: how will such an index be useful? First, the public index needs to be a reliable guide to a 'body of knowledge' (collection of films or even one film). Secondly, it would facilitate the analysis of media and enable the dissemination of that analysis. It may be that most people will not need such deep knowledge nor be interested in indexing in such detail. However, there are groups such as students of film and historians who would find such information to be invaluable. Within the framework, information from the superficial through to 'personal responses' may be recorded.

The relationship between the creator and the receiver in the process of making meaning is one which Democratic Indexing attempts to capture. The use of private and public indexes and reconciliation will capture the dynamic of responsibility in meaning-making. This approach would allow the individual viewer to make links between scenes which for them have a particular resonance and meaning when combined. As in the image retrieval system, our film retrieval system would reconcile the user-driven syuzet to construct a public set of linked scenes. Essentially these linked scenes would constitute a hypertext approach to film retrieval.

CONCLUSION

Multimedia indexing faces all of the problems encountered by text-based IR, namely:

- user modelling
- content analysis and modelling
- interface design
- costs (of development and take-on)
- performance (retrieval and take-on).

However, in addition multimedia objects cause extra difficulties:

- representation and storage
- more complex content analysis and modelling.

Multimedia indexing exists in the real world and, therefore, issues about costs and time are always likely to be raised. However, it is always worth considering if a cheap system that does not satisfy user needs is better than a more expensive system that does. If this view has any merit, any MMIR system needs to be measured in terms of its value to its users. Chowdhury (1999, p. 180) refers to research by Guinchat and Menou (1983) who employ two categories of criteria to define users:

- *Objective criteria*, such as the socio-professional category, specialist field, nature of the activity for which information is sought, and reason for using the information system.
- *Social and psychological criteria*, such as the users' attitudes and values in regard to information in general and their relation with information units in

particular, the reasons behind their particular information-seeking, and their professional and social behaviour.

Chowdhury (1999, p. 181) makes a number of observations as an introduction to a discussion about information needs:

1. Information need is a relative concept. It depends on several factors and does not remain constant.
2. Information needs change over a period of time.
3. Information needs vary from person to person, from job to job, subject to subject, organization to organization, and so on.
4. People's information needs are largely dependent on the environment. For example information needs in an academic environment are different from those in an industrial, business or government/administrative environment.
5. Measuring (quantifying) information need is difficult.
6. Information need often remains unexpressed or poorly expressed.
7. Information need often changes upon receipt of some information.

The MMIR systems that attempt to fix a single perspective on the information they record are unlikely to succeed except in the narrowest of applications and, even then, if one accepts Chowdhury's analysis only for a relatively short time.

Salton (1989, p. 409) discusses knowledge-based processing and states that 'knowledge representations all rest on a rationalistic tradition'. He goes on to discuss the interpretation of 'objects':

> There is a substantial antirationalist tradition, however, which denies the idea of objective reality, and does not accept the existence of objects that bear properties independent of particular interpretations. In this view, one cannot coherently talk about an external world without also furnishing the background and contexts that control the events in each circumstance. Knowledge and understanding are not believed to result from formal operations on mental representations of particular objects, but to require each individual's immediate participation, controlled by a socially shared background of concerns, actions and beliefs.

Philosophical 'Rationalism' usually refers to the view that you can gain knowledge by human reason alone, without reference to the external world. It is, perhaps, unfortunate that Salton used the term 'antirationalist' to describe a position that, in our view, is entirely rational and consistent. Is it unreasonable to believe that individuals see the world differently and report those perceptions in different ways? Is it unreasonable to believe that demanding a single 'one size fits all' approach to indexing is unlikely to satisfy all interested parties? Rationalism is based on 'human reason': our concern is that existing approaches assume that there is only one authoritative form of 'human reason'. Salton did not appear to be opposed to the 'antirationalist' perspective per se but was sceptical about the development of systems that could account for those variations.

Salton (1989) was primarily concerned with text documents whereas we have focused our attention on other media types. It is worth reiterating a key difference between text documents and multimedia 'texts' as the objects to be indexed namely that interpretation of the meaning and content of the latter is more open than the former. This is not to trivialize the interpretation of language; clearly understanding the meaning of words and texts is far from straightforward. However, the words are themselves a starting point, in a multimedia document words are often only secondary, used as a model of the meaning and content. Thus, it is our view that the only starting point for multimedia indexing (of meaning and content) is Salton's 'antirationalist' one.

The argument in this book has been that there are many approaches to multimedia indexing which we believe are limited in their scope because they are built on the assumption that communication is a straightforward process. In this book we have attempted to demonstrate that the issues relating to subject analysis and subsequent design and construction of retrieval tools are more complicated than this by drawing on models of communication and meaning from the domain of semiotics and communication studies to explore philosophical questions about meaning and communication.

We have described and critiqued information retrieval models drawn from the domains of information science and computer science. In Chapter 5, a variety of non-textual documents were interpreted using a 'reading' model based on insights drawn from the literature of semiotics. These objects were then indexed using specialist multimedia retrieval tools, and although we do not claim that our indexing is exhaustive or authoritative, indeed our claim would be more likely to echo Mai's (2000) conclusions about the uncertainty necessarily inherent in the indexing process, it is clear that using a controlled vocabulary does not offer the indexer the richness of the free description that was possible in the semiotics-based interpretations. Rich description is always lost in adhering to controlled vocabularies and classification schemes, but such systems are possibly more cost-effective.

It seems unlikely that a single MMIR system could be developed to store and adequately retrieve all the multimedia in existence, but it is an ideal if impractical solution. Almost certainly such a unified system would require a variety of user interfaces tailored for different purposes. Content and meaning may have to be described in many different ways depending on users' needs. However, this might be the only way that multimedia could be retrieved with any degree of certainty. Do the Internet and marked-up documents offer this possibility? Only as far as the storage and (technical) retrieval is concerned, not yet in terms of the content and meaning problem as we have discussed earlier in this book.

Bibliography

Amazon (2003), *Amazon.co.uk website*, http://www.amazon.co.uk, accessed 6 August 2003.

Ang, I. (1985), *Watching Dallas: Soap Opera and the Melodramatic Imagination*, trans. D. Couling, London: Methuen.

Armitage, L.H. and Enser, P.G.B. (1996), 'Information need in the visual document domain', *British Library Research and Innovation Report*, **27**, London: British Library Research and Innovation Centre.

Art and Architecture Thesaurus (AAT) Online Homepage (2000), *Art and Architecture Thesaurus Online Homepage*, http://www.getty.edu/research/tools/vocabulary/aat/about.html, (accessed 11 July 2003).

Art, Design, Architecture and Media Information Gateway (ADAM) (2003), *ADAM The gateway to art, design, architecture and media information on the Internet*, http://www.adam.ac.uk/, (accessed 7 August 2003).

Baeza-Yates, R. and Ribeiro-Neto, B. (1999), *Modern Information Retrieval*, Reading, MA, and Harlow: Addison Wesley.

Barthes, R. (1973), *Mythologies*, trans. A. Lavers, London: Paladin.

Barthes, R. (1974), *S/Z*, trans. R. Howard, New York: Hill & Wang.

Barthes, R. (1977), *Image-Music-Text*, ed. S. Heath, London: Fontana/Collins.

Barthes, R. (1985 [1967]), *The Fashion System*, trans M. Ward and R. Berkeley, London: Cape.

Beghtol, C. (1989), 'Access to fiction: a problem in classification theory and practice, part 1', *International Classification*, **16** (3), 134–40.

Beghtol, C. (1990), 'Access to fiction: a problem in classification theory and practice, part 2', *International Classification*, **17** (1), 21–7.

Beghtol, C. (1994), *Fiction Classification: The Development of a System Based on Theoretical Principles*, Metuchen, NJ: Scarecrow Press.

Beghtol, C. (1995), 'Domain analysis, literary warrant, and consensus: the case of fiction studies', *Journal of the American Society for Information Science (ASIS)*, **46** (1), 30–44.

Benjamin, W. (2000 [1937]), *The Work of Art in the Age of Mechanical Reproduction*, http://pages.emerson.edu/Courses/spring00/in123/work ofart/benjamin.htm, (accessed 30 July 2002).

Benson, D. and Flick, G. (1992), 'Spatial and symbolic queries for 3-D image data', SPIE/IS&T Symposium on the Electronic Imaging Science and Technology, vol. 1662, pp. 134–45.

Berwick Sayers, W.C. (1955), *A Manual of Classification for Librarians and Bibliographers*, London: Grafton.

Berwick Sayers, W.C. and Maltby, A.M. (1967), *A Manual of Classification for Librarians*, 4th edn, London: Andre Deutsch.

Besser, H. (2002), *Image Metadata: Important Recent Activities*, JISC International Image Meeting, 20 June 2002, http://sunsite.berkeley.edu/Imaging/Databases/JISC02-imaging/ (accessed 5 August 2003).

Bliss, H.E. (1939), *The Organization of Knowledge in Libraries and the Subject Approach to Books*, New York: Wilson.

Bodleian (2003), *Bodleian Library University of Oxford*, http://www.bodley.ox.ac.uk/, (accessed 7 August 2003).

Bordwell, D. (1989), *Making Meaning: Inference and Rhetoric in the Interpretation of Cinema*, Cambridge, MA: Harvard University Press.

Brown (Rafferty), P. and Hidderley, G.R. (1994), 'Deconstructuring pictures', *Proceedings of the Annual Conference of UK Media Librarians*, Birmingham, June 11, London: AUKML, pp. 39–50.

Brown (Rafferty), P. and Hidderley, G.R. (1995), 'Capturing iconology: a study in retrieval modelling and image indexing', *Proceedings of the 2nd International Elvira Conference, De Montfort University*, May 1995, London: ASLIB, pp. 79–91.

Buckland, W. (2000), *The Cognitive Semiotics of Film*, Cambridge: Cambridge University Press.

Burke, M.A. (1999), *Organization of Multimedia Resources: Principles and Practice of Information Retrieval*, Aldershot: Gower.

Burnard, L. (1996), *What is SGML and How Does It Help?* http://www.oasis-open.org/cover/burnardw25-index.html#W25B, (accessed 3 May 2002).

Carroll, N. (1997), *The Philosophy of Mass Art*, Oxford: Oxford University Press.

Chandler, D. (1995), *Semiotics for Beginners*, http://www.aber.ac.uk/media/Documents/S4B/semiotic.html, (accessed 23 May 2003).

Chandler, D. (2002), *Semiotics: The Basics*, London: Routledge.

Chen, H. (1993), *Machine Learning for Information Retrieval: Neural Networks, Symbolic Learning, and Genetic Algorithms*, http://ai.bpa.arizona.edu/papers/mlir93/mlir93.html, (Accessed 10 November 2003).

Chicago History Society (CHS) (2001), *Chicago Historical Society*, http://www.chicagohs.org, (accessed 7 August 2003).

Chowdhury, G. (1999), *Introduction to Modern Information Retrieval*, London: Library Association.

Cleverdon, C.W., Mills, J. and Keen, M. (1996), *Factors Determining the Performance of Indexing Systems*, Cranfield (Beds): College of Aeronautics.

Collingwood, R.G. (1924), *Speculum Mentis or The Map of Knowledge*, Oxford: The Clarendon Press.

Constable, J. (1821), *The Hay Wain*, at the National Gallery, http://www.nationalgallery.org.uk/cgi-bin/WebObjects.dll/ CollectionPublisher.woa/wa/work?workNumber=NG1207, (accessed 6 August 2003).

Corbis (2003), *Corbis*, http://www.corbis.com/, (accessed 7 August 2003).

Courtauld (2003), *Courtauld Institute of Art University of London*, http://www.courtauld.ac.uk/index.html, (accessed 7 August 2003).

Cover, R. (1999), *SGML: General Introductions and Overviews*, http://www.xml. coverpages.org/general.html, (accessed 30 April 2002).

Cover, R. (2001a), *About the Cover Pages Web Site*, http://xml.coverpages.org/ AboutXMLCoverPages.html, (accessed 6 August 2003).

Cover, R. (2001b), *Image Metadata Aggregation for Enhanced Searching (IMAGES)*, http://xml.coverpages.org/umnImages.html, (accessed 6 August 2003).

Cover, R. (2001c), *MPEG 21 part 2: Digital Item Declaration Language DIDL*, http://xml.coverpages.org/mpeg21-didl.html, (accessed 6 August 2003).

Cover, R. (2002a), *Extensible Markup Language (XML)*, http://xml.coverpages. org/xml.html#overview, (accessed 3 May 2002).

Cover, R. (2002b), *Moving Picture Experts Group: MPEG-7 Standard*, http://xml.coverpages.org/mpeg7.html, (accessed 10 May 2002).

Cover, R. (2002c), *DIG35: Metadata Standard for Digital Images*, http://xml.coverpages.org/dig35.html, (accessed 6 August 2003).

Cover, R. (2002d), *SMDL – Standard Music Description Language, ISO/IEC DIS 10743:1995*, http://xml.coverpages.org/gen-apps.html#smdl, (accessed 6 August 2003).

Cover, R. (2002e), *Chemical Markup Language (CML)*, http://xml.coverpages. org/cml.html, (accessed 7 August 2003).

Cover, R. (2003a), *XML Applications and Initiatives*, http://xml.coverpages.org/ xmlApplications.html, (accessed 6 August 2003).

Cover, R. (2003b), *Synchronised Multimedia Integration Language (SMIL)*, http://xml.coverpages.org/smil.html, (accessed 6 August 2003).

Cronin, B. (2000), 'Semiotics and evaluative bibliometrics', *Journal of Documentation*, **56** (3), 440–53.

Cronin, B. (2001), 'The scholar's spoor', in Perron, P., Danesi, M., Umiker-Sebeok, J. and Watanabe, A. (eds), *Semiotics and the Information Sciences*, Ottawa: Legas Press, pp. 55–75.

Date, C.J. (2000), *An Introduction to Database Systems*, Reading, MA, and Harlow: Addison Wesley.

Dawson, E. and Rafferty, P. (2001), '"Careless Talk Costs Lives": a case study examining the operation of information in British domestic posters of the Second World War', *The New Review of Information and Library Research*, **7**, 129–55.

Dublin Core Metadata Initiative Home Page (2003), http://dublincore.org/documents/dcmi-terms/, (accessed 30 June 2003).

Eakins, J.P. and Graham, M.E. (1999), *Content-based Image Retrieval: A Report to the JISC Technology Applications Programme*, Institute for Image Data Research, University of Northumbria at Newcastle, January 1999, http://www.unn.ac.uk/iidr/report.html, (accessed 6 August 2003) and http://www.jisc.ac.uk/uploaded_documents/jtap-039.doc, (accessed 1 November 2003).

Eco, U. (1976), *A Theory of Semiotics*, Bloomington, IN: Indiana University Press; London: Macmillan.

Eco, U. (1979), *The Role of the Reader: Explorations in the Semiotics of Texts*, Bloomington, IN: Indiana University Press.

Enser, P.G.B. (1991), 'An Indexing-free Approach to the Retrieval of Still Images', in McEnery, T. (ed.), *Proceedings of the 13th British Computer Society Information Retrieval Specialist Group Research Colloquium, University of Lancaster*, 8–9 April 1991, London: British Computer Society, pp. 41–55.

Enser, P.G.B. (1993a), 'Analysis of user need in image archives', *Journal of Information Science*, **23** (4), 287–99.

Enser, P.G.B. (1993b), 'Query analysis in a visual information retrieval context', *Journal of Document and Text Management*, **1** (1), 25–52.

Enser, P.G.B. (1995a), 'Image databases for multimedia projects', *Journal of the American Society for Information Science*, **46** (1), 60–64.

Enser, P.G.B. (1995b), 'Pictorial information retrieval', *Journal of Documentation*, **51** (2), 126–70.

Enser, P. (2000), 'Progress in visual information access and retrieval', *Journal of Documentation*, **56** (6), 697–9.

Enser, P. and Cawkell, A.E. (1994), 'Indexing collections of electronic images: a review', *Program*, **28** (4), 445–6.

Enser, P.G.B. and McGregor, C.G. (1992), *Analysis of Visual Information Retrieval Queries*, British Library Research and Development Report, no. 6104, London: British Library.

Enser, P.G.B. and Orr, H.P. (1993), 'Creative picture research using the Hulton Deutsch CD collection', *Program*, **27** (4), 389–98.

Evans, R. (1997), *In Defence of History*, London: Granta.

Faloutsos, C. (1999), 'Multimedia IR: Indexing and Searching', in Baeza-Yates, R.

and Ribeiro-Neto, B., *Modern Information Retrieval*, Reading, MA, and Harlow: Addison Wesley, pp. 345–65.

Fidal, R. (1997), 'The image retrieval task: implications for the design and evaluation of image databases', *The New Review of Hypermedia and Multimedia*, **3**, 181–99.

Fisher, R. (2001), 'Cvonline Applications', in Fisher, R. (ed.), *CVonline: On-Line Compendium of Computer Vision*, http://www.dai.ed.ac.uk/CVonline/applic.htm, (accessed 5 August 2003).

Flanagan, M. (1998), *Bakhtin and Film*, http://www.shef.ac.uk/uni/academic/A-C/bakh/flanagan.html, (accessed 28 June 2003]).

Fletcher, G. (2000), 'Indexing digital skating images', unpublished MSc dissertation, University of Central England.

Flickner, M. et al. (1995), 'Query by image and video content: the QBIC system', *IEEE Computer*, September, 23–32.

Floridi, L. (2002), 'On defining library and information science as applied philosophy of information', *Social Epistemology*, **16** (1), 37–49.

Fogg (2003), *Harvard University Art Museums Fogg Art Museum*, http://www.artmuseums.harvard.edu/fogg/index.html, (accessed 7 August 2003).

Foucault, M. (1970), *The Order of Things: An Archaeology of the Human Sciences*, London: Tavistock.

Foucault, M. (1991), 'What is an Author?,' in Rabinow, P. (ed), *The Foucault Reader*, Harmondsworth: Penguin, pp. 101–20.

Garfield, E. (1979), *Citation Indexing: Its Theory and Application in Science, Technology, and Humanities*, New York: Wiley.

Gary, J.E. and Mehotra, R. (1992), 'Shape similarity-based retrieval in image database-systems', *SPIE Proceedings*, vol. 1662, pp. 2–8.

Gennette, G. (1980), *Narrative Discourse*, Oxford: Blackwell.

Giannetti, L. (1993), *Understanding Movies*, Englewood Cliffs, NJ: Prentice Hall.

Goodrum, A.A. (2000), 'Image information retrieval: an overview of current research', *Informing Science*, **3** (2), http://209.68.25.5/Articles/Vol3/v3n2p63-66.pdf, (accessed: 5 August 2003).

Goodrum, A.A. and Spink, A. (2001), 'Image searching on the Excite web search engine', *Information Processing and Management*, **37** (2), 295–311.

Google (2002), *Google Image Search*, http://www.google.com/help/faq_images.html#use, (accessed 16 April 2002).

Gramsci, A. (1971), *Selections from the Prison Notebooks of Antonio Gramsci*, Q. Hoare and G. Nowell Smith (eds), London: Lawrence & Wishart.

Greene, T.C. (2001), 'Face recognition useless for crowd surveillance', *The Register*, http://theregisiter.co.uk/content/archive/21916.html, (accessed 14 July 2003).

195

Guinchat, C. and Menou, M. (1983), *General Introduction to the Techniques of Information and Documentation Work*, Paris, UNESCO.

Gunning, T. (1991), *D.W. Griffith and the Origins of the American Narrative Film*, Urbana, IL: University of Illinois Press.

Hall, S. (2001), 'Encoding/decoding', in Durham, M.G. and Kellner, D. M. (eds), *Media and Cultural Studies: Keyworks*, Oxford: Blackwell, pp. 166–77.

Harvey, D. (2000), 'The Great Train Robbery', *Film Monthly*, 8 March, http://www.filmmonthly.com/Silents/Articles/GreatTrain/GreatTrain.html, (accessed: 5 August 2003).

Hedstrom, M. (2002), *Digital Preservation: A Time Bomb for Digital Libraries*, http://www.uky.edu/~kiernan/DL/hedstrom.html, (accessed 5 August 2003).

Heitkötter, J. (2000), *The Hitch-Hiker's Guide to Evolutionary Computation*, http://www.cs.bham.ac.uk/Mirrors/ftp.de.uu.net/EC/clife/www/, (accessed 10 November 2003).

Heo, J. et al. (2003), 'Face recognition: evaluation report for FaceIt ® identification and surveillance', *Proc. of SPIE*, **5132**, 551–8, http://imaging.utk.edu/publications/papers/2003/150.pdf, (accessed 14 July 2003).

Hidderley, R. and Rafferty, P. (1997a), 'Democratic indexing: an approach to the retrieval of fiction', *Information Services and Use*, **17** (2–3), 101–11.

Hidderley, R. and Rafferty, P. (1997b), 'Democratic indexing: an approach to the retrieval of film', *Library and Information Studies: Research and Professional Practice. Proceedings of the 2nd British-Nordic Conference on Library and Information Studies*, Queen Margaret College, Edinburgh, 1997, London: Taylor Graham, pp. 90–103.

Hodge, R. and Kress. G. (1988), *Social Semiotics*, Cambridge: Polity.

Hodge, R. and Tripp, D. (1986), *Children and Television: A Semiotic Approach*, Cambridge: Polity.

Holdcroft, D. (1991), *Saussure: Signs, System and Arbitrariness*, Cambridge: Cambridge University Press.

Huber, D. (2002), *The Computer Vision Homepage*, http://www-2.cs.cmu.edu/afs/cs/project/cil/www/vision.html, (accessed 6 August 2003).

Hulton (2003), *Hulton Archive*, http://search.hultongetty.com/, (accessed 4 August 2003).

Hunter, E.J. (2002), *Classification Made Simple*, Aldershot: Ashgate.

Hunter, E.J. and Bakewell, K.G.B. (1991), *Cataloguing*, London: Library Association.

Huron, D. (1999), *Music Research Using Humdrum*, http://dactyl.som.ohio-state.edu/Humdrum/guide.toc.html, (accessed 4 December 2001).

Iconclass Official Homepage (2002), http://www.iconclass.nl/index.html, (accessed 11 July 2003).

Institute of Museum and Library Services (IMLS) (2001), *A Framework of Guidance for Building Good Digital Collections*, Institute of Museum and Library Services, 6 November 2001, http://www.imls.gov/pubs/forumframework.htm, (accessed 7 May 2002).

Jakobson, R. (1960), 'Closing Statement: Linguistics and Poetics', in Sebeok, T.A. (ed.), *Style in Language*, Cambridge, MA: MIT Press, pp. 350–77.

Joint Steering Committee for Revision of AACR (2002), *Anglo-American Cataloguing Rules*, 2nd edn prepared under the direction of the Joint Steering Committee for Revision of AACR, a committee of the American Library Association, the Australian Committee on Cataloguing, the British Library, the Canadian Committee on Cataloguing, Chartered Institute of Library and Information Professionals, the Library of Congress, Chicago, IL: American Library Association; London: Facet.

Keep, C., McLaughlin, T. and Parmar, R. (2001), *The Electronic Labyrinth*, http://www.iath.virginia.edu/elab/elab.html and http://www.iath.virginia.edu/elab/hfl0037.html (accessed 6 August 2003).

Krause, M. (1988), 'Intellectual problems of indexing picture collections', *Audiovisual Librarian*, **14** (2), 73–81.

Kress, G. and Van Leeuwen, T. (1996), *Reading Images: The Grammar of Visual Design*, London: Routledge.

Kuhns, R.J. (1988), 'A news analysis system', *Proceedings of the International Conference on Computational Linguistics, Coling '88, Budapest,Vol 1*, pp. 351–5, http://acl.ldc.upenn.edu/C/C88/C88-1072.pdf, (accessed 20 July 2003).

Kunst Indeks (2003), *Kunst Indeks Danmark + Weilbachs Kunstnerleksikon*, http://www.kid.dk/Root.asp, (accessed 7 August 2003).

Kunze, S. (1993 [1984]), 'Beethoven's symphonic language', *Beethoven, 9 Symphonien, Ouvertüren Karajan*, (booklet accompanying audio recording on compact disc), Hamburg: Deutsche Grammophon, pp. 53–79.

Lagoze, C. (2001), 'Keeping Dublin Core simple: cross-domain discovery or resource description?', *D-Lib Magazine*, **7** (1), January, http://www.dlib.org/dlib/january01/lagoze/01lagoze.html (accessed 30 June 2003).

Langridge, D.W. (1989), *Subject Analysis: Principles and Procedures*, London and Munich: Bowker-Saur.

Layne, S.S. (1994), 'Some issues in the indexing of images', *Journal of the American Society of Information Science*, **45** (8), September, 583–8.

Lévi-Strauss, C. (1986 [1967]), *Introduction to a Science of Mythology – 1: The Raw and the Cooked*, Harmondsworth: Penguin.

Library of Congress Thesaurus for Graphic Materials I: Subject Terms (TGM 1), (1995), http://www.loc.gov/rr/print/tgm1/toc.html, (accessed 11 July 2003).

Lober, B. (2000), *Image Markup Language*, http://faculty.washington.edu/lober/iml/, (accessed 14 May 2002).

Lye, J. (1996), *Reader-Response: Various Positions*, http://www.brocku.ca/ english/courses/4F70/rr.html, (accessed 30 July 2002).

Mai, E.J. (2001), 'Semiotics and subject indexing: an analysis of the subject indexing process', *Journal of Documentation*, **57** (5): 591–622.

Mai, J.-E. (2000), 'The subject indexing process: an investigation of problems in knowledge representation', PhD dissertation, University of Texas at Austin, May 2000, http://www.ischool.washington.edu/mai/abstract.html, (accessed 28 June 2003).

MARC 21 (2000), *Specifications for Record Structure, Character Sets, and Exchange Media: Record Structure*, January 2000, http://www.loc.gov/marc/ specifications/specrecstruc.html, (accessed 30 June 2003).

Martinez, J.M. (ed.) (2001), *Overview of the MPEG-7 Standard*, ISO/IEC JTC1/SC29/WG11, http://mpeg.telecomitalialab.com/standards/mpeg-7/mpeg-7.htm, (accessed 7 July 2002).

Metz, C. (1974), *Film Language: A Semiotics of the Cinema*, trans. M. Taylor, Oxford: Oxford University Press.

Morley, D. (1999), *The Nationwide Television Studies*, London: Routledge.

National Art Library (2001), *National Art Library*, http://www.nal.vam.ac.uk/, (accessed 7 August 2003).

Neural-net-faq (1995), *Neural-net-faq*, http://www-2.cs.cmu.edu/afs/ cs.cmu.edu/project/ai-repository/ai/html/faqs/ai/neural/faq.html, (accessed 5 August 2003).

Neural-net-faq (2001) *Neural-net-faq*, http://www.faqs.org/faqs/ai-faq/neural-nets/part1/index.html, (accessed 5 August 2003).

New York Public Library (NYPL) (2003), *The New York Public Library*, http://www.nypl.org/, (accessed 7 August 2003).

O'Connor, B., O'Connor, M.K. and Abbas, J.M. (1999), 'User reactions as access mechanism: an exploration based on captions for images', *Journal of the American Society for Information Science*, **50** (8), 681–97.

Omissi, L. (1998), 'The murder in the library: an analysis of narrative structure and detective fiction used as a critique of fiction classification within a library environment', unpublished MSc dissertation, University of Central England.

Pabst, G.W. (dir.) (2001 [1929]), *Diary of a Lost Girl* (video recording), Berlin: Pabst-Film; USA: Kino Videos.

Panofsky, E. (1993a), *Meaning in the Visual Arts*, Harmondsworth: Penguin.

Panofsky, E. (1993b), 'Iconography and iconology', in *Meaning in the Visual Arts*, Harmondsworth: Penguin, pp. 26–41.

Pathe (2003), *British Pathe*, http://www.britishpathe.com/index.cfm, (accessed 4 August 2003).

Pejtersen, A.M. (1978), 'Fiction and library classification', *Scandinavian Public Library Quarterly*, **11** (1), 5–12.

Pejtersen, A.M. (1979), 'The meaning of 'about' in fiction indexing and retrieval', *Aslib Proceedings*, **31** (5), 251–7.

Pejtersen, A.M. (1993), *'Book House Search and Write' for Classification and Retrieval of Fiction Literature. A Library System for Adults' and Children's Literature in Public Libraries*, produced by APPLE A/S and Risø National Laboratory for Machintosch, Denmark.

Pejtersen, A.M. (1994), 'A framework for indexing and representation of information based on work domain analysis: a fiction classification example', *Knowledge Organization and Quality Management. Proceedings of Third International ISKO Conference. Advances in Knowledge Organization*, Frankfurt/Main: Indeks, pp. 251–64.

Piggott, M. (1988), *A Topography of Cataloguing: Showing the Most Important Landmarks, Communications and Perilous Places*, London: Library Association.

Radway, J. (1991), *Reading the Romance: Women, Patriarchy, and Popular Literature*, Chapel Hill, NC: University of North Carolina Press.

Rafferty, P. (2001), 'The representation of knowledge in library classification schemes', *Knowledge Organization*, **28** (4), 180–91.

Rafferty, P., Cronin, B. and Carson, J. (1988), 'Corporate citizenship and monopolistic practices in the information industry: a study of IBM', *Aslib Proceedings*, **40** (3), March, 69–77.

Ranganathan, S.R. (1951), *Philosophy of Classification: Vol. 2*, Copenhagen: Munksgaard.

Rasmussen, E. (1997), 'Indexing images', *Annual Review of Information Science and Technology*, **32**, 169–96.

Rijksmuseum (2003), *Rijksmuseum Amsterdam*, http://www.rijksmuseum.nl/, (accessed 6 August 2003).

Rowley, J.E. and Farrow, J. (2000), *Organizing Knowledge: An Introduction to Managing Access to Information*, Aldershot: Gower.

Saarti, J. (1999), 'Fiction indexing and the development of fiction thesauri', *Journal of Librarianship and Information Science*, **31** (2), 85–92.

Saarti, J. (2000a), 'Fiction indexing by library professionals and users', *Scandinavian Public Library Quarterly*, **33** (4), 6–9.

Saarti, J. (2000b), 'Taxonomy of novel abstracts based on empirical findings', *Knowledge Organization*, **27** (4), 213–20.

Saarti, J. (2002), 'Consistency of subject indexing of novels by public library professionals and patrons', *Journal of Documentation*, **58** (1), 49–65.

Salton, G. (1989), *Automatic Text Processing*, Reading, MA, and Harlow: Addison Wesley.

Salton, G. and McGill, M. (1983), *Introduction to Modern Information Retrieval*, New York: McGraw-Hill.

Saussure, F. de (1974 [1915]), *Course in General Linguistics*, ed. J. Culler, trans. W. Baskin, London: Fontana.

Saussure, F. de. (2003a [1915]), *Speech Circuit Diagram 1*, http://www.this publicaddress.com/archives/000357.php, (accessed 1 July 2003).

Saussure, F. de. (2003b [1915]), 'Speech Circuit Diagram 2', in Ipsen, G. *Linguistics for Beginners*, http://www.uni-kassel.de/fb8/misc/lfb/html/text/6.html, (accessed 28 June 2003).

Schmidt, C. and Over, P. (1999), 'Digital video test collection', *Proceedings of the Twenty-Second Annual International ACM SIGIR Conference, Berkeley, California, USA*, http://www.itl.nist.gov/iad/894.02/works/papers/digital.video.html (accessed 8 August 2003).

Shannon, C.E. and Weaver, W. (1949), *The Mathematical Theory of Communication*, Urbana, IL: University of Illinois.

Shatford, S. (1984), 'Describing a picture: a thousand words are seldom cost effective', *Cataloging & Classification Quarterly*, **4** (4), 13–30.

Shatford, S. (1986), 'Analyzing the subject of a picture: a theoretical approach', *Cataloging & Classification Quarterly*, **6** (3), 39–62.

Shatford-Layne, S. (1994), 'Some issues in the indexing of images', *Journal of the American Society of Information Science*, **45** (8), 583–8.

Slaughter, L., Marchionini, G. and Geisler, G. (2000), 'Open video: a framework for a test collection', *Journal of Network and Computer Applications*, **23** (3), http://ils.unc.edu/%7Egeisg/info/Jnca0112.pdf, (accessed 5 August 2003).

Sonesson, G. (1988), *Methods and Models in Pictorial Semiotics*, http://www.arthist.lu.se/kultsem/pdf/rapport3.pdf, (accessed 28 June 2003).

Sonesson, G. (1999), *Pictorial Semiotics: The State of the Art at the Beginning of the Nineties*, http://www.arthist.lu.se/kultsem/sonesson/pict_sem_1.html, (accessed 28 June 2003).

Stam, R. (1992), *New Vocabularies in Film Semiotics: Stucturalism, Post-Structuralism and Beyond*, London: Routledge.

Stam, R. (2000), *Film Theory: An Introduction*, Oxford: Blackwell.

Svenonius, E. (1994), 'Access to nonbook materials: the limits of subject indexing for visual and aural languages', *Journal of the American Society for Information Science*, **45** (8), 600–606.

Tagg, P. (1999), *Introductory notes to the Semiotics of Music*, http://www.theblackbook.net/acad/tagg/teaching/analys/semiotug.pdf, (accessed 28 June 2003).

Tagg, P. (2003), personal correspondence with Philip Tagg.

TEI (2001), *Text Encoding Initiative*, TEI Consortium 2001, http://www.tei-c.org/, (accessed 3 May 2002).

Thomas, C. (2001), *IMAGES DTD*, http://xml.coverpages.org/UMN-imagesDTD.txt, (accessed 14 May 2002).

Thomas, D. (1998 [1954]), *Under Milk Wood* (audio recording on compact disc), Richard Burton, London: Polygram Film Entertainment.

Turner, G. (1996), *British Cultural Studies: An Introduction*, London: Routledge.

Turner, J. (1990), 'Representing and accessing information in the stock-shot database at the National Film Board of Canada', *Canadian Journal of Information Science*, **15**, 1–22.

UML (2000a), *Contributing Data to the IMAGES Database*, University of Minnesota Digital Collections and Services, http://digital.lib.umn.edu/ IMAGES/IMAGESelements.html, (accessed 14 May 2002).

UML (2000b), *Image Metadata AGgregator for Enhanced Searching*, University of Minnesota Digital Collections and Services, http://digital.lib.umn.edu/ IMAGES/IMAGESexplanation.html, (accessed 14/5/2002).

Van den Berg, J. (1995), 'Subject retrieval in pictorial information systems', *Proceedings of the 18th International Congress of Historical Sciences, Round Table 34: Electronic Filing, Recording, and Communication of Visual Historical Data*, Montreal, 1995, 21–9, http://www.iconclass.nl/texts/history05.htm, (accessed 5 August 2003).

Van den Berg, J. (1995), 'Subject retrieval in pictorial information systems', *Proceedings of the 18th International Congress of Historical Sciences, Round Table 34: Electronic Filing, Recording, and Communication of Visual Historical Data*, Montreal, http://www.iconclass.nl/texts/history05.htm, (accessed 5 July 2004).

Van Horik, R. (2001), *Archives and Photographs: The 'European Visual Archivei Project (EVA)*, Cultivate Interactive, http://www.cultivate-int.org/issue3/eva/, (accessed 7 June 2002).

Voisey, K.M. (2001), 'In the car', unpublished A level artwork.

Volosinov, V.N. (1973), *Marxism and the Philosophy of Language*, trans L. Matejka and I.R. Titunik, Cambridge, MA: Harvard University Press.

Webmuseum (2002), *Webmuseum Paris Kandinsky Wassily*, http://mirror. oir.ucf.edu/wm/paint/auth/kandinsky/, (accessed 7 August 2003).

West, S. and Norris, M. (1997), *Media Engineering: A Guide to Developing Information Products*, New York: Wiley.

whichbook.net (2003), *whichbook.net*, http://www.whichbook.net/index.jsp, (accessed 22 January 2003).

Wieblut, V. (1995), *Image Content Searching is Here*, http://sunsite.berkeley.edu/ Imaging/Databases/Fall95papers/vlad2.html, (accessed 5 August 2003).

Wilson, E. (1985), *Adorned in Dreams: Fashion and Modernity*, London: Virago.

Wong, T. and Wong, H. (1996a), 'Overview', in *Applications of Genetic Algorithms*,

SURPRISE '96, http://www.doc.ic.ac.uk/~nd/surprise_96/journal/vol4/tcw2/report.html#Overview, (accessed 4 December 2001).

Wong, T. and Wong, H. (1996b), 'Robot Vision', in *Applications of Genetic Algorithms*, SURPRISE '96, http://www.doc.ic.ac.uk/~nd/surprise_96/journal/vol4/tcw2/report.html#Vision (accessed 4 December 2001).

Wyner, B. S. (1980), *Introduction to Cataloguing and Classification*, Littleton, CO: Libraries Unlimited.

W3C (2003), *The World Wide Web Consortium*, http://www.w3.org/, (accessed 6 August 2003).

Zinkham, H. and Parker, E.B. (eds) (1986), *Descriptive Terms for Graphic Materials: Genre and Physical Characteristic Headings*, Prints and Photographs Division, Library of Congress, Washington: Cataloging Distribution Service, Library of Congress.

Index